Sisters

Sisters

NINE FAMILIES OF SISTERS
WHO MADE A DIFFERENCE

Edited by Siobhán Fitzpatrick and Mary O'Dowd

Acadamh Ríoga na hÉireann
Royal Irish Academy

First published 2022
Royal Irish Academy, 19 Dawson Street, Dublin 2
ria.ie

Text © the contributors 2022

ISBN
978-1-911479-83-3 (PB)
978-1-911479-99-4 (pdf)
978-1-911479-54-3 (epub)

British Library Cataloguing in Publication Data. A CIP catalogue record
for this book is available from the British Library.

Copyeditor: Neil Burkey
Book design: Fidelma Slattery
Index: Eileen O'Neill
Printed in Ireland by Walsh Colour Print

Cover illustration after Victor Brown, Cuala Press hand-coloured print no. 84 –
'Silver Apples'. Courtesy of Dublin City Library and Archive.
Illustration on title page and throughout is a detail taken from
Elizabeth Corbet Yeats, *Brush-work* (London, 1896).

Royal Irish Academy is a member of Publishing Ireland,
the Irish book publishers' association.

5 4 3 2 1

FSC
www.fsc.org
MIX
Paper from
responsible sources
FSC™ C165815

A NOTE FROM THE PUBLISHER

We want to try to offset the environmental impacts of carbon produced during the production
of our books and journals. For the production of our books this year
we will plant 45 trees with Easy Treesie.

The Easy Treesie – Crann Project organises children to plant trees. Crann – 'Trees for Ireland' is
a membership-based, non-profit, registered charity (CHY13698) uniting people with a love of
trees. It was formed in 1986 by Jan Alexander, with the aim of 'Releafing Ireland'. Its mission is
to enhance the environment of Ireland through planting, promoting, protecting
and increasing awareness about trees and woodlands.

In fond memory of Margaret MacCurtain (1929–2020)

Contents

Archival Abbreviations

BL	British Library
CHT	Chatsworth House Trust
IAA	Irish Architectural Archive
KBR	Koninklijke Bibliotheek van Belgie/Bibliothèque Royale de Belgique/Royal Library of Belgium
TNA	National Archives, Kew
NAI	National Archives Ireland
NLI	National Library of Ireland
PRONI	Public Record Office of Northern Ireland
RCB Library	Representative Church Body Library
UCD-OFM	University College Dublin-Order of Friars Minor

Editorial Note

The editors have distinguished between pagination or foliation in the case of manuscripts, and emphasised pagination as distinct from letter numeration in the Ashford–Jennings edition of Katherine Conolly's correspondence; as well as in all references to the National Folklore Collection, UCD and www.duchas.ie. The family trees in this volume reflect immediate family relationships only, including grandparentage (where known).

Introduction

The stories of the sisters included here extend over three hundred years, from the 1600s through to the 1900s. Despite the many changes in society during that time span, one characteristic remained constant: the importance of family in the formation of women's political or public activities. It is also striking how many of the women whose lives are documented here came from families in which a number of sisters were involved in the public world outside the home. Some siblings bonded in defiance of the social norms imposed by their families, while others grew up in households where the public engagement of daughters as well as sons was applauded and often expected.

In pre-democratic society, women in aristocratic families were often perceived as representatives of their wider kin network. This is clear, for example, in the manner in which the bardic poets wrote about Nualaidh, Máire and Mairghréad Ní Dhomhnaill as they dealt with the consequences of the departure of the Ulster lords to the continent in 1607. As Pádraig Ó Macháin tells us, the poets praised the women's family loyalty but also lamented their grief at the shattering of their lives with the destruction of Gaelic aristocratic power. In a later period – the eighteenth century – petitioners seeking political favours perceived Katherine Conolly as the means through which they could reach her husband William Conolly, Speaker of the Irish House of Commons (1715–29). Gaye Ashford describes how Katherine Conolly relished the political influence that she wielded as the wife of one of eighteenth-century Ireland's most prominent politicians.

In the nineteenth century, active engagement in public life could also be a family affair. Encouraged by their American mother, Anna and Fanny Parnell established the Ladies' Land League, in order, as Diane Urquhart notes, to support the political campaign of their brother, Charles. Margaret Ward documents the political environment in which Hanna Sheehy Skeffington and her sisters grew up. Their aunt was a member of the Ladies' Land League, while their uncles joined the Irish Republican Brotherhood, and their father, David Sheehy, was a member of parliament. Hanna remembered, as a child, visiting both her father and her uncle in prison. Ward also notes that a favourite game of the Sheehy children was 'Evictions and Emergency men', reflecting their awareness of the Land War agitation in which their father participated.

The involvement of Susan (Lily) and Elizabeth (known in the family as Lolly) Yeats in the Arts and Crafts Movement and their decision to establish the Dun Emer craft collective emerged from the artistic and literary world in which they had been raised. As Lucy Collins explains, the sisters' brothers – poet William Butler and artist Jack Butler – were also centrally involved in the enterprise. The first book published by the new printing press was a collection of poems by William and, later, drawings by Jack were printed on broadsheets to boost the commercial viability of the business.

The family could also, of course, be a source of tension and conflict, and many of the studies presented here tell stories of the falling out of siblings and parents, often because the women endeavoured to widen their public role in defiance of the restraints imposed by society on women's lives. Urquhart traces the growing hostility of Charles Stewart Parnell and his political allies to the Ladies' Land League, a dispute that led eventually to the disbandment of the League and a lifelong separation between sisters and brother. Constance and Eva Gore-Booth famously rejected the aristocratic society into which they were born, although, as Sonja Tiernan's analysis indicates, the philanthropic impulses of their parents had a stronger influence on their adult daughters' activities than has been hitherto recognised. Elizabeth, Lily and William Yeats also argued over the direction of the Cuala Press, with Lily opposing what she perceived as her brother's undermining of her role as the sole director of the press. The Yeats sisters also found it difficult to live together, and Lily eventually succumbed to illness under the constant strain of living and working so closely with her sibling. The Quaker framework within which the Shackleton family conducted their lives gave women many opportunities for participating in the public world of meetings and travelling ministries. Richard Shackleton was proud of his daughter Mary's literary skills, but both he and his wife Elizabeth were concerned that she spent too much time on her writing and not enough on her spiritual life. Even in later life, Mary smarted at the memory of her mother's disapproval of her literary pursuits.

Throughout the long time period covered by the essays in the volume, the family remained the predominant location for the imposition of patriarchal values. Richard Boyle, 1st earl of Cork, exercised a controlling influence over his adult children, partly because he was the source of much of his extended family's wealth. Ann-Maria Walsh's careful reading of the Boyle sisters' letters to their father reveals the tactics they used to work around his patriarchal assumptions. Almost three hundred years later, the woman-centred nature of the Sheehy household did not prevent David Sheehy from asserting his authority when he refused to welcome Hanna's husband to the family home because of the couple's decision not to baptise their son. David was also bitterly opposed to Kathleen's choice of agnostic Francis Cruise O'Brien as her husband. This paternal opposition led to family divisions and the estrangement of father and daughters. However, as Ashford reminds us, women too could hold a dominating role in the family, as she describes Katherine Conolly's tendency to critique and give unsolicited advice to her sisters.

Before the enfranchisement of women in 1918, philanthropic and charitable work was the most common means through which women entered into the public sphere. From the almsgiving of Máire Ní Domhnaill, through to the employment by Katherine Conolly of poor men to build a folly on the Castletown estate; the herbal cures provided to the poor by the Shackleton sisters; the assistance of Constance and Eva Gore-Booth to working-class men and women in Dublin and Manchester; and the training of girls in arts and craft work in Dun Emer, women's participation in assisting the less well-off sections of society remained the most acceptable form of public engagement that they could undertake. The chronological framework of the volume enables us to trace the gradual movement of women into a broader engagement with the public sphere. A key factor was the expansion of education for women. In the seventeenth century, Protestant families such as the Boyles and the Shackletons ensured that their daughters as well as their sons could read and write. In both families too, the girls developed literary interests that went beyond the reading of religious texts. As Walsh explains, Mary and Katherine Boyle both penned religious texts, and Mary kept a journal and wrote a memoir of her childhood. Writing for publication was, however, considered an unseemly public activity for women, and none of these writings were published during the sisters' lifetimes. By the eighteenth century, the figure of the published woman writer had become more acceptable, and Mary Shackleton Leadbeater and Sydney Owenson were the authors of commercially success-ful books. Both relished their public images as women writers, and both were also keen to conduct their own negotiations with publishers rather than doing so through a male intermediary. As Connolly documents, Owenson's novels also communicated a political awareness, and were recruited as part of the evolv-ing nationalist movement of early nineteenth-century Ireland. Through her writings, therefore, Owenson made an overt politi-cal contribution to the public sphere.

The establishment of the Ladies' Land League by the Parnell sisters marked another milestone in women's participation in public affairs. It was the first Irish political organisation to be founded and run by women. Not surprisingly, it drew condem-nation from Catholic clergy and other male authority figures. The League was an important training ground for Irish women, and left a legacy that historians are only beginning to explore. Stories of their aunt's work in the League must have made an impression on the Sheehy sisters when they were children. Hanna, Kathleen and Mary Sheehy also assisted in strengthen-ing the social acceptance of the woman politician. They success-fully advocated for women to be admitted to the youth branch of the United Ireland League (where all four sisters met their husbands); and were strong supporters of the suffrage campaign. The ultimate goal of a female member of parliament was achieved by Constance Markievicz in 1918, but prior to that date, her aristocratic background facilitated her entry into organisations that had not hitherto admitted women. In the post-suffrage era, Mary and Hanna Sheehy continued to expand women's political role. Mary was elected to Dublin City Council, and in 1928 she became its first female chair. Mary also joined Hanna in forming the first Irish political party established by women in 1938: the Women's Social and Progressive League.

The contributors to this volume utilised a variety of sources for their analyses. Many note the importance of letters as a means of communication between sisters, particularly in adulthood, when they were frequently living geographically apart. Some drew on poetry, memoirs and other literary works. A striking feature of all of these sources is how little they have been used by other scholars. Walsh is the first researcher to trawl through the extensive Boyle/Cork family archive and identify letters by women, while Ashford was the first to draw attention to the correspondence of the Conyngham sisters as a source for studying sibling relationships in an eighteenth-century Irish family. The vast archive of Quaker families in Ireland also remains virtually unexplored by historians, and O'Dowd's contribution points to its potential for studying Irish family relationships more generally. Other contributors have made use of more well-known sources, but the focus on sisters and sibling relations has resulted in a new analysis. Ó Macháin's forensic analysis of references in bardic poetry to the Ní Dhomhnaill sisters has resulted in an original study of the lives of three women who do not feature strongly in other sources. Similarly, Connolly's exploration of Sydney Owenson's published memoir and correspondence has revealed a great deal of new information about her sister Olivia and Sydney's relationship with her.

Family connections are complex, often loving and supportive, but also frequently stressful and disruptive. In this volume, there are stories of family rivalries; tensions between sisters; and siblings in agreement on engaging with the public world outside the home but disagreeing on how to do it. There are also stories of sisters who remained loyal to one another throughout their lives, who tolerated each other's differences, recognising that sibling bonds are for life. Despite the central role of the family in Irish society, historians have not explored the history of sibling relationships, nor have they been a major theme in literary studies. We hope that this collection of essays will, therefore, inspire the reader to look again at the importance of family bonds in the lives of the women who feature in it.[1]

The volume originated as a series of lunchtime lectures hosted by the Royal Irish Academy Library between 2019 and 2022. The talks formed part of the Academy's celebration of the centenary of the granting of the parliamentary vote to women in Ireland in 1918 and the subsequent Sex Disqualification (Removal) Act (1919). The enfranchisement of women and the removal of gender barriers for entry to many professions were, of course, significant milestones in the history of women in Ireland, richly deserving of commemoration. The aim of the Academy's lecture series was, however, to demonstrate that the new legislation did not mark the beginning of women's engagement with public life. Rather, as all the contributors document in different ways, it was the culmination of a long history of women breaking through the legal, political and social restrictions imposed on their lives, making their mark on Irish life.

SIOBHÁN FITZPATRICK AND MARY O'DOWD
16 MARCH 2022

---

[1] Shannon Devlin has recently completed a thesis in Queen's University Belfast entitled 'Sibling relations in Protestant middle-class Ulster families, 1850–1900'.

Nualaidh and her sisters, Máire and Mairghréad: the daughters of Aodh Ó Domhnaill and An Inghean Dubh

Pádraig Ó Macháin

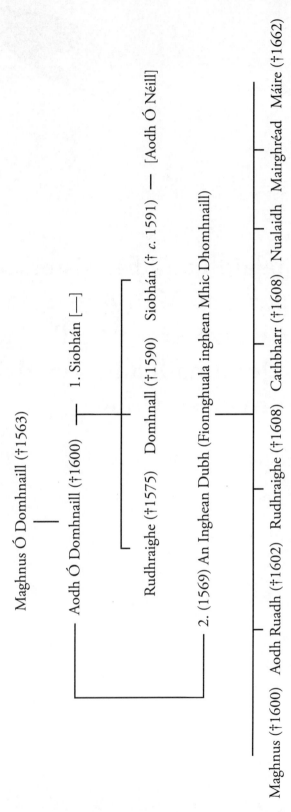

Maghnus Ó Domhnaill (†1563)

Aodh Ó Domhnaill (†1600) ———— 1. Siobhán [—]

Rudhraighe (†1575)   Domhnall (†1590)   Siobhán († *c.* 1591) — [Aodh Ó Néill]

2. (1569) An Inghean Dubh (Fionnghuala inghean Mhic Dhomhnaill)

Maghnus (†1600)   Aodh Ruadh (†1602)   Rudhraighe (†1608)   Cathbharr (†1608)   Nualaidh   Mairghréad   Máire (†1662)

'The Flight of the Earls'

Nualaidh, Máire and Mairghréad were the daughters of Aodh (son of Maghnus) Ó Domhnaill and Fionnghuala inghean Mhic Dhomhnaill.[1] They had four brothers: Aodh Ruadh, who succeeded his father as head of the Í Dhomhnaill (O'Donnells) and died in Spain in 1602; Rudhraighe, earl of Tyrconnell (d. 1608 in Italy), who succeeded Aodh Ruadh; Cathbharr, who also died in Italy in 1608, and Maghnus. Maghnus had been slain in battle in 1600 by his cousin and brother-in-law, Niall Garbh Ó Domhnaill. Two of the sisters, Nualaidh and Mairghréad, also died abroad, probably in the late 1620s, and are buried in the chapel of St Anthony's College, Louvain, in what was then Spanish Flanders. The third sister, Máire, remained in Ireland and died in Mayo at an old age in 1662.

Primary evidence for the sisters' story is to be found, mainly but not exclusively, in some of the last formal bardic poetry to be composed by Irish poets. Bardic poetry was an elite art form practised in late medieval Ireland from the second half of the twelfth century until it went into decline in the seventeenth century. This poetry was used to praise, to honour, to advise and sometimes to caution or censure members of the Irish nobility. Many such poems also survive that were composed on moral and religious themes and in praise of God. Bardic poems, secular and religious, are distinguished by the intricate syllabic metres (as opposed to rhythmical metres based on beats to the line) in which they were composed. As compositions, the poems were built up as one might a painting or a symphony, and took a long time to assemble, to compose and to polish. For the secular poems at least, and probably also for much of the religious poetry, the poets expected to be rewarded. The high achievers among them were wealthy, distinguished, professional artists, possessed of property and status. Towards the close of the sixteenth century, just as this poetry was enjoying a period of strong growth, the Elizabethan conquest began to tear away at the roots of Gaelic society and erode the supports upon which the aristocratic arts depended. As this accelerated into the early years of the seventeenth century, a sense of common cause began to feature in some of the poetry. From this, new themes emerged that displayed the ability of the poets to use poetry to confront their new situation and to use their art to give voice to matters that were suddenly of concern to all.

This situation continued into the Jacobean era, and one event in particular seems to have crystallised and concentrated the efforts of some of the last of the bardic poets in the northern half of the country: the so-called 'Flight of the Earls'. Today we recognise this event as the watershed that it was, and we group it with the Battle of Kinsale and the Plantation of Ulster in a cluster of seminal events in the first decade of the seventeenth century. Unusually for something viewed in retrospect, the departure of the earls of Tyrone and Tyrconnell was recognised and recorded even in its own time, in the poetry especially, as a traumatic event. No doubt the reason for this was the sudden departure of the three strongest rulers in the north, heads of the three main families who, up to that point, had been equally outstanding in their resistance to conquest and in their sponsorship of bardic poetry and native learning in general: the Í Dhomhnaill, the Í Néill and the Clann Uidhir.

The 'Flight' is an event for which a number of physical symbols survive – in Ireland and on the continent – as memorials of its history and of the dramatis personae involved. From the aspect of the literature of the 'Flight', the most important survival is the contemporary account in Irish of the journey from Rathmullan to Rome that was undertaken by the chieftains and their retinues in September 1607 and completed in 1608. This eyewitness account of the journey was written by Aodh Ó Néill's secretary, Tadhg Ó Cianáin, and it follows the style of contemporary travel itineraries.[2] It was written in Rome in 1609, and most of it is a retrospective recording of what the writer presents as Ó Néill's triumphant progress to Rome. It is much more than that, however, and one of the most moving parts of the narrative is where Ó Cianáin recounts the death by fever in the autumn of 1608 of some of the most prominent members of the party who had left Donegal the previous year: Rudhraighe Ó Domhnaill (28/29 July 1608), his brother Cathbharr (15 September) and

Cú Chonnacht Mág Uidhir (12 August). Mág Uidhir was buried with the Franciscans in Genoa, where he died, and the two Ó Domhnaill brothers were buried in Rome, in the church of San Pietro in Montorio, where Ó Néill himself would be buried eight years later.

Ó Cianáin makes his own observation on this litany of death:

> Is inmesta immorro nach don degh-fhortún nó don degh-chinnemain iss ferr tárraidh Éire an aurdail sin do degh-roignib mhac Míledh Espáinne d'foghbháil bháiss go hobann diaigh a ndiaigh a n-echtar-chrích imchéin ainiúil a gcoimhfhégmhuiss a n-atharrdha bunaid badhdéin.

> *It may well be believed that it was not through good fortune or the best of fate that it happened to Ireland that so many of the choicest of the descendants of Míl Easpáinne died suddenly, one after another, in a foreign and strange land, far removed from their own native soil.*[3]

This epitaph, by a contemporary witness in Rome – who himself would be buried in San Pietro on 24 September 1610[4] – forms the frame for our consideration of the sisters. Upon the deaths of Rudhraighe and Cathbharr the three sisters were all that remained of Aodh and An Inghean Dubh's children.

The sisters came from a line of distinguished patrons of the arts. Their grandfather Maghnus Ó Domhnaill is best remembered in the scholarly tradition as a patron of poets, as a composer of light verse, and most famously as the deviser and creator of a new biography of Colum Cille in 1532. His son Aodh, father of Nualaidh and her sisters, was chief of his name from 1566 to 1592. Like his father before him, he too was a 'staunch patron of learning',[5] with many extant poems addressed to him by well-known poets. It may also be observed that, in addition to the three sisters in question here, this branch of the ruling line of the Í Dhomhnaill gives us a glimpse of some of the other remarkable women of contemporary Gaelic Ireland: An Inghean Dubh (Fionnghuala, daughter of Séamus Mac Domhnaill of Islay) for example, who effectively ruled Tír Conaill before Aodh Ruadh was able to take over from his father, and of whom Aodh Ruadh's biographer said that though she was 'much praised for her womanly qualities, she had the heart of a hero and the mind of a soldier';[6] or Cathbharr's wife and widow, Róise Ní Dhochartaigh, daughter of Seaán Óg Ó Dochartaigh of Inishowen, a woman who was one of the central figures of what was effectively the Irish court in exile at Louvain.[7]

Address to Máire and Mairghréad

We first encounter the sisters in a poem composed after their brothers' deaths in Rome. The poem is addressed to Máire and Mairghréad, the two who remained in Ireland after the third sister, Nualaidh, had left with the earls in 1607. It was composed by one of the most famous bardic poets of that era, Donegal poet Fearghal Óg Mac an Bhaird, who had enjoyed the patronage of the Í Dhomhnaill all his life, as well as patronage from many other noble families around Ireland. In many respects, the story of this poet embodies the experience of the time, as he himself would leave Ireland for Louvain some years later.[8]

This poem, which begins *Truagh liom Máire agas Mairghréag* ('I pity Mary and Margaret') is, by bardic standards, a brief one of only fifteen verses.[9] Despite this brevity, the poet is able to capture the situation, not just of the two sisters left in Ireland, but also of Nualaidh – then in Rome – and, in addition, he is able to lament the demise of the Í Dhomhnaill and to hint at the demise of Gaelic Ireland as a consequence. That is quite a lot to encompass in fifteen verses, yet the poet does so with great skill. The opening two verses and the closing four concern Máire and Mairghréad, and the nine verses in between talk about their four dead brothers, and also their sister Nualaidh in Italy. The poet says that she might as well be dead, but that her fame will live forever among the Irish. It is as if Fearghal Óg assumes that Nualaidh will never be heard of again, or that she has not long to live in solitude and grief in Italy.

San Eadáill na n-eas dtana,
ionann is éag Nualadha,
atá géis chnómhoighe Chuinn,
cróluighe dhá héis oruinn.

In Italy of the gentle waterfalls
is the swan of the fruitful plain of Conn –
it is the same as Nualaidh being dead –
we are debilitated without her.

Nualaidh dhuaislíonmhar, dóigh cháich,
mairfidh go laithe an luanbhráith,
tosach garma chrú gCriomhthain,
clú a hanma idir Éirionnchaibh.

Generous Nualaidh, hope of all,
first in line of the stock of Criomhthan,
her fame will live among the Irish
until the Day of Judgement.

To form an idea of what is being said to the two other sisters, we can read the opening and closing verses together:

1. Truagh liom Máire agas Mairghréag,
ní beó bláth na n-umhailghéag:
do chuir siad a nduilli dhíobh,
dá bhuime iad don imshníomh.

I pity Mary and Margaret:
the blossom has died from the drooping branches,
they have shed their leaves,
they are two wet-nurses to grief.

2. Far-íor, far-íor, nochan fhuil
braon 'na gcroidhibh ón chumhaidh:
dá sheisi shuadh fhóid Uladh,
truagh mar táid ar dtiormughadh.

Alas, alas, mourning has left
no drop in their hearts,
a pity how they have run dry,
the two patrons of the Ulster poets.

12. Iongnadh Máire do mharthain,
's na haibhne nach ionarthroigh,
is fiodhbhaidh chríon chraoi Uisnigh
do shíor ag caoi an cheathrair-sin.

A wonder Mary still lives
when the swollen rivers
and the withered trees of Uisneach's land
forever keen those four [brothers].

13. Ní filltear fiodhradh abhla
le hubhlaibh feadh fionnBhanbha,
ná fiodhradh chaillghéag le cnoibh,
iongnadh Mairghréag do mharthain.

A wonder Margaret still lives,
when throughout Ireland
no apple-trees bend with fruit
nor hazel trees with nuts.

14. Ní hí Mairghréag ná Máire
chaoinim, is cúis diombáighe,
acht an cor-sa ar cró na bhFionn,
mó sa mhó osna Éirionn.

Regrettably, it is not Margaret and Mary
I lament but the state the country is in:
the sighing of Ireland grows louder and louder.

15. A gceithre dearbhbhráithre ar ndol,
Máire is Mairghréag mhúir Chruachan,
cosg ag dol do shíor ar shuan,
a gcor fa-ríor is rothruagh.

With the death of their four blood-brothers,
Mary and Margaret of Cruacha
can never rest,
alas their plight is very pitiful.

Reading these six verses as a unit, we get an idea of the depth of feeling in the poem. Such is the weight of learning and formality in the style and language of bardic poetry that it is often difficult to get beyond that structural façade to appreciate the emotions that lie behind it. In this case, however, by collapsing the verses in the central section of the poem we sense the intensity of the loss that the poet himself feels, and how the case of the two sisters is interpreted as a microcosm of the state of Ireland after its most powerful leaders have left and died. The very conventionality of the language enables the poet to portray the two sisters in a startling way, as two women who have lost everything, who are drained of blood and who yet can never rest. They are the walking dead. Describing them in the opening verses as trees without flower or foliage links them to the withered state of the country in the closing verses, where the connection between land and people is made overt. This sense of connection between the barren and the bereft comes together in the remarkable image of the two drained women who suckle only grief, dehumanised by the sudden deaths of their brothers, and representing, in that condition, the state of Gaelic Ireland as a whole.

This poem is of course a work of art existing within its own parameters. Nevertheless, in the absence of a body of joined-up historical detail regarding the sisters, the poetic record takes on an added value for us today. A further consideration, as previously noted, is the fact that these poems were created in the expectation of patronage. Therefore we can infer that Máire and Mairghréad were still women of status, possessed of the wherewithal to reward the poet for his composition.

Máire: patron and lone survivor

We get an idea of the substance of one of the sisters – Máire – from a relic of a different type that survives from about ten years after the poem was composed (see picture section). This is a chalice that she had commissioned in memory of her husband, the chief of the Í Ruairc of west-Bréifne, County Leitrim today.[10] He was Tadhg Ó Ruairc, who had been successful in a struggle with his brother Brian before taking the chieftainship. Máire married him in 1599, and in March 1605, aged 27, he died of bladder disease and was buried in Craobh Liath, the Franciscan friary at Dromahair. The same poet who composed the address to the two sisters – Fearghal Óg Mac an Bhaird – also created a long elegy of 55 verses on Tadhg, no doubt under Máire's patronage.[11]

By 1619, when the chalice was made, the Franciscan community at Dromahair had been forced out of the friary, but, occupying accommodation nearby, they were enabled to maintain their presence there.[12] We can regard the creation and donation of this item of church plate as a form of sponsorship of religious orders that was not unusual and that paralleled the sponsorship of poets in the secular world. It is remarkable that this artefact has survived. The chalice is relatively plain, with a depiction of the crucifixion on one of the lower panels, and along the perimeter of the base an inscription that informs us that it was made for the monastery of Craobh Liath by Máire Ní Dhomhnaill, in memory of her husband Tadhg Ó Ruairc in 1619.[13]

The following year Máire, now known as Lady O'Rourke, received 1,600 acres of arable land in Dromahair barony, together with 3,411 acres of bog and mountain, under the plantation of Leitrim; by 1641 the arable land had increased to 2,400 acres.[14] Máire was also in receipt of a government pension of £100.[15] She was therefore a woman of some substance. She also formed a new marriage alliance, marrying a grandson of yet another formidable woman, Gráinne Ní Mháille. He was Daibhíth Búrc (d. 1677), son of Tiobóid na Long of the Clann Uilliam (Mac William Burkes) of Mayo.[16] At the time of her death in 1662, Máire was living on the Búrc holding near Manulla, County Mayo.

Máire's patronage of poetry and her connection to events on the continent were not over. Another poem of consolation addressed to her survives in the invaluable collection of bardic poetry compiled in the early eighteenth century for the Ó Domhnaill family of Larkfield, County Leitrim, descendants of Niall Garbh's brother, Aodh Buidhe.[17] This poem of 27 verses begins *Tinn liom do mhaoith, a Mháire* ('Painful to me, Máire, is your grief'), and was composed by another Mac an Bhaird poet, Uilliam Óg.[18] The subject of the poem is the death, around the year 1629, of Aodh Ó Domhnaill, aged in his early twenties. He was Máire's nephew, son of her late brother Cathbharr and Róise Ní Dhochartaigh. Aodh had been two and a half at the time of the departure in 1607, and following the tragic deaths in Rome great hope had been placed in the next generation represented by him and by his first cousin Aodh son of Rudhraighe.

The poem is not a lament for Aodh mac Cathbhairr. As stated in the heading to the poem in the unique manuscript copy, it laments the grief and sadness of the daughter of Ó Domhnaill (*ag eccaoine tuirsi agus dobroin inghine Ui Dhomhnuill*), when Máire was the only offspring of Aodh mac Maghnusa and An Inghean Dubh now left in Ireland. The theme is that Máire had only just recovered from the deaths of her brothers when those wounds were reopened by the news of the death of her nephew; this news will now be the final blow and the death of her.

> Rug oraibh go nua a-nosa,
> i dtráth fhuaraidh th'orchrosa,
> sgéal dá sgoiltear do chroidhe,
> fréamh ó n-oiltear th'eólchoire

> *Now, when [the fire] of your suffering was cooling,*
> *you have been overtaken anew*
> *by news that breaks your heart,*
> *a root that feeds your lamentation.*

> Cloch fhaobhair dod thuirsi truim
> oidhidh Aodha meic Cathbhairr
> sí 'na cneidh i gceann guine,
> ag sein earr bhar n-eólchuire.

The death of Aodh son of Cathbharr
is a whetstone for your great sorrow,
it is a wound on top of a wound,
there is the nadir of your lamentation.

Máire is represented as driven to distraction, so that she cuts a solitary figure in Ireland.

Uch as ionganta iná sin –
acht fíorghrása Dé dúiligh –
leith do chéille ar do chumus
gé bheith Éire ar t'fhearannus.

Alas, it is more surprising still –
were it not for the true grace of God of creation –
that you are in possession of half your senses
though all of Ireland were yours.

Fríoth i bhfogus dá chéile
iomad n-adhbhar neimhchéille
led dhreich maithmhigh dtláithghil dtinn
nach táirthir th'aithghin d'Éirinn.

Your forgiving, strong face, soft and bright,
has received in quick succession many a reason for insanity,
to the extent that there is
no one like you in Ireland.

This death blow to Máire from the loss of her siblings and her nephew means that whatever benefit she might have been to the country as the last survivor in Ireland of her branch of the Í Dhomhnaill will now be lost. The poem shares with *Truagh liom Máire agas Mairghréag* the theme of devastation and insufferable loss. Composed roughly twenty years after that poem, an additional element in this poem is a sense of pessimism, and a suggestion of criticism directed at Máire's deceased siblings. The author claims that her nephew may not be lamented for his noble lineage – an expected component in any elegy – because of God's displeasure with the Í Dhomhnaill. He may, however, be praised for his personal characteristics (*as a airrdheanaibh*), and so the poet accords him an almost backhanded, two-verse enumeration of his gentlemanly qualities: wisdom, martial skills, learning, charity, eloquence, manliness and courtliness.

The implicit criticism of the Í Domhnaill reappears later in the poem, where reference is made to their transgressions as being due to the exuberance of youth, the 'sins of fate' (*cionta cinneamhna*); that is, that the outcome of their actions – the loss of leadership and the confiscation of lands in Tír Conaill – had not been contemplated or intended by them. The theme of the misfortunes of the Irish being the result of God's displeasure with them for their sins was one that was developing at the time.[19] One has to think that the theme would not have been included in the poem were not Máire receptive to it in some way.

In the end, the only thing preserving Máire from lasting despair is the consolation of religion – *acht tú ar aithne an uird chrábhaidh* 'were it not for your acquaintance with the religious order'. This association of Máire with religious orders connects with her sponsorship of the Dromahair chalice, and with further references to her charitable deeds in her elegy, which will be discussed below. The representation of Máire as the lone survivor of the Aodh mac Maghnusa branch is another point of difference between this poem and the earlier *Truagh liom Máire agas Mairghréag*. Mairghréad features no further in the surviving poetic record of the time. Her fate was in contrast to that of Máire: while Máire prospered, the historic record suggests that Mairghréad did not.[20] Furthermore, Mairghréad had been more deeply invested in the departure of the earls, in that not only were two of her siblings on board, but also two of her sons. A third son, the youngest, Conn, then ten years old, would be helped to escape from Ireland by Mairghréad in 1616.[21] Mairghréad's husband, Cormac (Mac an Bharúin) Ó Néill, was brother of the earl of Tyrone, and had been arrested in the immediate aftermath of the departure of his brother from Rathmullan in 1607. He was sent to the Tower of London, whence he was never to return. From the Tower in 1611 he petitioned the Privy Council to provide assistance to his wife and children, whom he described as being in a state of destitution. English officials visiting her residence at Augher Castle in south Tyrone reported that she had to scavenge to provide provisions for them, as she had no 'bread, drink, meat nor linen to welcome them'.[22] Her reported condition was in contrast to the fate of her sister Máire, as we have seen. We do not know when her husband Cormac died, but we might assume that he had died by 1622, when Mairghréad eventually left Ireland to join the third sister, Nualaidh, in Louvain.[23]

Poems addressed to Nualaidh

Nualaidh's relation with Irish literature is deeper and more varied than that of her two sisters. For instance, we know that among her acquaintances in exile was an Irish poet who had made the journey with the Irish party in 1607. This poet may even have been in the mind of the author of *Tinn liom do mhaoith a Mháire* when referring obliquely to the desertion of Tír Conaill, for among the 99 who left Rathmullan on 14 September 1607 was Uilliam Óg's brother, Eóghan Ruadh Mac an Bhaird, one of the finest poets of the era.[24] There are three main points that emerge about Eóghan Ruadh from the surviving records: one was his dissatisfaction with the leader of the Í Dhomhnaill at the time, the earl of Tyrconnell, Rudhraighe Ó Domhnaill, brother of the three sisters being discussed here; the second was how Eóghan Ruadh prospered in exile; and the third was his attachment to Nualaidh, which may have been the reason for his leaving Ireland.[25]

Nualaidh, named after her mother, was probably the eldest of the sisters. She had been married to her cousin, Niall Garbh Ó Domhnaill, but had become estranged from him around 1600 after he killed her brother, Maghnus, an event that was interpreted as having hastened the death of their father, Aodh mac Maghnusa, shortly afterwards.[26] Niall Garbh's enmity towards Nualaidh's side of the family had been inherited from his father, Conn mac an Chalbhaigh, and so his turning openly against

Nualaidh's brother, Aodh Ruadh, was not necessarily the impulsive act of treachery in which terms it has often been portrayed,[27] but rather, in O'Donovan's words, the act of 'the excluded chief seeking to recover his ancient birthright'.[28] Nevertheless, Nualaidh returned to her immediate family, and was on board the ship that left Rathmullan in September 1607. She journeyed with the Irish party from Louvain to Rome in 1608, arriving there at the end of April. Within five months her two brothers, Rudhraighe and Cathbharr, aged 32 and 24 respectively,[29] were buried in the church of San Pietro. Rudhraighe's funeral was paid for by Philip III of Spain, and in the aftermath of the funeral the Spanish ambassador in Rome wrote to the king that Nualaidh and Cathbharr (who would die in September) 'were in great want and should perish' if not given money.[30] Two years later, in 1611, Nualaidh was permitted to return to Louvain, on condition that none of the Irish in Rome be allowed to accompany her.[31] She would remain in Louvain for the rest of her life.

It was in Louvain that the most impressive of her literary relics was created, a manuscript written for her and entitled 'Leabhar Inghine Í Dhomhnaill' ('the Book of O'Donnell's Daughter').[32] This title is found three times on the front cover, and once inside the back cover. The daughter of Ó Domhnaill, without any doubt, is Nualaidh. While other hands contribute material to the manuscript later on, at the outset it is written in a beautiful, formal, well-practised hand, in such a way that the purpose reveals itself as we read through the poems in this section. This is a *duanaire*, a poetry anthology and family dossier dedicated to the Í Dhomhnaill of a type with which we are familiar in respect of other families, and the later addition to the book of the prose origin-legend of their remote ancestor, Conall Gulban, emphasises this. There is an additional aspect to the book, however, in that it has the status of an act of memorialisation, more than any family house-book of the earlier vellum era. It is in the material written in the primary hand in the opening gatherings of the book that we detect this memorial element, which imparts to the manuscript an elegiac tone.

In any Gaelic manuscript that has survived intact, the opening text is always significant as expressing the scribe's intent at the beginning of the project. In this case the manuscript opens with a poem by Fearghal Óg Mac an Bhaird, who had composed the poem for Máire and Mairghréad discussed earlier. This opening poem is a full-blown bardic elegy on Aodh Ruadh Ó Domhnaill, who left for Spain after the Battle of Kinsale – thus creating a precedent for the 'Flight' in 1607 – and died there in 1602 at the age of 30. The positioning on the first page of the manuscript of the lament for Aodh Ruadh, eldest of the brothers, has a funerary aspect to it, recalling the inclusion of his name on the grave-slab in the church of San Pietro, even though he was buried in Valladolid. It is a reminder that the reversal in fortunes of Nualaidh and her family began in exile – not in Flanders or Rome, but in Spain itself. As the opening line of this poem says, *Teasda Éire san Easbáinn*, 'Ireland has died in Spain'.[33]

This opening poem is followed by two poems addressed to Aodh Ruadh's brother and successor, Rudhraighe, and these are followed by Fearghal Óg's address to Nualaidh's sisters, Máire and Mairghréad, *Truagh liom Máire agas Mairghréag*. We may wonder at what Nualaidh's reaction must have been to seeing herself mentioned in this poem; in truth there are many items in this book that must have resonated with her. In the opening nine leaves, the scribe has assembled material that memorialises, in one way or another, all of the children of Aodh mac Maghnusa and An Inghean Dubh. This comprehensiveness is continued through the inclusion of further poems on Aodh Ruadh and Rudhraighe; on their father Aodh mac Maghnusa;[34] on Nualaidh's nephew, Aodh son of Rudhraighe Ó Domhnaill,[35] whom she reared in Louvain; on her first cousin, Séamus Mac Domhnaill;[36] and on her estranged husband, Niall Garbh, and their son, Neachtain Ó Domhnaill, in prison in London.[37] And if we wonder at her reaction to the mention of herself in the poem to Máire and Mairghréad, what are we to make of the inclusion of the poem to her husband (*A bhráighe atá i dTor Lunndan* 'Prisoner in the Tower of London'), in which the poet claims that either God or King James will have him released? What, again, must her reaction have been to the verses at the end of that poem that were addressed to herself?

Mó an príosún fós ina bhfuil
inghean ríogh fhréimhe Dálaigh
a bhfuilnge ag crádh a cridhe
doilghe dál a daoirsine.

Greater still the prison
in which lies the daughter of the king of the Í Dhomhnaill;
all that you [sc. Niall Garbh] suffer torments her heart:
her captivity is more grievous

Dá mbeith nach biadh do dhochar
do chách uile it iarnochadh
acht an brón ina mbí soin
do budh mór an ní a-nalloin.

Even if your fettering caused no harm
to anyone other than
the sorrow that she feels,
it would still be a terrible thing.

Ní hionann tuirrse is tuirrse,
ní grádh grádh 'na fochairse,
ní himneadh as doghrainn dí
inghean Í Dhomhnaill Daoile.[38]

Not all sorrow is the same,
love is not the love that she feels,
no [ordinary] anxiety distresses her,
the daughter of Ó Domhnaill from the Deel.

As with the sentiments addressed to Máire in *Tinn liom do mhaoith*, we must assume that Nualaidh was receptive to this poem on Niall Garbh, and to the picture of herself paralysed by anxiety for her imprisoned husband. If so, the poem adds to the complex of evidence on which the career of Niall Garbh must be interpreted. The author of that poem was Eóghan Ruadh Mac an Bhaird, who, as already mentioned, was on the ship that left Rathmullan in 1607, and it would seem that he was an especial confidant of Nualaidh. He is also the poet with the most items in this manuscript, and it has been shown that his handwriting is also present in the book.[39] This book brings us closer than any other surviving *duanaire* to a view of the poet–patron relationship.

The culmination of the *speculum* effect of the references to herself in Nualaidh's manuscript must have been one of its most famous poems, that beginning *A bhean fuair faill ar an bhfeart* 'Woman who found the grave unattended', which was again composed by Eóghan Ruadh.[40] It depicts Nualaidh mourning alone at the graves of her two brothers in the church of San Pietro. The poet says that, had those in the graves died in Ireland, Nualaidh would not be alone in her mourning, but rather keening women would come from all over the country; and were San Pietro itself located in Ireland, the hill would be flattened by the number of horses that would assemble there for the funeral.

The opening of the poem is orchestral in its structure, alternately occupied with quiet and commotion. After establishing this dramatic, rhetorical setting, Eóghan Ruadh follows the traditional elegiac route of recording the genealogical affiliations of those being lamented, and of registering some of their martial victories. This serves to remind us of the reality behind the rhetoric, and underpinning this reality is the setting of the graves in the church of San Pietro, the earliest reference, certainly in Irish, to the two stones and their inscriptions.

> An dá chloichsin ósa gcionn
> dá bhfaicdís ógbhuidh Éirionn,
> ar aoi a líneadh do léaghadh
> caoi ar míleadh do mhoisgéaladh.

> *Did the fighting men of Éire*
> *see those two stones above (the grave),*
> *the reading of their lines*
> *would awaken the grief of our soldiers.*

The occupants of the graves beneath the stones are identified as Nualaidh's brothers Rudhraighe and Cathbharr, and, as the poet puts it, Nualaidh's father's grandson, Aodh Ó Néill, who was son of Siobhán, Nualaidh's half-sister by Aodh mac Maghnusa's first marriage. Had any of these died in one of their many martial engagements back in Ireland, their death would not have been treated with indifference: 'what Gael would not lament with you the flower of the race of Míleadh?'

Having discharged these traditional elegiac duties, the poet returns to the other reality of the poem, that of Nualaidh's isolation, hinted at in the Spanish ambassador's letter referred to earlier. She had been spared the disaster that overcame the Irish party in Rome, what Mac an Bhaird describes as the *loingbhriseadh* ('shipwreck'). Among the early metaphorical uses of this term was that describing the fall of the angels, and it carries some of that connotation here.[41] The poet also employs the word in a cleverly semi-literal sense, as he references implicitly the perilous journey of the earls and their retinues from Ireland to Spain a year earlier, when they were forced to change their plans by seeking refuge from a storm on the coast of Normandy. The figurative *loingbhriseadh* that occurred in Rome a year later was therefore a delayed shipwreck, and one that was caused by Divine providence:

> A ríoghan fhréimhe Dáluigh,
> tánuig ón tuinn iombádhuigh,
> nach rabh ní as sia a fherg ret' fhuil
> fagh ó Dhia, an Ceard rod chruthuigh.

> *O Queen of the O'Donnells,*
> *who escaped the drowning wave,*
> *implore God, the Creator who made you,*
> *that His anger should no longer be directed against*
> *your people.*

This is the only hint in the poem of God's anger towards the Í Dhomhnaill. It occurs in the penultimate verse, where the poet encourages Nualaidh to cast off her grief and seek the consolation of religion. This recalls *Tinn liom do mhaoith a Mháire*, the poem that was composed for Nualaidh's sister Máire some twenty years later by Eóghan Ruadh's brother Uilliam Óg. In the final verse of that poem, Eóghan Ruadh's *A bhean fuair faill* is referenced explicitly. It may be that in articulating God's displeasure with the Í Dhomhnaill, Uilliam Óg is taking this fragile hint in his brother's poem and developing it in a deliberate and powerful way.[42]

Nualaidh returned from Rome to Louvain in late 1611, and there she took over the tutelage of her nephew, Aodh mac Rudhraighe, who was now the titular earl of Tyrconnell.[43] It would appear that she remained in this role of tutor until her pupil left Louvain for Spanish service, returning again in 1621 to attend the university.[44] Thereafter, Nualaidh fades from view, appearing only sporadically in the record. We know that in 1627 Flaithrí Ó Maoil Chonaire, archbishop of Tuam in exile, was making representations for her with the Spanish king regarding her pension, and that seems to be the last known date for her.[45] We know that Mairghréad joined Nualaidh in Louvain around 1622, and there she fades from view also. The coincidence of the two sisters in exile while their husbands lay incarcerated in the Tower of London adds to the drama of a story that was already full of drama. Were it not for an entry on the flyleaf of another of the Louvain manuscripts preserved in the Royal Library in Brussels, we would not know that Mairghréad and Nualaidh were buried with their nephew Aodh son of Cathbharr on the gospel side of the high altar in the chapel of the College of St Anthony Louvain.[46] Róise Ní Dhochartaigh was laid with them on her death in 1660, and an inscribed stone commemorated herself and her son Aodh.[47] As a memorial to Nualaidh, to Mairghréad and to all the others involved in the calamitous aftermath of the departure of the earls, Nualaidh's manuscript of poetry is as fitting and as eloquent a monument as any tombstone.

Death of Máire

The only sister of the three whose date of death is known for certain is Máire. It will be recalled that she was a woman of substance, the only one of the sisters to remain in Ireland, and also the only one, as far as we know, to marry more than once. With her sisters she shared the pain of the knowledge of a family member confined in the Tower of London, where her son Brian ended his days in 1641.[48]

The final poem to be considered here is an elegy of 42 verses that was composed on Máire's death on the eve of the Feast of the Assumption, 1662.[49] The author was Cúchoigríche Ó Cléirigh, one of the Four Masters. Máire and her sister Mairghréad had been the recipients in 1608 of the earliest of the poems discussed here, a poem that lamented the deaths of their four brothers. With this elegy on Máire over 50 years later, matters were brought full circle, as her death marked the end not just of the children of Aodh mac Maghnusa and An Inghean Dubh but of all the children of Aodh mac Maghnusa inclusive of the three by his previous marriage.[50] The poem begins *Ní deireadh leóin do Leath Chuinn* ('The sorrow of the North is not over'). It survives in the Larkfield *duanaire*, and is as yet unpublished.[51]

The poem consists of two well-defined sections. The first half laments the demise of all the offspring of 'Aodh mac Maghnais mheic Aodha'. This demise is characterised by Ó Cléirigh as *díth deirbhfhine*, using a refined definition of the ancient four-generation kinship group to signify merely the family of Aodh Ó Domhnaill.[52] The poet first places this loss in the context of the decline of the northern families in general, and then enumerates the individuals involved:

> Aodh mac Maghnais meic Aodha
> or fhásadar úrchraobha
> ba croinn far ghnáth glóir gach tan
> snir dhóigh le cách a ccríonadh.

> *Aodh son of Maghnas son of Aodh,*
> *from whom new branches sprang;*
> *trees they were adorned always with glory,*
> *and no one ever thought that they would wither.*

> Clann fhear ardfhlatha Doire
> Aodh Ruadh rathmhar Rudhraidhe
> Mághnus is Cathbharr crádh linn
> rachlann ar ágh dob inghill.

The sons of the high prince of Derry
were prosperous Aodh Ruadh, Rudhraighe,
Maghnus and Cathbharr, whom we lament:
great sons supreme in war.

Clann oile do ghein on ghéig
do rigfidhe a leas a leithéid
conghlonn fa rúnghloine rath
Rúdhraidhe is Domhnoll diormach.

Other sons, whose kind would be needed,
sprang from the branch,
a pair whose success was clear and determined:
Rudhraighe and Domhnall of the battalions.

Siobhán chaithmheach do thuill toil
Contaois thréan thire heóghain
do bhuadhaigh gach báire an tréd
Núala, Máire agus Mairghréd.

Generous Siobhán who earned love,
mighty Countess of Tír Eóghain;
Nualaidh, Máire and Mairghréad,
a group that won every contest.

Only of Máire and her father could it have been said that they
lived very long lives.

Ionann do ghoir Día diobh soin
an tóg aobhdha is an társoidh
dream or síoladh gach méin mhaith
an Rioghain réidh, an Righfhlaith.

Of those, God summoned equally
the fair youth and the old man —
people from whom every good quality had been expected —
the mild queen and the prince.

Apart from references to the demise of the Í Dhomhnaill and of the Irish nobility being God's will, the author of this poem makes no attempt to apportion blame for the downfall. Instead, the second part of the poem is devoted entirely to elegising and eulogising Máire. He praises her gentleness (*réidhe*) and her intelligence (*ciall*), but it is her charity (*daonnacht*) that is his main focus, her discreet almsgiving in particular, and he references Matthew 6:3–4 as her inspiration.[53]

Do thuig tra agus tug da húidh
briathra beannaighthe an sgriobhtúir
is nir dhior tarsa a tobhach
biodh bhar nalmsa in ionfholach.

She understood and paid heed
to the blessed words of scripture:
'let your alms-giving be in secret';
and to censure her for them would be unjust.

Aingeal na láimhe clí cuil
beith da réir riamh nir aontuigh
Aingeal na deisi o dia ale
ba seisi gach dia dise

She did not give in to the will
of the angel on the left hand,
but she was devoted daily
to the angel of the right sent by God.

Do sgaoil go measardha a maoin
sni thug grádh don ghloir dhiomhaoin
leis an láimh chlí do ba chrádh
gach ní dar dháil a deaslámh

She spent her wealth in moderation,
and loved not vainglory:
a torment to the left hand
was everything the right hand dispensed.

Her almsgiving was practised during her time with Tadhg Ó Ruairc, and continued afterwards in Daibhíth Búrc's time.[54] Just as the other poems we have been discussing are located in their respective historical realities, the picture painted by Ó Cléirigh here of the people aided by Máire's charity is probably reflective of the reality of displacement and impoverishment caused by confiscation, plantation and by the Confederate and Cromwellian campaigns.

> Iomdha fear le a bhfríth a crodh
> iomdha bean fhíorbhocht uasol
> sdob iomdha seanóir gan sén,
> iomdha dearoil is deiblén

> *Many the man who received her wealth,*
> *many the impoverished noble woman,*
> *and many the unfortunate old person,*
> *many the wretch and pauper.*

> Na mná bochta baoi gan chuid
> dob isi a ccrodh sa ccaruid
> snir cheard bhaoísi acht bladh da rath
> don mhnaoisi car le a ccúmhdach.

> *The poor women with nothing,*
> *she was their sustenance and their friend,*
> *and it was no foolish undertaking but part of her goodness*
> *for this woman to try to shelter them.*

There may also be faint echoes in these verses of some of those earlier poems. For instance, in the verses from the poem on the imprisonment of Nualaidh's estranged husband, Niall Garbh, quoted above, Nualaidh's situation is itself likened to imprisonment. In the elegy on Máire, much play is made on the name of the place in Mayo where she lived, the area of An Príosún,[55] to which the poor came to her for assistance: *Tánaig gan tilleadh ar ccúl / dronga bochta don Phríosún* ('crowds of poor came

to An Príosún and never turned back'). Ó Cléirigh even provides the useful information that the name 'An Príosún' was a
forainm ('byname'), and that the real name was Baile Sléibhe
Cairn.[56] The remaining verses bring a symmetrical close to the
poem, as the names of the noble families who have declined, and
who were mentioned at the beginning of the poem, are again
invoked. In a clear echo of the argument of *A bhean fuair faill
ar an bhfeart*, the poet regrets that Máire's death did not occur
while those families were in their prime, so that she might be
mourned properly.[57]

The picture of Máire that emerges from this elegy is of a
woman of means who had done well in negotiating the vicis-
situdes of the time. Like her two sisters, Máire was a survivor.
Through her marriages, first to Tadhg Ó Ruairc and then to
Daibhíth Búrc, who would outlive her by fifteen years, she succeeded in retaining her noble status and the trappings that went
with it. One might say the same of Nualaidh in Louvain, though
the challenges that she faced both there and earlier in Italy were
very different. The third sister, Mairghréad, the sister about
whom we know least, went to Louvain much later. In her decline
in fortunes in Ireland, as commented on earlier, she might be
taken as an example of the type of *bean fhíorbhocht uasal* who
was one of the objects of her sister Máire's charity.

Conclusion

The poems concerning these three sisters are valuable windows
on the momentous events surrounding the decline of the
Í Dhomhnaill in the first half of the seventeenth century. In
addition to their value as historical documents, the poems convey
something of the personalities of the women they celebrate and
commemorate. They highlight the resilience of the sisters and,
in the minds of the poets, their characters as tragically lone sur-
vivors in Ireland and abroad. Though fragmented, the personal
narratives that underlie the poems are a unique lens of female experience through which we can glimpse aspects of the turbulent
times in which they lived.

These poems are among the literary relics of the events surrounding the 'Flight of the Earls', as potent as the physical relics of the Dromahair chalice or the grave-slabs of the church of San Pietro in Montorio. They are extraordinary bardic compositions, and it is possible for the modern reader to approach them as a single narrative of separation, loss and isolation. They speak to the time in which they were composed, and articulate a genuine and widely felt sense of devastation. That genuineness is due in no small part to the strength of the personalities of the three sisters that is captured and mirrored in the graceful syllabic metres and the elevated language of the master poets.

Endnotes

[1] Paul Walsh, *Irish men of learning*, ed. Colm Ó Lochlainn (Dublin, 1947), 187–8; see, genealogy of An Inghean Dubh in Paul Walsh, *Beatha Aodha Ruaidh Uí Dhomhnaill as Leabhar Lughaidh Uí Chléirigh* (2 vols; Dublin,1948, 1957), vol. 1, 203.

[2] Pádraig Ó Macháin, 'Observations on the manuscript of Tadhg Ó Cianáin', in Fearghus Ó Fearghail (ed.), *Tadhg Ó Cianáin: an Irish scholar in Rome* (Dublin, 2011), 171–205. The text survives in Ó Cianáin's autograph manuscript, formerly part of the Louvain library, now UCD-OFM, MS A 21.

[3] Paul Walsh (ed.), *The Flight of the Earls by Tadhg Ó Cianáin edited from the author's manuscript, with translation and notes* (Maynooth and Dublin, 1916), 242–3.

[4] Fearghus Ó Fearghail and Kieran Troy, 'The "Flight of the Earls": new light from a Roman necrology', *Ossory, Laois and Leinster* 4 (2010), 72–106.

[5] Brian Ó Cuív, 'The Earl of Thomond and the poets, A.D. 1572', *Celtica* 12 (1977), 125–45: 127.

[6] Walsh, *Beatha Aodha Ruaidh*, vol. 1, 38–9.

[7] Jerrold Casway, 'Rosa O Dogherty: a Gaelic woman', *Seanchas Ard Mhacha* 10 (1980–1), 42–62.

[8] Pádraig Ó Macháin, 'The iconography of exile: Fearghal Óg Mac an Bhaird in Louvain', in Pádraig A. Breatnach *et al.* (eds), *Léann lámhscríbhinní Lobháin: the Louvain manuscript heritage* (Dublin, 2007), 76–111.

[9] Osborn Bergin, *Irish bardic poetry: texts and translations, together with an introductory lecture*, eds David Greene and Fergus Kelly (Dublin, 1970), Poem 8; the text given here is Bergin's with minor regularisation of orthography; translation based on Bergin's.

[10] She had previously been married to Domhnall Ballach Ó Catháin: Paul Walsh, *Irish leaders and learning through the ages*, ed. Nollaig Ó Muraíle (Dublin, 2003), 331; Jerrold Casway, 'The decline and fate of Dónal Ballagh O'Cahan', in Micheál Ó Siochrú (ed.), *Kingdoms in crisis: Ireland in the 1640s, essays in honour of Dónal Cregan* (Dublin, 2001), 44–62: 48, 61. An earlier alliance of Mary with Maol Muire Mac Suibhne is referred to in Jerrold Casway, 'The last lords of Leitrim: the sons of Sir Teigue O'Rourke', *Breifne* 7(26) (1988), 556–74: 561–2. On the benefit to the Church of a wife's right, under Gaelic law, to hold property independent of her husband, see K.W. Nicholls, 'Irishwomen and property in the sixteenth century', in Margaret MacCurtain and Mary O'Dowd (eds), *Women in early modern Ireland* (Edinburgh, 1991), 17–31: 19.

[11] Pádraig Ó Macháin, 'A poem on the death of Tadhg Ó Ruairc, 1605', *Celtica* 28 (2016), 35–54.

[12] Liam Kelly, *The Diocese of Kilmore c.1100–1800* (Dublin, 2017), 231–40.

[13] 'Maria Ni Domnaill filia Hugonis Magoni pro anima Thaddei Ruairc sui mariti me fieri fecit monasterio Chrivelehae 1619': inscription published in Walsh, *Beatha Aodha Ruaidh*, vol. 2, 133; photographs of the chalice in Kelly, *Diocese of Kilmore*, 239; I am grateful to Msgr Kelly for providing me with further images for inspection.

[14] Brian Mac Cuarta, 'The Plantation of Leitrim, 1620–41', *Irish Historical Studies* 32 (127) (May 2001), 297–320: 309; Casway, 'Last lords', 574.

[15] Casway, 'Last lords', 574.

[16] Walsh, *Beatha Aodha Ruaidh*, vol. 2, 133; Anne Chambers, *Chieftain to knight: Tibbot-ne-Long Bourke (1567–1629)* (Dublin,1983), 147, 192.

[17] NLI MS G 167, pp 289–91; for the family and their manuscript see references in Pádraig Ó Macháin, 'Tadhg Ó Rodaighe and his school: aspects of patronage and

poetic practice at the close of the bardic era', in Seán Duffy (ed.), *Princes, prelates and poets in medieval Ireland: essays in honour of Katharine Simms* (Dublin, 2013), 538–51: 542.

[18] Eoin Mac Cárthaigh, 'Tinn liom do mhaoith a Mháire', in E. Mac Cárthaigh and Jürgen Uhlich (eds), *Féilscríbhinn do Chathal Ó Háinle* (Indreabhán, 2012), 159–86; the text given here is Mac Cárthaigh's, with minor regularisation of orthography; translation also based on Mac Cárthaigh's.

[19] Breandán Ó Buachalla, *Aisling ghéar: na Stíobhartaigh agus an tAos Léinn 1603–1788* (Baile Átha Cliath, 1996), 34–9.

[20] The basis for the identification of her with the 'Mairgarita' mentioned in the will of Fr Robert Chamberlain (UCD-OFM MS A 30/10) in 1611 is not clear; Felim O'Brien, 'Robert Chamberlain OFM', *Irish Ecclesiastical Record* 40 (1932), 264–80: 277 n.1.

[21] Micheline Kerney Walsh, *'Destruction by peace': Hugh O Neill after Kinsale* (Armagh, 1986), 60, 372–3.

[22] John McGurk, 'Irish prisoners in the Tower of London: prerequisites for plantation', in David Finnegan, Éamonn Ó Ciardha and Marie-Claire Peters (eds), *The Flight of the Earls: Imeacht na nIarlaí* (Derry, 2010), 237–46: 241–2.

[23] Kerney Walsh, *'Destruction by peace'*, 60.

[24] Canice Mooney, 'A noble shipload', *Irish Sword* 2 (1954–6), 195–204.

[25] Pádraig Ó Macháin, 'The flight of the poets: Eóghan Ruadh and Fearghal Óg Mac an Bhaird in exile', *Seanchas Ard Mhacha* 21–22 (2007–8), 39–58: 43.

[26] John O'Donovan, *Annála Ríoghachta Éireann. Annals of the kingdom of Ireland by the Four Masters, from the earliest period to the year 1616* (7 vols, Dublin, 1848–51), vol. 6, 2214–20.

[27] Paul Walsh, 'Hugh Roe O Donnell's sisters', *Irish Ecclesiastical Record* Ser. 5, 19 (1922), 358–64; Walsh, *Beatha Aodha Ruaidh*, vol. 2, 132.

[28] O'Donovan, *Annála Ríoghachta Éireann*, vol. 6, 2385.

[29] The respective ages of Rudhraighe and Cathbharr are given on their tombstone in the church of San Pietro: 'in the 33rd year of his life', and 'in the 25th year of his life' (translation). We tend to forget how young the members of this Ó Domhnaill family were: in 1600 none of them was aged over 30.

[30] Kerney Walsh, *'Destruction by peace'*, 230.

[31] Kerney Walsh, *'Destruction by peace'*, 273, 278.

[32] KBR, MS 6131–3 (recently digitised by Irish Script on Screen, www.isos.dias.ie): Kuno Meyer, 'A collection of poems on the O Donnells', *Ériu* 4 (1908–10), 183–90; Paul Walsh, 'The Book of O'Donnell's daughter', in Walsh, *Irish men of learning*, 179–205.

[33] Pádraig A. Breatnach, 'Marbhna Aodha Ruaidh Uí Dhomhnaill (†1602)', *Éigse* 15 (1973–4), 31–50.

[34] KBR MS 6131–3, f. 11v., *Maighean dioghla Druim Lighean*.

[35] KBR MS 6131–3, f. 25r-v., *Ionmhoin sgríbhionn sgaoiltear sonn* and *Cia re bhfáiltigh fian Éirne*.

[36] KBR MS 6131–3, f. 24r., *Ionmholta an tóglach nach diongnadh*. For Séamus see also, Bergin, *Irish bardic poetry*, Poem 43, and Ruairí Ó hUiginn, 'Captain Somhairle and his books revisited', in Pádraig Ó Macháin (ed.), *The Book of the O'Conor Don: essays on an Irish manuscript* (Dublin, 2010), 88–102: 92–4, 96–9.

[37] KBR MS 6131–3, f. 26r., *A bhráighe ata a ttor Lunndan*, and KBR MS 6131–3, f. 27r., *Mairg as bráighe ar mhacruidh Murbhuigh*. According to O'Donovan, *Annála Ríoghachta Éireann*, vol. 6, 2390, Nualaidh was mother of Niall's two sons, Neachtain (Séamus Pender, 'The O'Clery Book of Genealogies', *Analecta Hibernica* 18 (1951), 1–198: 13 §193) and Maghnus (Dubhaltach Mac Fhirbhisigh, *Leabhar Mór na ngenealach: The great book of Irish genealogies, compiled (1645–66)*, ed. Nollaig Ó Muraíle (5 vols, Dublin, 2003), vol. 3, 438 §1110.3).

[38] Láimhbheartach Mac Cionnaith (ed.), *Dioghluim dána* (Baile Átha Cliath, 1938), Poem 63.26–8; Tomás Ó Raghallaigh (ed.), *Duanta Eoghain Ruaidh Mhic an Bhaird* (Gaillimh, 1930), Poem 9. Translation developed from that in L. McKenna, 'To Niall Garbh O Domhnaill', *The Irish Monthly* 56 (657) (March 1928), 153–6.

[39] Pádraig A. Breatnach, 'A poet's autograph in the Book of O'Donnell's daughter', in Walter Bisang and Maria Gabriela Schmidt (eds), *Philologica et linguistica: historia, pluralitas, universitas. Festschrift für Helmut Humbach* (Trier, 2001), 377–84; Pádraig A. Breatnach, 'Scríbhinní i láimh Eoghain Ruaidh Mhic an Bhaird', *Éigse* 36 (2008), 43–62.

[40] Eleanor Knott, 'Mac an Bhaird's elegy on the Ulster lords', *Celtica* 5 (1960), 161–71; the translation of the verses cited here is based on that of Knott.

[41] *Dictionary of the Irish language L*: 200.33–6. The term is also used by Eóghan Ruadh in a literal sense in his poem on St Francis (Cuthbert Mhág Craith (ed.), *Dán na mBráthar Mionúr* (2 vols, Baile Átha Cliath, 1967, 1980), Poem 19.19). It is used in a combined sense of 'shipwreck' and 'utter destruction' by the Four Masters s.a.751 (*Annála Ríoghachta Éireann*, vol. 1, 354). Eóghan Ruadh's use of *loingbhriseadh* was consciously echoed by Dáibhidh Ó Bruadair 80 years later '*An longbhriseadh long sin tug Dia na ngrás / tré chionntaibh an ughdair ar fiannaibh Fáil*': John C. Mac Erlean (ed.), *Duanaire Dháibhidh Uí Bhruadair* (3 vols, London, 1910, 1913, 1917), vol. 3, 182.vii.

[42] In another poem Eóghan Ruadh lists the Í Dhomhnaill among many other Irish families who had incurred God's anger: *Féachadh clann Chonaill cia dhíobh / nachar thuill fearg an Airdríogh* (Ó Raghallaigh, *Duanta*, Poem 16.13). The legacy of *A bhean fuair faill* is to be seen (1) in the proto-*aisling* on the Confederate Wars, *Innisim fís is ní fís bhréige* (Cecile O'Rahilly, *Five seventeenth-century political poems* (Dublin, 1952), 12–32); (2) in the work of later vernacular Ulster poets (Seán Ó Gallchóir, *Séamas Dall Mac Cuarta: dánta* (Baile Átha Cliath, 1971), Poem 2, lines 19, 85–8; Liam Ó Caithnia agus Tomás Ó Fiaich (eag.), *Art Mac Bionaid: dánta* (Baile Átha Cliath, 1979), Poem 30.18); and (3) in Mangan's 'O woman of the piercing wail' (see, Owen Connellan, *Imtheacht na Tromdháimhe* (Dublin, 1860), 294), which gave to Nualaidh the persona of a *bean sidhe*, just as the seventeenth-century *aisling* had given her that of a *spéirbhean*.

[43] Brendan Jennings, 'The career of Hugh, son of Rory O Donnell, Earl of Tirconnel, in the Low Countries, 1607–1642', *Studies* 30 (118) (June 1941), 219–34: 226–7; Walsh, *Irish men of learning*, 182.

[44] Jennings, 'Career of Hugh, son of Rory', 227–8.

[45] Jerrold Casway, 'Heroines or victims?: the women of the Flight of the Earls', *New Hibernia Review* 7(1) (2003), 56–74: 67; Benjamin Hazard, *Faith and patronage: the political career of Flaithrí Ó Maolchonaire c. 1560–1629* (Dublin, 2010), 144.

[46] KBR MS 5095–96, front flyleaf, verso; James Henthorn Todd and William Reeves, *The martyrology of Donegal: a calendar of the saints of Ireland translated from the original Irish by the late John O'Donovan* (Dublin, 1864), xxiv; Walsh, *Irish men of learning*, 192.

[47] Jerrold Casway, 'Rosa O Dogherty: a Gaelic woman', *Seanchas Ard Mhacha* 10 (1980–1), 42–62: 62; inscription in C.P. Meehan, *The fate and fortunes of Hugh O'Neill, Earl of Tyrone, and Rory O'Donel, Earl of Tyrconnel* (Dublin, 1868), 474.

[48] Casway, 'Last lords', 573.

[49] The date is given in the last two verses: '*Se chéd déag se dheich sa dó...An lá ria bfhéil Muire mór*'.

[50] For the children of Aodh's first marriage, see, Walsh, *Beatha Aodha Ruaidh*, vol. 1, 24–5, and *Irish men of learning*, 188.

[51] NLI MS G 167, pp 292–5: transcript and translation by the present writer. For comment see Pádraig A. Breatnach, *The Four Masters and their manuscripts: studies in palaeography and text* (Dublin, 2013), 176–9.

[52] Fergus Kelly, *A guide to early Irish law* (Dublin, 1988), 12; later confusion as to the meaning of *derbfhine* is dealt with in D.A. Binchy, 'Irish history and Irish law: II', *Studia Hibernica* 16 (1976), 7–45: 31–8.

[53] Thus in the 1602 *Tiomna Nuadh*: '[6].3. Achd cheana an tan do ní tú deírc, na biodh a fhios ag ad laimh chlí créud do ní do lamh dheas. [6].4 Do chum go mbíadh do dhéirc a bfolach agus do bhéruidh hathair do chí a nuaigneas lúaghuigheachd duit gós aírd'. This is augmented here by reference to the scholastic tradition of personal angels and demons (see, for example, Marcia L. Colish, 'Early scholastic angelology', *Recherches de Théologie Ancienne et Médiévale* 62 (1995), 80–109).

[54] Ó Cléirigh does not mention any other marriage as occurring between the death of Ó Ruairc and her marriage to Búrc, so that it is difficult to accommodate the supposed intervening marriage to Gerald Nugent (Walsh, *Irish men of learning*, 191 n.22, Casway, 'Last lords', 570 n. 56).

[55] Now the townlands of Prison North, Prison South and Prison East, all in the civil parish of Manulla, County Mayo.

[56] '*Baile súthach sleibhe caírn / Priosún a ainm ger fhorainm*' 'The fertile Baile Sléibhe Cairn, is called Príosún, though a byname'. The first line here is an echo of a twelfth-century poem, *Baile suthach síth Emhna* (Brian Ó Cuív, 'A poem in praise of Raghnall, King of Man', *Éigse* 8 (1955–7), 283–301).

[57] '*do bhiadh cúmha ag cailg gach cinn /sa gubha in gach aird déirinn*' 'grief would pierce every head and she would be mourned in every part of Ireland'.

Writing family and voicing the female: Alice, Sara, Lettice, Joan, Katherine, Dorothy and Mary Boyle, daughters of the earl of Cork

ANN-MARIA WALSH

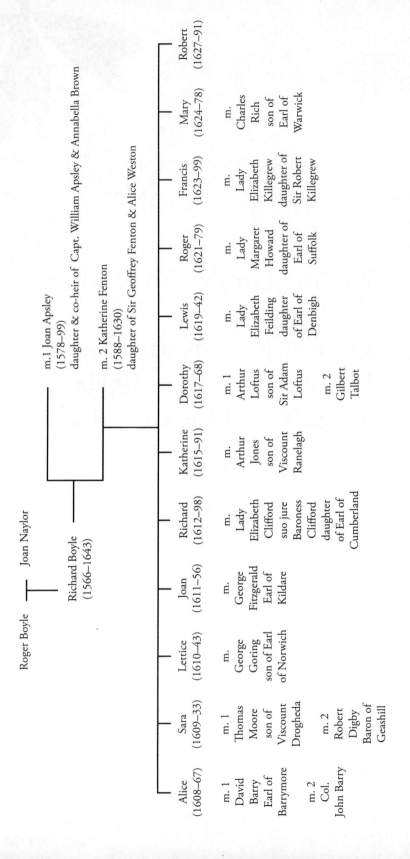

BOYLE FAMILY TREE

Roger Boyle —⊤— Joan Naylor

Richard Boyle (1566–1643)

m.1 Joan Apsley (1578–99) daughter & co-heir of Capt. William Apsley & Annabella Brown

m. 2 Katherine Fenton (1588–1630) daughter of Sir Geoffrey Fenton & Alice Weston

Alice (1608–67)
m. 1 David Barry Earl of Barrymore
m. 2 Col. John Barry

Sara (1609–33)
m. 1 Thomas Moore son of Viscount Drogheda
m. 2 Robert Digby Baron of Geashill

Lettice (1610–43)
m. George Goring son of Earl of Norwich

Joan (1611–56)
m. George Fitzgerald Earl of Kildare

Richard (1612–98)
m. Lady Elizabeth Clifford suo jure Baroness Clifford daughter of Earl of Cumberland

Katherine (1615–91)
m. Arthur Jones son of Viscount Ranelagh

Dorothy (1617–68)
m. 1 Arthur Loftus son of Sir Adam Loftus
m. 2 Gilbert Talbot

Lewis (1619–42)
m. Lady Elizabeth Feilding daughter of Earl of Denbigh

Roger (1621–79)
m. Lady Margaret Howard daughter of Earl of Suffolk

Francis (1623–99)
m. Lady Elizabeth Killegrew daughter of Sir Robert Killegrew

Mary (1624–78)
m. Charles Rich son of Earl of Warwick

Robert (1627–91)

Introduction

My first encounter with the seventeenth-century Boyle sisters happened during a chance visit to St Patrick's Cathedral in Dublin. Immediately inside the doors and dominating the western end of the cathedral stands the Boyle monument, which was originally erected in 1632 at the behest of Richard Boyle, 1st earl of Cork (1566–1643), to honour his wife, Katherine, 1st countess of Cork, who had died on 16 February 1630.[1] Hailing from Preston in Kent, Richard Boyle first travelled to Ireland in 1588 as part of the Munster plantation scheme, and, using his legal training, he was quickly put to work checking land titles and overseeing confiscations and forfeitures to the Crown.[2] During the course of those Munster-based activities, Boyle also took advantage of any opportunity that arose to acquire his own lands. On 25 July 1603 he married Katherine Fenton, and together they had fifteen children, twelve of whom survived into adulthood, comprising seven daughters (Alice, Sara, Lettice, Joan, Katherine, Dorothy and Mary) and five sons (Richard, Lewis, Roger, Francis and Robert) (see opposite). While the effigy in St Patrick's is an impressive marker of this family's powerful dynastic strength in early modern Ireland, I was more visibly struck by the six female statues, representing Boyle's daughters, who are positioned at the base of this enormous tomb (see picture section). Kneeling in prayer and facing forward, each daughter is dressed in a floor-length, red robe with long hair lying veil-like down her back. Since the seventeenth century, the Boyle women have remained anonymous and largely ignored, with the exception of limited scholarship focused on two of the sisters, the intellectual, Viscountess Katherine Ranelagh (see picture section), and the spiritual diarist, Mary Rich, countess of Warwick.[3] In contrast, the women's father and brothers have provoked numerous biographical studies, as well as receiving recognition in the mainstream histories of the period. While the line of statues suggests a uniform female piety and passivity, the women's surviving papers reveal a much more complex view of how they as writers sought to differentiate themselves, how they imagined themselves as a sisterly collective, and how they wished to be remembered as strong, able participants in the momentous happenings of that period.

The sheer size and geographic spread of the Boyle archive is proof of the family's impactful presence throughout seventeenth-century Ireland and Britain. An unusually large amount of the surviving papers relate to the women in the family, and the range and intergenerational character of those writings reflect the extent to which the Boyle women were directly involved in safeguarding the family's property, power and privilege at a time when all of those elements were under threat.[4] The noticeably smaller numbers of female-to-female correspondence within the Boyle archive is a salient reminder of the kind of safekeeping policies that prevailed in the past, and which required the retention and preservation of the senior men's papers as a priority. Archival evidence does, however, also show that certain key women in the family were actively involved in that system of conservation.[5] It therefore could be argued that the shape and appearance of today's archive is in some measure a reflection of the different forms of custodial interventions that particular Boyle sisters undertook for the sake of the family and its future reputation.

In the last 40 years scholars have begun revisiting and exploring existing historical sources with a specifically gendered focus, so that fresh insights might be gleaned about women as historical actors.[6] As part of that research trajectory, experts in women's writing have increasingly engaged with less traditional literary sources, such as familial letters, private diaries, recipes, accounts and commonplace books – materials more commonly associated with the household and their original female user. Through close analysis of those domestic papers, scholars have identified the layered quality of those texts and the innovative devices that early modern women writers developed for self-expression, while still adhering to the patriarchal strictures of that time. In the case of the Boyle archive, it is noticeable that the female correspondents frequently reference the sibling tie as a way of affirming a sense of selfhood and their place within the family. Taking into account that the sisters were the largest cohort within the natal Boyle group, it therefore seems entirely appropriate to explore the familial letters from a sisterly perspective. At different stages in the female life cycle, these daughters, sisters, wives and mothers similarly inscribed and availed of the umbilical qualities of the natal family. These female correspondents exploited the elastic, sustaining and rooting properties of the family link in order to carve out identities of their own, to pursue their separate agendas and, at the same time, to signal their loyalty and attachment to the kinship circle.

Upbringing, education and marriage

The speed with which Richard Boyle became one of the largest and most successful property owners in Ireland and Britain can be partially attributed to his two wives. In 1595 Boyle's marriage to the heiress Joan Apsley provided him with lands around Limerick at Dungrott and Galbally.[7] Four years after Joan's death from childbirth in 1599, Boyle married Katherine Fenton, who brought with her a dowry of £1,000.[8] Boyle used that money to purchase Sir Walter Raleigh's 42,000-acre estate near Fermoy, County Cork, and with that move established the centrepiece of his valuable property portfolio. Katherine Boyle was also quick to immerse herself in the business of creating and sustaining another kind of substantive legacy with her seven surviving daughters and five sons. A sense of the countess of Cork's maternal character is indicated in one of her few surviving letters. Writing from Lismore Castle, late on 22 October 1623, Katherine updated her husband Richard about the spread of smallpox that had infiltrated the local area and the Boyle household. She offered him reassurance that two of their daughters, Alice and Lettice, 'are i hope now past the worste' and 'the rest of the childerne ar, blessed bee god for it, in good health:'.[9] The letter also confirms that while the countess and the majority of the children were staying together at Lismore, the eldest son and heir, 'dicke [Richard]' had remained at the family's other residence, which was situated in the town of Youghal nearly 30 kilometres away from his two infected sisters. Katherine further disclosed that she had sent 'worde' to the servants in Youghal to keep the boy 'from colde' and 'too get Mr goden to teche him att my lady parsones house till your retourne home'.[10] The letter thus draws attention to Katherine's careful oversight of all her children, but more particularly the report of her handling of the smallpox outbreak demonstrates to the reader that, in spite of all the internal pressures and the external dangers, her focus remained firmly fixed on the family's future prospects.

The custom of fostering out children was a practice commonly associated with early modern aristocratic households, and sisters Alice, Mary and Margaret spent part of their childhoods with Sir Randall and Lady Anne Clayton, who were also neighbours and close associates of the Boyles.[11] Mary, who later became the countess of Warwick, acknowledged in her autobiography that, while her mother had died when she was very young, Lady Clayton had ensured that she was 'soberly educated'.[12] Apart from being provided with a religiously themed education, noble daughters in Anglo-Irish families like that of the Boyles were also instructed how to compose and write letters, to speak and write in the French language, to occupy themselves with needlework, to engage in polite conversation and, most importantly, how to manage multiple residences and landed estates.[13] The family records confirm that professional tutors were a constant presence in the Boyle household, and it is therefore plausible that the three Boyle girls who remained in the natal home, Sara, Lettice and Joan, might have inadvertently benefited from the kind of 'text-based learning' that was taking place within that same domestic space.[14] While noble sons and daughters may have been educated apart and with different objectives in mind, what is sometimes ignored or forgotten is the 'relationship *between* those separately educated sons and daughters'.[15] In the case of siblings Sara and Richard, three letters illustrate how they availed of that medium to maintain their close affinity, irrespective of their actual geographic distance.[16] The colourful content and the shortened intervals between those particular letters reflect Richard's determination to include Sara, albeit remotely, in his educational grand tour of Europe. More generally, the letters underscore how the practice of family writing might have helped to transform childhood friendships into fruitful adult relationships. Diary notes and correspondence exchanged between three of the other Boyle siblings, Katherine, Mary and Robert, highlight how they seemingly encouraged and stimulated each other's overlapping interests in religion, medicine, science and writing.[17]

Patrick Little notes how Richard Boyle started planning his daughters' futures as early as their infanthood, by studying genealogies and employing antiquarians to research the pedigree of families with potential suitors.[18] Five out of the seven daughters were strategically matched with Irish-based nobles, while the third and seventh daughters, Lettice and Mary, married the sons of influential English lords. All of those marital manoeuvres increased the Boyles' landed presence across the territories of Britain and Ireland, as well as broadening the family's network of noble alliances and important political contacts. For the Boyle daughters, most of their marriages resulted in misery and unhappiness, but the archival evidence also reveals the different ways in which the women came to rely on their pens to adjust and to cope with adversity. A letter from Sara, dated late October 1623, illustrates how she adapted to the changed reality of her life.[19] Two years earlier Sara had been married to Sir Thomas Moore, heir to Garrett Moore, 1st viscount Drogheda, but in the intervening period Sara remained with the natal family until Sir Thomas returned from his European grand tour and was ready to escort his new wife the two hundred miles north to their marital home. When Sara wrote to her father reassuring him of her safe arrival at Mellifont Abbey, County Louth, she used the opportunity to signal her continuing filial duty through the carefully ornate italic script and deferential tone. Sara also included in the letter a request to retain her father's 'gildinge [gelding]' that had carried her with great 'ease' to Mellifont, so that she could work towards becoming a 'beter horsewoman'. The reference to the horse that Sara had grown familiar with over the course of the journey from Lismore suggests that she was conscious of the need to put on record her intention to self-improve, and to take on the responsibilities associated with her new role as a landed noblewoman. The letter thus perceptibly marks in an official sense that pivotal moment of change in a woman's life, when she transitioned from child and dependent on her father to adult married woman. The consequences of the move to Mellifont also meant that the link between Sara and her siblings would necessarily become stretched. The importance of the letter is thus reinforced as a physical point of contact with the natal family, and as a mechanism to track the writer's progress while she adjusted to both her alien surroundings and to her new identity as Lady Sara Moore.

Constructions of sisterly relations

Writing was used by Sara and all of her sisters as a means of mediating the kinds of life crises which those women variously experienced as wives, as mothers and as widows: preparing a young son for departure from home in Ireland for school in England; dealing with invalided and sometimes abusive husbands; and having to become financially astute in the aftermath of a husband's death.[20] The enabling powers of the pen offered the sisters an instrument through which they could try to plan ahead and to call for help in times of need. In 1633 four of the Boyle sisters, Alice, Sara, Joan and Katherine, were pregnant at roughly the same time. Patricia Crawford pointed out that, in the early modern period, 'childbirth was the female rite of passage *par excellence*', but Clodagh Tait also observes that 'women were conditioned to fear labour and to expect the worst'.[21] On 9 July 1633, Sara died from complications after the birth of her fourth child.[22] However, that sad event does not seem to have altered the earl of Cork's optimistic outlook when he wrote to his son Richard in November advising that he shortly expected to hear of his daughter Katherine's 'safe delivery of a goodly boy'.[23] Cork reported how Katherine had recently written to her eldest sister Alice, pleading that 'she should die if she [Alice] were not with her at the time of her travail'. The presence of female-only attendees during childbirth was routine from a modesty perspective; sisters would also have commonly wished to offer their experience and support at the final stages of the lying-in period.[24] According to Cork, in response to Katherine's request, Alice 'most affectionately and Sister like' promptly 'left her house and children and all', and having parted from her husband at Clonmel, she took 'the shortest way to Athlone'. Yet, rather than focusing on the likely ordeal Katherine would have to face, the reader's attention is instead directed towards Alice and her show of sisterly solidarity, which is framed as an outward sign of Boyle strength and unity at a time of necessity. The idealising of maternity to publicise the family's flourishing posterity is echoed in the earl's autobiography, 'True remembrances', when he characterises his wife Katherine as, 'the happy mother of all my hopefull children'.[25] Cork's account of his daughter Katherine's birthing preparations is also telling in terms of her instinctive urge to write and to call upon a sister when confronted with the prospect of a perilous labour. Moreover, Katherine's cry for help and Alice's prompt answer together demonstrate how the Boyle sisterhood was enacted in real and practical terms, while also illustrating how that sibling bond seems to have superseded any prior claim or consideration.

The sibling tie was further tested during an incident in 1639 that involved the third Boyle sister, Lettice, and her husband, George Goring, when they sought and subsequently were refused a loan of £500 from the earl of Cork.[26] Rather than accepting her father's decision as final, Lettice pens an urgent appeal to her eldest brother, Richard, requesting that he mediate on her behalf with their father regarding the matter of the loan. Written in early August while Lettice was visiting Bath, her letter reached Richard, who, along with most of the other Boyle siblings, was staying with their father at the family's English country seat at Stalbridge Manor in Dorset.[27] In addition to contacting Richard, Lettice's husband, George Goring, also wrote to her father, begging him to reconsider the loan.[28] The dense and lengthy content of Lettice's letters to her father and brother, combined with the close intervals between and the tense undertones of the correspondence, are all features consistent with an increasingly desperate situation. The decision to approach her eldest brother about the matter of the loan can be explained by Richard's elevated position within the family as the Boyle heir and his father's closest confidant, suggesting that he was well placed to wield influence.[29] Lettice opens her letter to Richard by asserting that the refusal of the money was 'testamoney' of her father's 'littell affection for mee'. The desired effect of this claim was presumably to arouse her brother's sympathy and his sense of care towards his sister.[30] Yet, in addition to exercising the usual obligatory bonds associated with the sibling relationship, Lettice's expectations of Richard are also more specifically gendered. In contrast with the practical support that Alice was able to offer her younger sister Katherine some years previously, Richard, as the eldest brother, was far more likely to have access to the kind of material help that Lettice urgently required. Predicting that without the loan of money from their father she would be forced to 'live missorably' and in 'Great nessecatey', Lettice builds on the idea that as a powerful figure within the family, Richard had both a responsibility and an opportunity to help ease his sister's afflictions. This persuasive tactic gains in intensity when the material and the emotional threads become increasingly entangled. Thus, capitalising on their close relationship, Lettice reveals to Richard her fears concerning her own vulnerability, but more especially her husband Goring's unpredictability, and the 'dee[s]prat corce' he might take in response to the perceived paternal slight and to their worsening financial situation. Richard is therefore being pressed to save his sister from ruin on several different fronts. But additionally, the real strength of Lettice's plea for help lies in the notion of interdependency and the future implications for the Boyles in reputational terms if their sister was knowingly allowed to suffer neglect or harm.

In an attempt to cement her argument that she was being treated unequally in comparison with her sisters, Lettice disclosed how she felt aggrieved remembering that, while she had sought 'so small a Sume as fife hundred pound', her father 'hath lent some of my Sistars' ... 'maney thousands'.[31] Cork, undoubtedly, invested heavily in his Irish-based daughters, both in terms of equipping them with generous dowries and through various other methods, such as restructuring mortgaged lands, rebuilding their marital homes and paying, in some instances, for the creation of their aristocratic titles.[32] Admittedly, while some of those monetary interventions led to improvements in the standard of living for particular sisters, the majority of the investments were geared towards promoting and consolidating the Boyles' economic, political and social interests in Ireland. Lettice and George Goring, in contrast, had neither children nor property of any substance to show in return for either the original dowry of £10,000 or the thousands more in Boyle monies they had received in the intervening ten years of their marriage.[33] By the early 1640s conservative estimates suggest that Cork was one of the richest men in Ireland and England, and therefore it seems likely that he could easily have afforded to give Lettice the £500.[34] More significantly, Lettice's correspondence with her father and brother sheds important light on one Boyle woman's attitude to money: as a practical necessity; as a key measure of self-worth; as a source of sisterly rivalry; and as the competitive spur for paternal attention.

A letter written by Lettice's younger sister, Joan Fitzgerald, countess of Kildare, illustrates how she also deployed the concept of interdependency in her appeal for help from their father. On this occasion, rather than playing up the potential threat to the wider family, as was hinted by Lettice, Joan focuses on the positive benefits that might accrue from fulfilling the overlapping requests of two Boyle sisters. Joan's letter, dated 8 February 1642, begins with an account of the dramatic events that led up to her sudden departure from her home at Maynooth Castle in County Kildare during the Irish rebellion and her subsequent arrival in London. By immediately focusing the reader's attention on the wartime context, the request for help is given legitimacy and a sense of urgency.[35] In contrast to Lettice's self-serving agenda, Joan asserts from the outset that her letter is a collaborative endeavour, representing the needs of not just herself and her five children, but also her 'Sister Loftus [Dorothy] and her three children'. By alluding to her sister Dorothy in this way, Joan widens the remit of the letter, making it more difficult for Cork to refuse help to no fewer than ten family members. Halfway down the letter, however, there is a switch in direction, when the writer emphasises her isolation and vulnerability in London, with 'nether money nor frends hear to releeve me nor Counsell me what to doe'. Adjectives like 'miserable', nouns like 'pitte [pity]', and verbs such as 'troubling' help to consolidate this picture of female frailty and dependency. Yet, rather than being an 'uncontrolled' product of 'desperation', Joan's letter and her use of such self-deprecatory devices were entirely consistent with a writing formula typically associated with this kind of entreaty for help.[36] Parallels can also be drawn between Joan's and Lettice's attitude towards their male relatives and the gendered expectation that the senior Boyle men had the capacity to alleviate material distress, and to provide the necessary protection to their female kin.

One particular difference in terms of approach between Lettice and Joan lies with the extent of paternal support which they each sought. Thus, while Joan asks her father for help, she also presents a number of alternative solutions that are self-revealing. For example, Joan requests that the rental income from 'my Cousen Peirsey Smith [Sir Percy Smith] and Mʳ Perry' might instead be diverted for her use.[37] The effect of naming those two tenants, one of whom was a kinsman, allows Joan to re-affirm the familial bond by underlining her knowledge of the inner workings of the Cork estates. Re-routing the rent proceeds to another branch of the family was an innovative way of raising cash, a scarce commodity during those 'troublesome times'. Joan makes a further suggestion that the earl send over 'three gilt bolds [gilt bowls]' which he had previously redeemed on his daughter's behalf at a cost of '40ˢ'. Recalling his recent involvement in redeeming the bowls also works to remind the earl of a pattern of paternal assistance. Therefore, while the idea of recycling both the rent and the bowls is pragmatic and inventive, those particular items also serve as points of connection that help to unify rather than expose weaknesses within the family.

Having offered various suggestions as to how she might receive assistance, Joan attaches a further request, that her father write and 'give order to tome mury [Tom Murray]', who was the head steward at Stalbridge, that if the sisters 'desiar to live there' that they could make 'use of the house and garden'.[38] Before Joan expands this idea of a longer-term refuge for herself and Dorothy, she first makes the request contingent upon establishing whether their 'Sister dungarvant [Elizabeth Boyle, Viscountess Dungarvan] has doe not intend to live at Stalbridg'. By drawing attention to the pecking order among the sisters, and by affirming her willing compliance in that regard, Joan enacts the part of a model, obedient daughter and sister, and hence presents herself as a worthy candidate for her father's support.

Joan's petition noticeably evolves and transforms over the trajectory of the letter: starting off as a basic plea for money, developing into a request for the use of Stalbridge plus the 'garden' and eventually escalating to an inquiry about whether the sisters might also have access to 'any land belonging to the house'.[39] This process of inflation is facilitated through the varying shifts in perspective offered by the writer as she reconfigures her identity to synchronise with and strengthen the petition. For instance, the besieged countess becomes the wartime refugee in the city of London, whereas the suggested move to the countryside prompts a further transformation into 'any other' tenant, willing to pay rent and ready to work the land. Casting herself in the role of labouring tenant contradicts the earlier depiction of female helplessness, while the importance previously attached to familial proximity is seemingly reversed to create distance and a reluctance to be seen receiving any undue favour. Joan's solitariness is underlined in London, while a familial but also gendered harmonious community is imagined in relation to Stalbridge, which may have been (perhaps deliberately) designed to conjure up happier memories when the sisters had congregated around their father and enjoyed his hospitality.[40] Lettice's earlier individualist approach provided her with a basis from which to decry, rather than accept, the perceived favouritism shown to her sisters. In contrast, Joan's mention of Dorothy at the very beginning and at the postscript stage of the letter allows her as writer to remind the reader of the sisters' common purpose as mothers and as protectors of the Boyles' long-term interests. As the letter draws to a conclusion, Joan urges her father to send a speedy answer, so that she and Dorothy 'may know how to provide for our selfe', and by using that remaining space to reiterate the focus on self-sufficiency and sisterly solidarity, Joan ensures that the favours being sought from the recipient had the best chance of being remembered and acted upon.

Conclusion

One final archival gem showcases how writing about the sibling tie had the potential to simultaneously bind and differentiate the Boyle sisters. On 9 July 1637, twelve-year-old Mary Boyle (later Mary Rich, Countess of Warwick) (see picture section) wrote, on the entreaty of her foster mother, Lady Clayton, to inform her father, the earl of Cork, about the circumstances in which the youngest member of the family, Margaret Boyle, had died on 30 June.[41] According to Mary's account, Margaret had suffered from a 'tedious sicknes', but in a touching attempt to reassure and comfort her father, Mary informs him that 'ther was nothing waniting' in the care and attention which Margaret had received, either from the Claytons or from her doctors. The letter goes on to express the sense of grief and loss that both Mary and the Claytons felt in the aftermath of Margaret's passing, while also interpreting her death as a sign of God's will. Yet, while the reader is afforded a fleeting glimpse of young Margaret and her 'swete sobrietty', the bearer of the sad news and the holder of the pen, Mary, is much more fulsomely and favourably portrayed. Thus, availing of her proximity to the occasion of Margaret's death, and using the facility of the letter, a version of Mary emerges, espousing filial duty, sisterly devotion and a pious inclination. The letter also serves as another reminder of how the Boyle women used writing to deal with catastrophe, to call for help, to vent their emotions, to reflect on their lived experiences and to ensure that their memory of a person or a special event was embedded in the written record.

Returning to the Boyle monument in St Patrick's Cathedral, an observer might wonder why there are only six daughters, and assume that neither Mary nor her younger sister Margaret were figuratively represented, perhaps, because of their youth and unmarried status at that point in time. The answer is most likely that the final two statues were damaged during the various moves to which the monument was subsequently subjected. It is even more significant, therefore, that while Mary Boyle's 1637 letter was registered and preserved because it was addressed to her father, its survival also increased the possibility that the two youngest Boyle sisters might be remembered by posterity. The fragile condition of the letter, with the disintegrating paper and the faded, barely legible script, also materially reinforces the vulnerability of those kinds of ephemeral materials in contrast to the monument and its gigantic solidity. Yet, by looking afresh at the line of red-robed sisters in St Patrick's, it is also possible to better appreciate and more clearly understand the fundamental importance of the blood tie in the Boyle women's life writings. The blood tie afforded the sisters all kinds of support and a sense of belonging at a time of huge uncertainty, but it also allowed them the scope to imagine themselves as individuals who had the capacity to make a difference and to contribute not only to their communities but also to the course of Irish and British history.

Endnotes

[1] For more on the Boyle monument see, Clodagh Tait, 'Colonising memory: manipulations of death, burial and commemoration in the career of Richard Boyle, first earl of Cork (1566–1643)', *Proceedings of the Royal Irish Academy* 101C (2001), 107–34.

[2] Toby Barnard, 'Boyle, Richard, first earl of Cork (1566–1643)', *ODNB Online*.

[3] For a list of publications on both Rich and Ranelagh and the Boyle men see the bibliography in, Ann-Maria Walsh, *The daughters of the first earl of Cork: writing family, faith, politics and place* (Dublin, 2020), 160–8.

[4] For a survey of the Boyle archive, see, Ann-Maria Walsh, 'The Boyle women and familial life writing', in Julie A. Eckerle and Naomi McAreavey (eds), *Women's life writing in early modern Ireland* (Lincoln, 2019), 79–98.

[5] TDC, C, CM/22.146, Joan Fitzgerald, Countess of Kildare to Richard Boyle, 1st earl of Cork, 8 February 1642. Joan reports to her father that she had deposited her family's papers in Dublin Castle before fleeing from the Irish rebellion and escaping to London.

[6] Walsh, *Daughters*, 160–8.

[7] David Edwards, 'The land-grabber's accomplices: Richard Boyle's Munster affinity, 1588–1603', in David Edwards & Colin Rynne (eds), *The colonial world of Richard Boyle, first earl of Cork* (Dublin, 2018), 170–3.

[8] Barnard, 'Boyle'.

[9] TDC, C, CM/14.173, Katherine Boyle, 1st countess of Cork to Richard Boyle, 1st earl of Cork, 22 October 1623.

[10] Lady Anne Parsons, née Maltham, wife of Sir Lawrence Parsons (d. 1628), who was deputy judge of the admiralty court in Munster and a close neighbour and cousin of Richard Boyle. See, Judy Barry, 'Parsons, Sir Lawrence (d. 1628), lawyer and planter', *DIB Online*. Accessed 6 July 2020.

[11] Dorothea Townshend, *The life and letters of the great Earl of Cork* (London, 1904), 58.

[12] Mary Rich, *Autobiography of Mary Boyle, Countess of Warwick* (London, 1848), 2.

[13] See example of child's letter in, TDC, C, CM/24.107, Katherine Jones to Richard Boyle, 1st earl of Cork [?1638–41].

[14] A.B. Grosart (ed.), *The Lismore Papers*, 1, ii, (5 vols; London, 1886), 249. On 16 May 1629 the earl of Cork records that 'Mr ffrye' had come to Lismore to be his son Richard's tutor. On the subject of women's literary skills within families see, Rebecca Krug, *Reading families: women's literate practice in late medieval England* (Ithaca and London, 2008), 12–13.

[15] Naomi J. Miller and Naomi Yavneh, 'Introduction: Thicker than water: evaluating sibling relations in the early modern period', in Miller and Yavneh (eds), *Sibling relations and gender in the early modern world: sisters, brothers and others* (Aldershot, 2006), 1–14: 2.

[16] TDC, C, CM/17.146,151,154, Three letters from Richard Boyle, Viscount Dungarvan to his sister, Lady Sara Digby, 8 June, 6 July, 30 July 1633.

[17] Mary Rich, *Memoir of Lady Warwick* (London, 1847), 243. Rich references numerous occasions when she enjoyed meeting with her siblings.

[18] Patrick Little, 'The Geraldine ambitions of the first earl of Cork', *Irish Historical Studies* 33(130) (November 2002), 151–68.

[19] TDC, C, CM/14.189, Lady Sara Moore to Richard Boyle, 1st earl of Cork, endorsed 1 November 1623. Sara's marriage to Sir Thomas Moore was short-lived; he

died of smallpox a month after their arrival at Mellifont. Three years later Sara married Sir Robert Digby.

[20] Claydon House Trust, Verney Letters 1639, Alice Barry, née Boyle, 1st countess of Barrymore to Sir Ralph Verney, 18 February [?1641]. In this letter Alice arranges for a tutor to be sent to Castlelyons to prepare her eldest boy for school in England.

[21] Patricia Crawford, *Blood, bodies and families in early modern England* (Abingdon and New York, 2014), 95. Clodagh Tait, 'Safely delivered: childbirth, wet-nursing, gossip-feasts and churching in Ireland *c*.1530–1690', *Irish Economic and Social History* 30 (2003), 1–23: 1, 7–10.

[22] Grosart, *LP*, 1, iii, 192–3, 199. The child's death is noted on 23 May and on 9 July 1633; the event of Sara's passing is described by her father as, 'A moste lamentable daye to me'.

[23] TDC, C, Misc. Book 2, Hardwick/78, ff 712–14. Richard Boyle, 1st earl of Cork to Richard Boyle, Viscount Dungarvan, 24 November 1633. A. Clarke, B. McGrath and D. Edwards (eds), *A lord justice's letterbook: the earl of Cork's letterbook, 1629–1633* (Dublin, forthcoming). Sincere thanks to Dr Bríd McGrath for bringing this letter to my attention.

[24] Crawford, *Blood*, 95, 218.

[25] BL, Add. MS 19,832, Boyle Papers, Copy of 'True remembrances', autobiography of the 1st earl of Cork, ff 23–30: f.28r.

[26] TDC, C, CM/20.90, Lady Lettice Goring to Richard Boyle, 1st earl of Cork, 4 August [1639].

[27] TDC, C, CM/20.91, Lady Lettice Goring to Richard Boyle, Viscount Dungarvan, [4 August 1639].

[28] TDC, C, CM/20.89, Colonel George Goring to Richard Boyle, 1st earl of Cork, 5 August 1639.

[29] See n. 23 above, which shows that Cork kept his son well-informed about family matters.

[30] TDC, C, CM/20.91, Lady Lettice Goring to Richard Boyle, Viscount Dungarvan, 4 August [1639].

[31] TDC, C, CM/20.91, Lady Lettice Goring to Richard Boyle, Viscount Dungarvan, 4 August [1639].

[32] Townshend, *Life*, 475, Cork supplied Alice and David Barry with 'the Sum of Seven hundred Sixty-Seven pounds English' for the renovation of their home at Castlelyons; Grosart, *LP*, 1, iv, 6. A diary note for 2 January 1633[34] states that '1530[li] ster' had been paid by Cork for 'making' a house at Maynooth for his daughter [Joan] and her husband, the earl of Kildare.

[33] Grosart, *LP*, 1, iii, 105; v, 81. Cork documents substantial loans of money paid out to the Gorings.

[34] Terrence O. Ranger, 'Richard Boyle and the making of an Irish fortune, 1588–1641', *Irish Historical Studies* 10(39) (1957), 257, 295–6.

[35] TDC, C, CM/22.146, Joan, Countess of Kildare to Richard Boyle, 1st earl of Cork, [at Youghal], 8 February 1642. Joan married George Fitzgerald on 15 August 1630; two of their sons and four daughters survived. See, Jane Ohlmeyer, 'Fitzgerald, George, sixteenth earl of Kildare', *ODNB Online*.

[36] Lynne Magnusson, 'A rhetoric of requests: genre and linguistic scripts in Elizabethan women's suitors' letters', in James Daybell (ed.), *Women and politics in early modern England, 1450–1700* (Aldershot, 2004), 51–66: 57.

[37] TDC, C, CM/22.146, Joan, Countess of Kildare to Richard Boyle, 1st earl of Cork, 8 February 1642.

[38] TDC, C, CM/22.146, Joan, Countess of Kildare to Richard Boyle, 1st earl of Cork, 8 February 1642.

[39] TDC, C, CM/22.146, Joan, Countess of Kildare to Richard Boyle, 1st earl of Cork, 8 February 1642.

[40] Grosart, *LP*, 1, v, 98–9. Cork's diary for 26 July 1639 notes that his daughters Alice and Katherine, and daughter-in-law Elizabeth Dungarvan, were all present with him at Stalbridge.

[41] TDC, C, CM/19.19, Mary Boyle to Richard Boyle, 1st earl of Cork, 9 July *s.a.* [endorsed 1637].

'Ties that endure':
the lives and letters of
three eighteenth-century
Irish sisters, Katherine, Jane
and Mary Conyngham

GAYE ASHFORD

CONYNGHAM FAMILY TREE

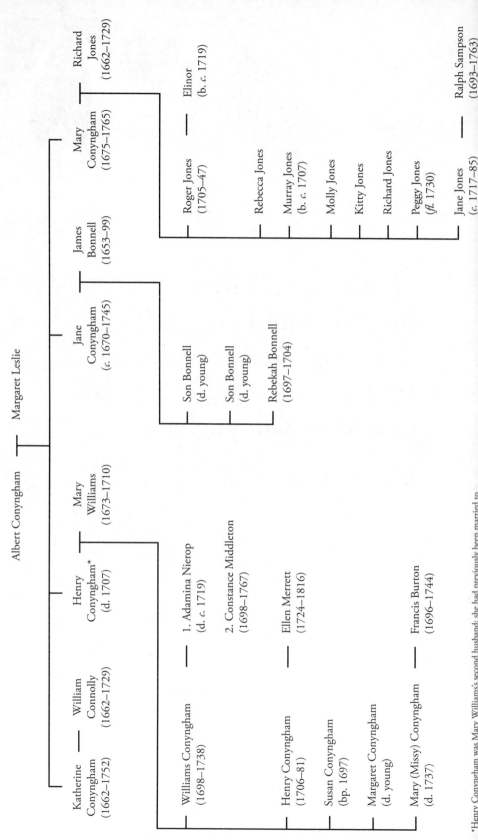

Albert Conyngham — Margaret Leslie

Katherine Conyngham (1662–1752) — William Connolly (1662–1729)

Henry Conyngham* (d. 1707) — Mary Williams (1673–1710)

Jane Conyngham (c. 1670–1745) — James Bonnell (1653–99)

Mary Conyngham (1675–1765) — Richard Jones (1662–1729)

Williams Conyngham (1698–1738) — 1. Adamina Nierop (d. c. 1719)
2. Constance Middleton (1698–1767)

Henry Conyngham (1706–81) — Ellen Merrett (1724–1816)

Susan Conyngham (bp. 1697)

Margaret Conyngham (d. young)

Mary (Missy) Conyngham (d. 1737) — Francis Burton (1696–1744)

Son Bonnell (d. young)

Son Bonnell (d. young)

Rebekah Bonnell (1697–1704)

Elinor (b. c. 1719)

Roger Jones (1705–47)

Rebecca Jones

Murray Jones (b. c. 1707)

Molly Jones

Kitty Jones

Richard Jones

Peggy Jones (fl. 1730)

Jane Jones (c. 1717–85) — Ralph Sampson (1693–1763)

*Henry Conyngham was Mary Williams's second husband; she had previously been married to

'Letters are among the most significant memorial a person can leave behind them'
– JOHANN WOLFGANG VON GOETHE

The correspondence between the three Conyngham sisters – Katherine Conolly (1662–1752) of Castletown, County Kildare; Jane Bonnell (*c.* 1670–1745), living in London and later in Essex; and Mary Jones (1675–1765), who was based in County Meath – are an important source for the history of the family. The letters reveal the dynamics of the relationships between the sisters: the role of Katherine as matriarch, and her financial power; Mary Jones's particular position within their family; and Jane's status as family mediator. Furthermore, they document the sisters' collective response to their involvement in the Conolly family guardianship of various nieces and nephews. In short, the sisters' letters illustrate the trials, tribulations, failures and successes of an elite eighteenth-century Irish family, while also providing a credible alternative to the traditional eighteenth-century female stereotype.[1]

The Conyngham family and their letters

The sisters' paternal grandfather, Rev. Alexander Conyngham (*c.* 1580–1660), settled at Mountcharles, County Donegal in the early seventeenth century, and his descendants and collateral relations are among the many cousins referred to throughout the sisters' letters. Their father, Sir Albert Conyngham (d. 1691), married Margaret Leslie, and they had nine children, four of whom survived to adulthood: Katherine, who married William 'Speaker' Conolly (1662–1729) in 1694; Jane, who married James Bonnell (1653–99) in 1693; Mary, who married Richard Jones (1662–1729) of Dolanstown, Kilcock, County Meath in 1707; and their brother Henry Conyngham (d. 1707), who married Mary Williams, Lady Shelburne, in 1696. The eldest Conyngham sister, Katherine, and her husband, William Conolly, accumulated sufficient wealth to build Castletown House, the great Palladian mansion in County Kildare, and to ensure that she held a controlling position within the Conyngham family.

The regular exchange of letters was an important part of eighteenth-century domestic and political life. It helped to maintain family ties, and was also politically valuable in enabling the correspondents to keep abreast of the latest developments and appointments. As was the case with the Boyle sisters, the letters that the Conyngham sisters wrote functioned on a number of different levels, depending on the writer and the sister to whom the letter was directed. Furthermore, the meanings inherent in the use of words and the way in which the letters were circulated were also of importance. The letters of the Conyngham sisters were not written with a view to publication. The sisters' functional literacy is reflected in the immediate, unpolished, even unformed character of their letters. In their directness they detail the minutiae of everyday life, and the writers' complaints, commissions, advice, solutions and scandal.

Although the sisters' handwriting is fairly clear, they used little punctuation, their spelling is often erratic and many of the letters were undated. This was particularly the case with the letters of Mary Jones, who promised Jane that she would rectify this omission, but she never did.[2] Girls in eighteenth-century wealthy families were taught to read, but there was less emphasis on developing writing skills; Jane Lovell Edgeworth (1696–1764) of County Longford, for example, was taught enough to read the bible and cast up a week's household accounts. According to her mother, that was enough education for any woman![3]

For Katherine, Jane and Mary, the correspondence they exchanged constituted a crucial part of their daily lives; through it each sister developed and adopted her own strategy for negotiating her place within their family. For Jane Bonnell, this was to act as an intermediary not only between her sisters Katherine and Mary, but also between her wayward Conyngham and, more agreeable, Conolly nephews. The recipient of most of Katherine's letters (279 survive, written between 1707 and 1747) was her widowed sister Jane. Their other sister, Mary, was also more inclined to correspond with Jane than with Katherine, which is not surprising, given that she and Katherine lived relatively close to each other and met frequently, while Jane was based in London.

Letters were never really considered private; when received they were commonly read aloud or passed around to the assembled company, perhaps satisfying a need for gossip or a public recognition of benevolence. Mary and Jane both used this custom for their own ends; Mary would suggest to Jane to write and tell Katherine that she, Jane, had received a letter from Mary 'owning great kindness received from [Katherine]'.[4] Sometimes Mary would write to inform Katherine that a hogshead of wine had been sent to Jane in London that Katherine had offered to purchase for her. But while the wine may not actually have been dispatched, Katherine's payment for it was received and pocketed by Mary.[5] Although letters were commonly read aloud in company, there were also occasions when a degree of privacy was required, and Jane sometimes addressed her letters to Mary care of Mary's son-in-law Ralph Sampson, particularly when Mary was staying with Katherine in Castletown.[6]

Katherine Conolly: the matriarch

Following her marriage to William Conolly of Ballyshannon, County Donegal in 1694, Katherine, as eldest sister, automatically assumed the role of matriarch of the family. Although he was not her social equal, Conolly was ambitious; he was determined to make a name for himself politically and financially. With money from his marriage settlement to Katherine he bought confiscated Jacobite estates, and in 1715 he was unanimously elected speaker of the Irish House of Commons. By the time of his death in 1729, Conolly's combined income from lands and government positions amounted to c. £32,000 per annum, giving him the reputation of being the richest commoner in Ireland.[7] Even if Conolly's marriage was for strategic and financial reasons, there is no doubt that Katherine admired and cared deeply for her husband; her references to him in her letters both when he was alive and after his death are full of affection and respect. She rarely left his side during his final illness, and her growing distress is evident in letters sent to her sisters at this time. As the wife, and later the widow, of 'Speaker' Conolly, Katherine's financial and social position guaranteed her – at least outwardly – respect and deference from her sisters and those within the extended Conyngham and Conolly families.

Initially the Conollys lived modestly at Rodenstown, County Meath, and in 1707 William purchased a substantial house on Capel Street, Dublin. In addition to a townhouse, the Conollys also desired a more imposing country home, not too far from Dublin, where they could entertain and William could court his political connections. Consequently, Conolly purchased the Castletown estate in Kildare in 1709, and in 1722 construction of the great Palladian mansion that survives today commenced.

The building of Castletown was not complete when Speaker Conolly died in 1729. The remaining development, building and furnishing of the house, and the management of the estate, each a formidable task, were carried out under Katherine's direction. Contemporary reaction to the mansion, however, was not always favourable. Katherine's sister Mary wrote disparagingly of Castletown as 'the Grey Tower my sister has made', and she disliked staying there.[8] Nevertheless, Katherine enjoyed Castletown. The house, 'never designed as a place of rural seclusion', came fully into use as a centre of public and private functions by the 1730s, all overseen by the widowed but still formidable matriarch of the family, Katherine (see picture section).

As the wife of 'Speaker' Conolly, Katherine was a channel for people seeking favours; those who sought positions at Dublin Castle, government employment or clerical appointments often approached William Conolly through his wife. As evidenced in their correspondence, Conolly, with Katherine's support, dispensed favours and ruthlessly promoted their family's political interests. Power, position and wealth gave Katherine a strong sense of her own importance, particularly when her husband was living; following William's death she mourned her loss of political influence and clung to what power she had. As a widow, Katherine remained an influential figure, and lords lieutenant continued to visit her in Castletown; in 1740 she wrote elatedly to her sister Jane that she had entertained 'the gover[n]m[en]t and 100 more' over the Christmas period there.[9]

It was the combination of Katherine's social, financial and political status that permitted her to intrude and meddle in her family's business and welfare, whether they liked it or not. She would severely reprimand members of the extended family if they acted without consulting her first, or when she disagreed with their actions. When Katherine offered unsolicited advice on the subject of choosing servants for her nephew's house, his wife, Lady Anne Conolly (1714–97), responded that when she hired servants it should be to please herself, not her husband's aunt.[10] Katherine wrote offering a constant stream of advice to her sister Jane during her long-running legal dispute with their nephew, Williams Conyngham (c. 1698–1738), and, after Williams's death, with his brother Henry (1706–81) concerning the mortgage Jane held on the Conyngham's Donegal estate.

Given the political involvement of the extended Conolly/Conyngham family, it was inevitable that the sisters would be drawn into political disagreements between family members. When these occurred, Katherine was swift to communicate her political opinions. Mary's husband, Richard Jones, who was a member of parliament for Killybegs, a seat in William Conolly's gift, infuriated Conolly in 1709 by failing to vote as desired by the lord lieutenant. Over the years the disagreement between the families festered. Conolly subsequently refused to support Richard in the 1713 election. Attempting to resolve the situation, Mary wrote pleading letters to William Conolly and her sister Katherine, but to no avail. To Mary's dismay, Katherine sided with her husband. Mary then wrote to her sister Jane begging her to 'use her utmost endeavours to soften Brother Conolly for I am sure nobody has a greater influence on him than you'.[11] But Jane's efforts were also to no avail. The political divisions left lingering bad feelings on all sides.

While Katherine's wealth allowed her to reward deference and obedience to her, particularly within the family, many considered her fickle in her choice of favourites. Colonel Robert Dalway (1669–1740) noted that Katherine was 'governed and imposed upon by those about her', and her friends and relations were quick to solicit her for gifts of money or favours.[12] When her nephew, Frank Burton, approached Katherine for a loan, he obsequiously claimed that he had declined to avail of money from others, as he was afraid Katherine would 'take it ill should [he] ask money from anybody but her'.[13] As her sister Mary observed, they 'know very well how to make … court to my sister'.[14] But while Katherine was usually generous, she was also careful not to appear too charitable. According to Mary, Katherine's assertion that she was short of money was simply 'for fear I should aske her the lone of some'.[15] Nonetheless, Katherine did help the 'deserving' poor. During the famine crisis of 1739–41 she built the obelisk (later called Conolly's Folly) to provide paid work for tenants on the estate, and sent weekly cartloads of bread from Dublin to feed 100 Castletown tenants.[16]

Katherine claimed that she led a quiet life writing and sewing, but Mary's letters suggest differently. She noted that Castletown was constantly filled with relations and political and social guests. Katherine, 'the robust and ruddy faced widow' as the historian Toby Barnard has described her, was 'secure in her ample wealth to behave as she chose rather than as fashion decreed'.[17] Fond of gambling, she and her nephew by marriage, Frank Burton, incurred considerable losses playing the card game basset. Though the game was banned at Dublin Castle, Katherine defiantly continued to play it in Castletown.

Furthermore, some of the invited company were of doubtful social and moral character and, in her sister Mary's view, unsuitable. At one dinner in Castletown, Katherine seated the Drury Lane actress Kitty Clive (1711–85) at her own table, where there was 'company of the first ranke', an act that shocked her sister's sensibilities.[18] Perhaps it was the eclectic guest list and the random nature of the dining arrangements that resulted in Katherine never becoming a serious political hostess.[19]

Mary Jones, the aggrieved sister

While Katherine's ability to hold a grudge was legendary, it was her force of personality and superior wealth that particularly upset the equilibrium between her and her sister Mary, a frustration that is especially noticeable in Mary's letters. The youngest of the three Conyngham sisters, Mary married Richard Jones of Dolanstown, County Meath in 1707. Her financial position was never as secure as Katherine's, and after her husband's death in 1729, became less so. Although he had been amply provided for, Mary transferred to her son Roger (1705–47) her husband's bequests, leaving her with just a small annuity of £200, an action Katherine pointedly criticised in her letters to Jane in London. While Katherine's estimated income of £5,000 *p.a.* allowed her to support her sister Jane during times of particular hardship, she rarely extended meaningful financial assistance towards Mary.

It is evident that Mary and her extended family were not counted among Katherine's favourites. Possessed of a more retiring personality than her sisters, Mary found Katherine increasingly difficult as the years passed. Indeed, her letters reveal her mounting reluctance to stay with Katherine, while their disagreements sometimes spilled over into the public domain. Having failed to invite Mary to the wedding of their niece, Alice Burton, Katherine claimed publicly that Mary had refused to attend. But, as a feisty Mary wrote to Jane, 'as meney as asked me about it, I cleared myself'.[20]

Katherine's dislike of Mary's daughter Jane (*c.* 1717–85) and her husband's family, the Sampsons, was particularly noticeable; her gift to Jane of old linen aprons to make baby clothes was not appreciated by Mary, who wrote that she would have been ashamed to give them to her maid.[21] Katherine's extravagant and expensive gifts and purchases for those nieces and grand-nieces living with her were listed in great detail in Mary's letters to Jane in London. According to Mary, Katherine 'layed out 1000 or 1200 pound'[22] on Alice Burton's wedding, and in 1741 reported that 'Mis Burton gote a fine pair of eaire rings. I beli[e]ve they are worth 100 pound at least,' adding, perhaps slightly enviously, 'No young lady in Ierland is kept so fine nor at so great expence'.[23] A garden and grotto with statues and walks was also cut into the woods at Castletown for the nieces' enjoyment. But no matter how generous Katherine was to her family, she remained erratic in her meagre gifts to the Jones and Sampson families. It was at times like these that Mary, feeling slighted by Katherine, relied on supportive letters from Jane in London to restore her equilibrium. As she wrote ironically to Jane, 'I am a very good begger for you but the worst in the world for myself'.[24]

In life and in death Katherine had her favourites, and not all children's deaths were equally mourned. The marriage of Mary's daughter, Jane to Ralph Sampson produced at least fifteen children, most of whom died in early childhood. Despite the worry expressed by Mary in letters to both her sisters about the deaths of the children, Katherine rarely expressed sympathy for the bereft parents, declaring rather heartlessly that 'they ear all the most miserable rotten childrin as ever was boorn. She [Jane Sampson] is a great and foull b[ree]der'. Harsh comments indeed.

Jane Bonnell, family mediator

Although Mary and Katherine's relationship was frequently fraught, their sister Jane fared better. As well as being possessed of a more moderate personality and temperament, Jane's astuteness with money also garnered respect from the Conollys. The distance between Dublin and London (and later Chelmsford, Essex) allowed Jane the luxury of maintaining amicable relationships with both her sisters and their extended family. While Katherine felt closest to Jane, so did Mary. According to Mary, her temperament and outlook was due to the care Jane 'took of me when I was young. [It] was the greatest happyness of my life.'[25]

Jane Conyngham married James Bonnell in 1693; they had two sons who died young and a daughter, Rebekah, who died in childhood in Dublin.[26] In 1695, Bonnell was appointed secretary of the forfeitures commission, a position that would bring him into close proximity with his brother-in-law, William Conolly. Following her husband's death in 1699, and her daughter's death in 1704, Jane moved to live in England.

As a widow Jane was extremely vulnerable, socially and financially. Her late husband's estate provided her with a modest income that was reduced when the exchange rate between England and Ireland fell in 1701. She was, however, financially astute, abilities not normally attributed to eighteenth-century females. While William Conolly was alive Jane corresponded frequently with him on a diversity of financial matters. She invested in stocks and acted as a stockjobber for her friends while also buying lottery tickets for friends and family. She invested in South Sea Company stock and advised some of her women friends to purchase shares in the company; but when the South Sea bubble burst in 1721, she lost a significant sum of money.[27] Two long-running financial disputes, a loan she made to Sir John King (d. 1721),[28] and the mortgage she held on the Conyngham's Donegal estate, jeopardised her income even further.[29]

For Jane, letters to and from Ireland were of great importance, and her list of correspondents was extensive. She solicited jobs for friends and family directly through William Conolly and her reputation was such that she was one of a number of people consulted in 1710 when the issue of a viscountcy for Conolly was proposed.[30] Jane was willing to chase a debt or inheritance in England for someone based in Ireland, or to pay their London debts, as her sister Mary did for Jane in Ireland. Family and kinfolk who travelled into or through England often visited Jane; she was entrusted with the care of children going to and from school in England, and her home was a refuge for nephews sent away from school when ill. When asked, she was also able to furnish her sisters with detailed pedigrees of English visitors to Ireland. In addition, Jane acted as a conduit for parcels of goods and the purchase of linen, jewellery and furniture, and was the first to relay the latest London fashions to her sisters. She was also able to satisfy her sister Katherine's insatiable desire for drinking chocolate or 'jackalet' as Katherine called it. Indeed, Katherine rarely omitted in her letters to urge her sister to 'hasten my jack-alet'. Katherine also charged Jane with more personal requests. For example, she asked Jane to purchase for her a diamond ring in memory of her beloved Conolly niece, Anne (Nancy) Pearson (1712–36). In her letter Katherine enclosed a lock of Nancy's hair and requested that it be set into the ring. Poignantly, some of Nancy's soft brown hair remains pinned to that letter today.[31]

A trusted and reliable intermediary, time and again Jane was the first to be informed by her nephews and grand-nephews of their latest debts or transgressions; their letters appealed to her to plead their case with their aunt or uncle Conolly. In July 1721 her nephew, Williams Conyngham, admitted to Jane that he did not dare acquaint his uncle Conolly with the true extent of his debts, because 'if I had told him the [w]hole, I am convinced he would be in such a passion that I shou[l]d never been able to have brought him to temper ... I thought it was better not to risk it'.[32] Williams had acknowledged half his actual debts to his uncle, though he confidentially admitted the total amount to his aunt Jane.

Sisters, children and family guardianships

Of special significance in the lives of the three sisters was the guard-ianship of a succession of Conyngham and Conolly nieces and nephews, first by William and Katherine, and later by Katherine on her own. The correspondence between the sisters reveals their collective responses to the difficulties and delights of caring for these children and their perception of the latters' behaviour. Though childless, Katherine exhibited an overwhelming desire for children in her life. She pressed the newly married Alice Burton to visit Bath in the hope of a resulting pregnancy, for, as Mary Jones observed, 'she wo[ul]d so faine have a littell child of the[i]rs'.[33]

Particular attention was paid by the three women to the chil-dren of their brother, Lieutenant Colonel Henry Conyngham, who died in 1707: Williams (1698–1738); Henry (Harry) (1706–81); and Mary, referred to in the family as 'Missy' (d. 1737), who came under the Conollys' legal guardianship from a young age. In the early 1700s the eldest, Williams, was presumed to be William Conolly's heir, but his subsequent disreputable behaviour eventually ruled him out. Throughout their early correspondence, the sisters expressed deep concern about Williams's behaviour; they generally referred to him as 'our unhappy' and 'worthless nephew', while Katherine claimed he was born just to 'trouble the quiet of my days'.[34] Indeed, Williams epitomised the stereotypical unreliable rakish young man of the eighteenth century. By the age of fourteen he had contracted venereal disease and his many subsequent infec-tions confirmed that he behaved without any concern for his health and welfare, or anybody else's.[35] In an effort to remove him from bad company, Williams was dispatched on a grand tour of Europe with his tutor, but he quickly ran up exorbi-tant debts, all drawn on his uncle Conolly's account. When he arrived in Amsterdam, Williams met a young woman, Adamina Wilhelmina Nierop, and to the dismay of his tutor they entered into an engagement to marry, which they did in London in 1718, though both were under age.[36] Relying on Jane's position as family mediator, Williams wrote to her first with news of his marriage, pleading his case and imploring her to intervene on his behalf with his uncle and aunt Conolly. Jane duly obliged, but her entreaties did not dilute the wrath of William and Katherine, and letters full of anger and frustration from all sides flew between Ireland and London.

Shortly after the marriage Adamina died, and, again without consulting the Conollys, Williams married Constance Middleton (1698–1767) in August 1719.[37] The three sisters were dismayed by this behaviour. The couple's marital difficulties and Williams's continuing rowdy lifestyle were a constant subject of discussion among them. Writing to Jane, a weary Katherine wondered 'how he can hold out'.[38] Needless to say, Williams did not 'hold out'; he died at Slane in 1738, his death a relief to his aunts.

Growing up, Williams's brother and, subsequently, his heir, Henry Conyngham, posed fewer challenges. Katherine described him as 'tall as most men', 'good natured', but also lazy. Similar to those of his age and status, Henry was taught dancing, fencing and 'the matthamaticks', which according to Katherine was the limit of his abilities. Nonetheless, Henry developed into what Katherine believed to be 'a sober, managing, young man'.[39] The reality, however, was very different.

The marriage of Henry to Ellen Merrett (c. 1718/19–1816)[40] of London in 1744 caused another flurry of concerned letters between the sisters, and again Jane was the first to be informed of the event. The shortness of Henry's letter to Jane announcing his impending marriage, and Katherine's surprise at the news, suggests that there was little family involvement in his decision to marry. According to Katherine, Henry's expectations of marrying a fortune should have 'made him wiser, for that is what he has most at heart'.[41] Indicative of the sisters' reliance on their collective correspondence, Katherine cautioned Jane that she would 'be une[a]sey till I hear again from you of this matter'.[42]

Raising her niece, Williams's and Henry's sister Missy, was a more tender affair; Katherine lavished love and attention on Missy. She and Jane were intimately involved in the negotiations surrounding Missy's marriage to Frank Burton of Buncraggy, County Clare.[43] The night before the marriage, Katherine gave Missy a personal and practical letter of advice regarding the conduct expected of a married woman.[44] She advised that a wife should make a comfortable and peaceful home for her husband and, with a certain degree of foresight, emphasised how to behave towards her future mother-in-law, with whom Missy subsequently had a difficult relationship.

In this particular affair, Katherine exploited her correspondence with Missy to make her point; when Missy moved to the Burton family home in Clare, her mother-in-law Alice (d. *post* 1765) was firmly entrenched in the house and playing havoc with the marriage. Knowing that Alice opened and read Missy's letters first, Katherine deliberately wrote a pointed letter to Missy concerning her mother-in-law. Alice opened it, read it, flew into a passion, railed at her son Frank and departed the house in a temper. As Katherine admitted to Jane, it was exactly the result she had expected.

As the years progressed, Katherine's letters to her sisters, always deeply personal, became more so. Her loneliness and vulnerability, not really apparent in her early correspondences, is much more noticeable in her later ones. Unlike her sister Mary, who was surrounded by her own loving family, in older life Katherine was alone and relied heavily on the emotional support of her nephew William Conolly and his family. Conscious of her sometimes overpowering affection for their children, Lady Anne controlled Katherine's access to them. Of all the Conolly children, the eldest, Katherine or Kety (1733–71), was Katherine's favourite, perhaps because she carried her name, and her notes and postscripts to Kety are poignant in their simplicity.

Over the years the sisters, united in widowhood, mourned the deaths of their sons and daughters, nieces, nephews and grandchildren. Perhaps the greatest blow for Katherine and Mary was Jane's death in England in 1745. Unsurprisingly, the ongoing correspondence and relationship between the two remaining sisters never reflected the closeness that both had with Jane. Katherine herself died at Castletown on 23 September 1752, aged 90. Thirteen years later, on 9 May 1765, the *Gentleman's & London Magazine* announced the death of 'Mary Jones, relict of Richard Jones of Dollanstown, Co. Meath, and sister of Mrs Catherine Conolly deceased'.[45] Even in death the ties that bound Mary and Jane to their more famous sister Katherine endured.

Conclusion

Collectively the three Conyngham sisters' letters afford a picture of life within the extended Conyngham and Conolly families. Their content was overwhelmingly determined by their social and financial status, and because of the informality in the sisters' letters to each other the topics discussed were wide ranging. They highlight the many facets of female life in eighteenth-century Ireland; the domestic, the political, and the intricacies and difficulties of family relationships. The letters illustrate the values that guided the sisters' lives and reveal the strategies each adopted in order to negotiate her position within a highly charged family environment. Even though Jane and Mary's social and financial position could not match that of Katherine, it was their position as members of an elite family that enabled them to maintain this crucial family connection and correspondence. The letters between the three Conyngham sisters, Katherine Conolly, Jane Bonnell and Mary Jones, always poignant and deeply personal, provide an unrivalled window onto the lives of three remarkable eighteenth-century women and sisters.

Endnotes

1 See, Mary O'Dowd, *A history of women in Ireland 1500–1800* (Harlow, 2005); Gabrielle M. Ashford, Childhood: studies in the history of children in eighteenth-century Ireland. Unpublished PhD thesis, Dublin City University (2012).

2 NLI, MS 41,577/1, Mary Jones to Jane Bonnell, 15 April 1736.

3 R. L. Edgeworth and Maria Edgeworth, *Memoirs of Richard Lovell Edgeworth, begun by himself and concluded by his daughter Maria Edgeworth* (2 vols, Shannon, 1969; reprint of 1820 edition), 1, 106.

4 NLI, MS 41,577/3, Mary Jones to Jane Bonnell, 9 April [*ante* 1737].

5 NLI, MS 41,577/3, Mary Jones to Jane Bonnell, 18 December [*c.* 1737].

6 NLI, MS 41,577/3, Mary Jones to Jane Bonnell, 4 November *s.a.*

7 Patrick Walsh and A.P.W. Malcomson (eds), *The Conolly Archive* (Dublin, 2010), ix–x.

8 NLI, MS 41,577/3, Mary Jones to Jane Bonnell, 31 July *s.a.*

9 Katherine Conolly to Jane Bonnell, 15 January 1740, in Marie-Louise Jennings and Gabrielle M. Ashford (eds), *The letters of Katherine Conolly, 1707–1747* (Dublin, 2018), p. 190.

10 NLI, MS 41,755/3, Mary Jones to Jane Bonnell, 11 April 1734.

11 IAA, Castletown papers, A/1, Mary Jones to Jane Bonnell, 1713.

12 NLI, MS 41,477/5, Mary Jones to Jane Bonnell, 22 October [1737].

13 NLI, MS 41,577/3, Mary Jones to Jane Bonnell, 3 May *s.a.*

14 NLI, MS 41,577/5, Mary Jones to Jane Bonnell, 24 May *s.a.*

15 NLI, MS 41,755/3, Mary Jones to Jane Bonnell, 11 April [1734].

16 Jennings and Ashford, *Letters*, p. 190.

17 Toby Barnard, *Irish Protestant ascents and descents, 1641–1770* (Dublin, 2004), 270.

18 NLI, MS 41,577/5, Mary Jones to Jane Bonnell, 27 October (*post* 1737; *ante* 1743).

19 Rachel Wilson, *Elite women in ascendancy Ireland 1690–1745* (Woodbridge (Suffolk), 2015), 110.

20 NLI, MS 41,577/5, Mary Jones to Jane Bonnell, 1 December *s.a.*

21 NLI, MS 41,577/2, Mary Jones to Jane Bonnell, 24 February 1734.

22 NLI, MS 41,577/3, Mary Jones to Jane Bonnell, 9 September *s.a.*

23 NLI, MS 41,755/5, Mary Jones to Jane Bonnell, 14 March [1741?].

24 NLI, MS 41,577/3, Mary Jones to Jane Bonnell, 3 March *s.a.*

25 NLI, MS 41,577/4, Mary Jones to Jane Bonnell, 19 August *s.a.*

26 RCBL, Dublin, Registers of St Michan's and St John the Evangelist churches, Dublin.

27 Anne Laurence, 'Women investors, "that nasty South Sea affair" and the rate to speculate in early eighteenth-century England', *Accounting, Business and Financial History* 16(2) (July 2006), 255–9; NLI, MS 41,580/31, Jane Bonnell to Dr Francis Dickens, 15 September 1725.

28 NLI, MS 41,580/31, Henry King to Jane Bonnell, 25 January 1723.

29 In 1702 Jane invested most of her capital, £1,500, in a mortgage on the Conyngham's county Donegal estate. This formed the basis for the subsequent long-running dispute between Jane and her Conyngham nephews. NLI, MS 42,579/1, Brigadier Henry Conyngham to Jane Bonnell, 4 July 1702.

30 Patrick Walsh, *The making of the Irish Protestant ascendancy: the life of William Conolly, 1662–1729* (Woodbridge (Suffolk), 2010), 24.

31 Katherine Conolly to Jane Bonnell, 17 Mar. 1733, in Jennings and Ashford, *Letters*, p. 95.

[32] NLI, MS 41,579/1,Williams Conyngham to Jane Bonnell, 22 July 1721.

[33] NLI, MS 41,577/3, Mary Jones to Jane Bonnell, 19 March [1744?].

[34] Katherine Conolly to Jane Bonnell, 11 June 1719, in Jennings and Ashford, *Letters*, p. 11.

[35] Katherine Conolly to Jane Bonnell, 25 July 1719, in Jennings and Ashford, *Letters*, p. 15.

[36] NLI, MS 41,579/1, Christopher Caldwell, Amsterdam to William Conolly, including Williams Conyngham to Katherine Conolly, 17 September [1718].

[37] Constance Middleton (1698–1767), daughter of Elizabeth (*c.* 1677–1742) and Thomas Middleton (1676–1715), Stansted Mountfitchet, England.

[38] Katherine Conolly to Jane Bonnell, 4 February 1729[/30], in Jennings and Ashford, *Letters*, p. 62.

[39] Katherine Conolly to Alexander Murray, Scotland, 17 January 1728, in Jennings and Ashford, *Letters*, p. 42.

[40] NLI, MS 41,579/4, Henry Conyngham to Jane Bonnell, 6 September 1744.

[41] Katherine Conolly to Jane Bonnell, 1 January 1745, in Jennings and Ashford, *Letters*, 261.

[42] Katherine Conolly to Jane Bonnell, 18 April 1730, in Jennings and Ashford, *Letters*, 72.

[43] Katherine Conolly to Jane Bonnell, 20 February, 15 March 1720, in Jennings and Ashford, *Letters*, 18–20.

[44] Katherine Conolly to Molly Burton, 12 June 1720, in Jennings and Ashford, *Letters*, 20–2; see also, Gabrielle M. Ashford, '"Advice to a daughter": Lady Frances Keightley to her daughter Catherine, September 1681', *Analecta Hibernica* 43 (2012), 17–46.

[45] *The Gentleman's & London Magazine or Monthly Chronologer* 35 (1765), 320.

The Shackleton sisters –
Deborah, Margaret,
Mary and Sarah –
and the Society of Friends

Mary O'Dowd

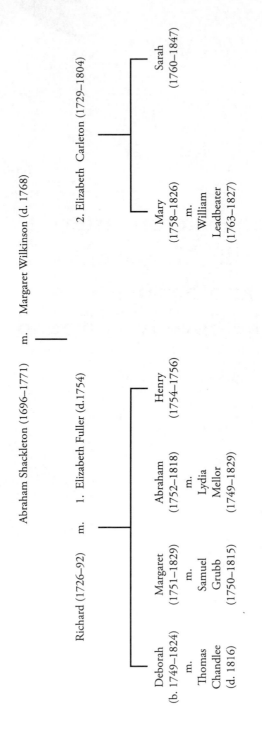

SHACKLETON FAMILY TREE

Abraham Shackleton (1696–1771)   m.   Margaret Wilkinson (d. 1768)

Richard (1726–92)   m.   1. Elizabeth Fuller (d.1754)

2. Elizabeth Carleton (1729–1804)

Deborah
(b. 1749–1824)
m.
Thomas
Chandlee
(d. 1816)

Margaret
(1751–1829)
m.
Samuel
Grubb
(1750–1815)

Abraham
(1752–1818)
m.
Lydia
Mellor
(1749–1829)

Henry
(1754–1756)

Mary
(1758–1826)
m.
William
Leadbeater
(1763–1827)

Sarah
(1760–1847)

In February 1824 the writer Mary Leadbeater (1758–1826) and her sister, Sarah Shackleton (1760–1847), visited a third sister, Margaret Grubb (1751–1829), in her home in Clonmel, County Tipperary. The women were in mourning for their eldest sibling, Deborah (b. 1749), who had recently died. They were all in their sixties, and Deborah's death had heightened their awareness of their advancing years. Their only brother, Abraham, had died some years earlier, and Mary and Sarah (known in the family as Sally) were suffering from ill health. They both would have found the journey from their home in Ballitore, County Kildare to Clonmel physically demanding. Margaret (known in the family as Peggy) warmly welcomed her sisters. Mary later described in her journal how Margaret had 'folded me in her arms, rejoicing over me, the three remaining children of my dear father were now together'.[1]

Although Mary's account suggests a strong bond of affection between all the Shackleton siblings, they never lived together as a family unit. Their father Richard Shackleton had married twice. Deborah, Margaret and Abraham were the children of his first marriage to Elizabeth Fuller, who had died in childbirth in 1754.[2] The following year, Richard married Elizabeth Carleton, who gave birth to two daughters, Mary and Sarah. Richard managed the famous Quaker school in Ballitore. There were usually over 50 pupils in the school, some of whom lodged with the master and his wife. Elizabeth had, therefore, charge of a large household, as well as managing the family farm. She was also a convert to the Society of Friends, and was eager to play an active role in its affairs. Elizabeth's daughter, Mary, later suggested that her mother had not wanted to be either a stepmother or a teacher's wife. It may have been for these reasons that, shortly after Richard Shackleton's second marriage, his two daughters by his first wife were sent to live with other relatives. Margaret went to stay with her stepmother's sister and mother in Dublin, while Deborah was brought up by her maternal grandmother until she was twelve years of age. Both girls also spent time as teenagers in a Quaker boarding school in Edenderry, County Offaly. Subsequently, Deborah returned to live in her father's house, and seems to have taken on the role of housekeeper, assisting her stepmother until she married in 1780 and moved to Athy. Margaret returned from boarding school to live with her aunt Deborah, who had moved to Ballitore following her sister's marriage to Richard Shackleton. When Margaret married in 1776 she went to live in Clonmel. Mary and Sally also left the Shackleton household as young children, and were brought up mainly by their aunt Deborah. Of the five Shackleton siblings, only Abraham spent his whole childhood in his father's house.[3]

Despite their geographical distance from one another, the sisters and brother remained in contact through letter writing and occasional visits. The sisters, in particular, wrote regularly to one another with news of family life, social events and their engagement with meetings and events organised by the Society of Friends. Much of this correspondence has survived, although it is now scattered in public and private archives in Ireland and the USA.[4] In addition, the journals of two of the sisters, Mary and Sally, are extant. Mary began her journal in 1769 when she was eleven years of age, and wrote the last entry days before her death at the age of 68 in 1826. For over 50 years, therefore, Mary wrote about her daily life, her childhood and teenage years, her marriage and the birth and rearing of her six children. The journal presents a unique record of an Irish woman who lived in the late eighteenth and early nineteenth centuries.[5] Sally Shackleton's journal writing was more limited. In imitation of her older sister, Sally kept a journal when she was a young girl, from the age of ten to fourteen. Later, as an adult, she recorded her travels while on a number of Quaker missions in Ireland and England in the 1790s.[6]

This private family archive of correspondence and journals is supplemented by the surviving records of Quaker meetings that all of the sisters attended on a regular basis.[7] The documentation on the extended Shackleton family is, therefore, one of the largest to survive for any Irish family in the eighteenth or nineteenth centuries. It is a very rich source for a study of familial relations, including those between siblings.

Historians of women have praised the Society of Friends for its attitude to women.[8] From its foundation in the seventeenth century, women were perceived as spiritually equal to men within the Society. Women were permitted to speak at meetings, preach in public and participate in travelling ministries to promote the Society in different parts of the world. In the 1670s the Quaker organisation established separate women's meetings. The women were given responsibility for certain aspects of Quaker society, particularly in relation to marriage and the supervision of the personal lives of members in the local community.

At the core of the Society's regulations was a focus on following a 'plain' or simple lifestyle. Members were advised to avoid ostentation in their choice of clothes, house design and furnishings. The education of children was also strictly controlled to avoid what were perceived as frivolous subjects, such as music or art.[9] Adherence to these rules varied, with some members interpreting them more rigidly than others. The large Shackleton family archive enables us to explore how the sisters responded to the regulations of the Quaker framework within which they lived, and the impact that these had on their lives.

Childhood and testing Quaker regulations

As children, the sisters would all have been very aware that they lived in a Quaker community. In the earliest entries in her journal at the age of eleven, Mary recorded her attendance at the local meetings in Ballitore twice or sometimes thrice a week. Her mother adhered closely to the Society's regulations and, much to her daughters' dismay, insisted that they wear 'plain' clothes and read a limited range of books.[10] The children were also forbidden from participating in other forms of children's amusements. Mary wrote of how she and some Quaker friends stood on the back of a horse to catch a glimpse of a drummer making his way through Ballitore village to announce a puppet show. She noted wistfully that 'that's our share of it for we would not be let go to it'. 'Nor,' she added a little unconvincingly, 'would we desire it'.[11]

Fortunately, Deborah Carleton was more flexible in her attitude to the Society's regulations than Mary's and Sally's mother. She allowed her young charges to read books that would not have been approved by the Society's authorities. Mary described how her aunt would hide under a cushion books that she had been reading with her nieces when their mother visited. In later life, Mary recalled that her mother had burnt a copy of Samuel Richardson's *Pamela*, her daughter having read one volume of it.[12]

Although Elizabeth Shackleton disapproved of what she perceived as frivolous reading material, she nonetheless, like her husband, believed strongly in the benefits of a formal education for children. As parents, Richard and Elizabeth ensured that all of their daughters received a structured school education. Deborah and Margaret, as noted already, attended Edenderry School in County Offaly as teenagers. It is likely that they had also attended a school for younger children in Ballitore. Their stepsisters Mary and Sally went to a small school run by a local woman in the village before they enrolled in their father's school when they were eleven years of age.[13]

The encouragement to Society members to keep a daily journal also testifies to the emphasis that the Quakers placed on the importance of literacy for girls and boys. The main purpose of the Quaker journal was for the author to record his or her daily spiritual actions and thoughts, particularly following attendance at a meeting. The journals kept by the Shackleton sisters did not, however, follow in this tradition. While the girls recorded their attendance at meetings, their main focus was on more secular activities. Their journals testify to the ways in which, as pre-teens and later as young teenagers, Mary and Sally stretched the rules of the Society of Friends as far as they could. Their preoccupations in their journals would be familiar to many girls of a similar age in today's society. They wrote about their conversations with girl friends, their changing hairstyles and about boys!

The Quaker hierarchy of meetings included weekly local meetings, quarterly provincial meetings and an annual (later changed to biannual) national meeting in Dublin. Attendance at meetings, particularly those at provincial and national levels, fostered personal connections between Friends across Ireland. Mary wrote with enthusiasm about meeting up with her young female friends before and after meetings. The Leinster provincial meetings rotated around meeting houses in Carlow, Enniscorthy, Edenderry and other towns. The Shackleton sisters sometimes stayed overnight when they attended meetings and, when they were in their late teens, visits to the annual meetings in Dublin usually entailed spending a week in the city. The sisters shared lodgings and often beds with their girl friends and Mary described how they frequently stayed awake until late in the night talking and catching up with each other's news.[14]

Mary also recorded in her diary her acute embarrassment and self-consciousness about the dress that they were compelled to wear as children. As she recalled in later life, 'the fondness for dress so natural to youth was pretty much starved'.[15] The dark, plain clothes that their mother insisted her daughters wear made the Shackleton girls stand out, even within the Quaker community. When she was eighteen, Mary described attending a Quaker wedding where the bride and her attendants wore light-coloured clothes. Mary was dressed in a long black cloak and hood, and felt decidedly out of place. She thought that she 'was not a fit person to be in the train of girls' that followed the bride from the meeting house to her home, but was mortified at the thought of having to join the men instead.[16]

There were, however, no explicit Quaker regulations about hairstyles and, as teenagers, the Shackleton sisters experimented with cutting their hair in different ways. In her journal, Mary boasted that she and Sally had been the first to introduce a new style of fringe to Ballitore. The sisters also experimented with powdering their hair.[17]

Mary and Sally were aware that the content of their journals did not conform to the Quaker tradition of journal writing. Mary was concerned to hide hers from her aunt and her older sister, Margaret. She described how she took care to write where she would not be seen, often in the dark or in a hidden corner of the house, and took steps to ensure that her aunt or Margaret did not see her bringing ink up to her bedroom:

> I steal the ink up to bed at night and down in the morning but always forget to leave it in a convenient place to steal so I run the risk of being seen carrying it away. I steal Betty's ink into the boys' room where I have a pen but as I could not do either … (my aunt being in the Parlour and Sister Peggy in

the Kitchen), I went into the closet, put a pen in my bosom and the ink bottle in my pocket ...[18]

Mary also recorded in her journal her fear that her parents would discover her writing habit: 'I dread my father catching me writing'. She described dreams that she had of her journal being discovered: 'I dreamt last night that St Clair found this journal and carried it to my father and mother which vex'd me exceedingly'.[19]

St Clair was one of the boys who attended the school in Ballitore and lodged in Deborah Carleton's house (see picture section). Mary and Sally Shackleton were the only girls at their father's school. In their home and at school, therefore, they encountered teenage boys on a daily basis, and many of their regular playmates included boys from the school. It is not surprising that both girls developed adolescent crushes on some of the schoolboys and confided their feelings to their journals. As a fourteen-year-old, Sally wrote of how she got up early in the morning to walk along the path, where she might encounter her 'beloved' on his way to school. She would later record if he looked at her or spoke with her.[20]

Mary wrote in her journal about her affection for two of the schoolboys and her meetings and conversations with them. The historian Kevin O'Neill noted how Mary described the frequent physical contact between the teenagers.[21] The schoolboys, most of whom were not Quakers, flirted with the girls and played games with them that involved asking intimate questions with kissing as a reward for the answers. When they were on their own without adult company, kissing and sitting on each other's laps seem to have been a normal part of the horseplay between the two sexes: 'Sally and I left in the parlour. Bob pulled Sally on his lap and kissed her. Sally got up and ran out. Bob pulled her back'.[22] A favourite game was 'questions and commands', better known today as 'truth or dare'. The questions that Mary recorded in her journal have a modern air to them:

I had asked Elsey ... if he was a rose who would he have to pluck him. He said Sally. She commanded him to kiss her the next time ...

> … Playing questions and commands with Jack and
> Sally. Jack commanded me to kiss Rayner which I
> was obliged to do.[23]

Other commands requested the truth about the girls' and boys' feelings for one another: 'I made Sally tell that she had rather see Elsey return than any other of the boys who left [i.e. the school]'.[24]

Not surprisingly, two of the Shackleton sisters, Mary and Margaret, married men who had attended the Ballitore school. When Samuel Grubb came back to Ballitore in 1775 to court Margaret, her younger stepsisters looked on, fascinated by his regular visits to their household. Much of the courtship took place in the presence of Margaret's parents and aunt, but in the evening the couple were often unchaperoned. Deborah Carleton suffered from migraine headaches and frequently retired early to bed, leaving her young lodgers and nieces to entertain themselves. As her sister reported, Margaret spent long periods of time alone with Samuel in a room in her aunt's house.[25]

Advice books addressed to young women on how to behave in polite society flourished in the last quarter of the eighteenth century. They prescribed the appropriate curriculum for girls' education, with an emphasis on 'accomplishments' in music, drawing and an ability to converse in a foreign language, particularly French. The Quaker education of girls eschewed such advice and, perhaps, along with it, imposed less restraint on young women on how to behave in society.

Adulthood and new opportunities in the Quaker community?

As the girls moved into their late teens and early twenties, their activities conformed more to the Society's regulations. Sally ceased to keep a journal, while the tone and content of Mary's changed. While she continued to write about her daily life, Mary also began to keep an account of religious meetings that she attended, summarising the advice given by those who spoke and recording her own spiritual thoughts.[26]

All of the Shackleton sisters also availed of the opportunities that the Society of Friends offered to single women to play an active role in the Quaker organisation. Richard and Elizabeth Shackleton did not put pressure on their daughters to marry, but Richard did encourage them to participate in meetings and become 'useful' members of the Society. As well-educated women, the Shackleton sisters were frequently asked to take on the role of clerk at the women's meetings, or to represent the local meeting at a provincial or national meeting. Their names, along with those of their parents, occur regularly in the minutes of Quaker meetings.[27]

As already noted, women were permitted to speak at Quaker meetings, but not all women were comfortable at speaking in public. Mary Shackleton had a speech defect, and she found it particularly challenging to speak at meetings. She wrote in her journal about how nervous she was when called on, as clerk, to read reports of meetings: 'my heart beat, and my blood flashed in my face ... the sense of my infirmity of speech prevailed'.[28] Sally also had difficulties contributing to meetings. She described one of her attempts to speak at a meeting as 'hard beyond expression'.[29]

Travelling ministries for women: Sally Shackleton's experience

Although she participated in two travelling ministries, Sally never seemed to be at ease when speaking at meetings. In 1797 she accompanied an American minister, Sarah Taylor, as she travelled through England and Wales. For the duration of her travels with Taylor, Sally kept a journal, in which she gave a detailed description of the logistics involved in a travelling ministry, as well as her thoughts about the experience. The two women undertook a lengthy journey, starting in Liverpool and travelling through Wales, down to London and then northwards through the midlands and the north of England. Their mode of transport was mainly by horse and cart. They covered between ten and 30 miles a day, stopping at towns and villages where there was a small Quaker community. They lodged with a Quaker family or, if none was available, at an inn. In a relay system, a man from the local Society would usually accompany the two women to the next town or village. Sometimes, however, they travelled alone. Physically, it was a gruelling experience. Sally described in her journal how the roads were often bad and the weather wet and cold. She kept a record of the distances travelled and estimated that in total they had covered about 8,000 miles. As the senior minister, Sarah Taylor spoke at most of the meetings, which varied in size from a small private family meeting of Quakers to larger public meetings open to all denominations. The two women might attend up to seven meetings a day in a locality.[30]

As a companion to such an active minister, Sally Shackleton could be perceived as embracing the public role that the Society of Friends provided for women. The next stage might have been for Sally to take on the more senior role, and to embark on a new journey with her own companion. Sally's journal, however, suggests a different narrative. She did not enjoy her travels with Sarah Taylor. She was clearly exhausted by the demanding schedule, and noted rather wearily in her journal the indefatigable energy of her companion: 'she never tires'.[31] There was also tension between the two women, as Sally continued to find it difficult to speak in public, much to Sarah Taylor's annoyance.[32] More significantly, Sally confided in letters to her sister Margaret that she doubted the value of some of the meetings that Taylor addressed. In particular, she wondered about the purpose of large public meetings open to non-Quakers. On one occasion, she noted that Taylor addressed a group of Welsh speakers in English, while at another meeting, many people stood at the door, fascinated, perhaps, by the phenomenon of an American woman preacher but reluctant to enter the hall to join the meeting.[33]

Sally may also have suffered from a crisis of faith during her travels with Sarah Taylor. Her journal notes a number of occasions when she seemed to question her religious belief and the purpose of the Quaker mission. She listened with envy as Taylor and another minister talked about the satisfaction they received from preaching: 'Ah, I thought were I favoured with this feeling I would ask no more'.[34] When her travels with Sarah Taylor came to an end, Sally did not participate in any further travelling ministries. Instead, she returned to Ballitore and took on a more traditional role for a single woman, the care of her elderly mother, who was suffering from dementia. She also became involved in charity work, visiting and administering herbal medicine to the poor, a skill she had learnt from her aunt Deborah.[35] Sally did not, however, abandon her questioning of Quaker beliefs and practices. In 1807 and again in 1810 she wrote to Margaret that she had been requested by the elders of the Leinster quarterly meeting not to speak at meetings because her 'appearances … had given uneasiness'.[36] Sally did not specify in her letters what she had said that had caused concern, but the incidences may have reflected her own restlessness and self-doubt about her religious belief.

Margaret Shackleton Grubb: a Quaker preacher

Of all the Shackleton sisters, it was Margaret who most welcomed the opportunities to engage publicly with the Society of Friends. The Society did not distinguish between single and married women when it came to approving travelling ministers. Margaret and Samuel Grubb had a large family of eleven children, but this did not prevent Margaret from serving as a travelling minister. She was encouraged to do so by her mother-in-law, Sarah Grubb, who was a prominent preacher and travelled around Ireland with her daughters and daughters-in-law.[37] Richard Shackleton also approved of his daughter's travelling ministry. Two of Margaret's children died while she was away from home. But even after these tragic events, Richard encouraged her to continue with her ministry:

> I am not for dragging thee, my dear child, from thy domestic concerns, which are various and important; but if truth gently draw thee, and whisper that a duty is to be done, I would have thee follow its leadings and secret monitions … if thou has heard the call, go forth, though it may be weeping; bear and scatter the precious seed …[38]

Margaret did not, however, fully return to her ministry before her husband's death in 1815.

The Society of Friends: a challenge for married women

Before she married, Deborah Shackleton was also active in the Quaker organisation. Deborah, like her sister Mary, married relatively late, at the age of 31. Following her marriage in 1780 she moved to Athy, where her husband, Thomas Chandlee, had a linen business. The Chandlees were active in the small Quaker community in Athy. Thomas funded and oversaw the building of the new meeting house in the town.[39] Like her sisters, Deborah served as a clerk at the women's meetings, but she does not seem to have been as actively engaged with the Society's wider hierarchy of meetings as Margaret or Sally.[40]

Not all married women or mothers, therefore, welcomed the pressure to attend meetings away from the family home or become too actively involved even in local meetings. After she married, Mary, like Deborah, endeavoured to withdraw from activities that drew her away from caring for her six children for any length of time. In particular, she expressed her frustration that her attempts to resign as clerk were often ignored.[41]

Although Mary and her husband, William Leadbeater (see picture section), regularly attended Quaker meetings, they did not play a prominent role in the Quaker organisation. Instead, they developed a network of friends outside of the Quaker fold. William had established an inn in Ballitore that was on the mail coach route. Several visitors to the inn became long-term friends of the Leadbeater family. Among those who stayed at the hostelry were the author Melesina Chenevix Trench, as well as Thomas Lewis O'Beirne, bishop of Meath, and his wife, Jane, who encouraged Mary Leadbeater to publish her writing. This included Leadbeater's *Cottage dialogues*, which appeared in 1811 and was very successful, partly because her friends persuaded Maria Edgeworth to write the introduction (see picture section). Written in the form of a dialogue between two domestic servants, the volume offered moral as well as practical advice to young female servants and their employers. The popularity of the volume encouraged Mary to write a series of books with a similar format involving conversations between the husbands of the two servants, and between two landlords.[42]

Mary clearly relished the status and fame that her publications bestowed on her. She was also aware, however, that members of the Quaker community were more reserved about her literary success. When she was young, her parents had expressed concern that she was spending too much time on writing verse. Elizabeth Shackleton was fearful that Mary's mind was so absorbed by her literary endeavours that she was in danger of neglecting her religious duties.[43] For his part, Richard Shackleton was proud of his daughter's talent as a poet, but he too advised her to give priority to religion, citing the example of Moses, who, he suggested, would never have become a 'leader of the Lord's people' if he had devoted himself to honing his poetic skills.[44] Later in life, Mary noted that she was admonished by some of the elders for spending too much time on her writing, and that this had hindered her from being a 'useful' member of the Society.[45] Mary was clearly, therefore, aware of the constraints that the Quaker community imposed on her ability to develop her public status as a writer of secular literature.

Conclusion

Living within the Quaker community bestowed considerable advantages on the Shackleton sisters that women in other Irish communities did not share. They were well educated and encouraged to develop their self-confidence through speaking at meetings and serving as officeholders. They also travelled far more widely than most women of their time, particularly if they were nominated as visiting ministers. There were also restraints, however. Mary Shackleton recalled that, as children, she and her sisters 'had great awe, perhaps terror on our minds of committing offence against religion'.[46] As adults, they could speak at meetings but, as Sally Shackleton discovered, they could also be asked to be silent if their speech did not meet the approval of the elders. Mary Leadbeater was also conscious of the suspicions within the Quaker community of the time she spent on her writing, regardless of her publishing success. As married women, Mary and Deborah were also often torn between their duty to the Society and their concern to care for their children. Then, as now, not all married women and mothers wanted 'to have it all'.

Endnotes

[1] NLI, MS 9343, Journal of Mary Leadbeater, February 1823, 16.

[2] The child, Henry, died of measles before he was two years of age.

[3] Information drawn from new edition of Mary Leadbeater's 'Annals of Ballitore' in preparation by Magda Stouthamer-Loeber for the Irish Manuscripts Commission, forthcoming.

[4] In Ireland, the main collections of manuscripts relating to the extended Shackleton family are deposited in the Religious Society of Friends in Ireland Historical Library (I am grateful to the curator Christopher Moriarty for his help with access to this collection), and in the National Library of Ireland (hereafter NLI). Some collections remain in private possession. For a list of American libraries with Shackleton family papers see, Gerald J. A. Hodgett, 'The Shackletons of Ballitore: some aspects of eighteenth-century Irish Quaker life', *Journal of the Friends' Historical Society* 54(5) (1980), 217–34.

[5] NLI, MSS 9292–9346, Journal of Mary Leadbeater.

[6] Sarah Shackleton's Journal, Department of Special Collections, Davidson Library, University of California, Santa Barbara, Ballitore Collection, MS 4. Consulted on microfilm in NLI.

[7] Minutes of eighteenth- and nineteenth-century meetings of Irish Quakers are available on www.findmypast.co.uk.

[8] The most recent study on women and the Society of Friends is Naomi Pullin, *Female friends and the making of transatlantic Quakerism, 1650–1750* (Cambridge, 2018).

[9] Michael Ahern, The Quakers of county Tipperary 1655–1924. Unpublished PhD thesis, National University of Ireland Maynooth (2003), 338–81.

[10] Richard and Elizabeth Shackleton, *Memoirs and letters of Richard and Elizabeth Shackleton, late of Ballitore, Ireland*, ed. Mary Leadbeater (London, 1823).

[11] Cited in Mary O'Dowd, 'Mary Leadbeater: modern woman and Irish Quaker', in D.W. Hayton and Andrew R. Holmes (eds), *Ourselves alone?: religion, society and politics in eighteenth- and nineteenth-century Ireland* (Dublin, 2016), 137–53:139.

[12] O'Dowd, 'Mary Leadbeater', 140.

[13] Details from Leadbeater, *Annals of Ballitore*, ed. Stouthamer-Loeber.

[14] Based on an analysis of Leadbeater's diary. See also, O'Dowd, 'Mary Leadbeater'.

[15] Mary Leadbeater, *The Leadbeater papers: the annals of Ballitore* (2 vols; London, 1862), vol. 1, 62.

[16] Mary O'Dowd, 'Adolescent girlhood in eighteenth-century Ireland', in Mary O'Dowd and June Purvis (eds), *A history of the girl: formation, education and identity* (London, 2018), 63.

[17] O'Dowd, 'Adolescent girlhood' 63.

[18] O'Dowd, 'Adolescent girlhood', 62.

[19] O'Dowd, 'Adolescent girlhood', 62.

[20] Journal of Sarah Shackleton, 1774.

[21] Kevin O'Neill, '"Almost a gentlewoman": gender and adolescence in the diary of Mary Shackleton' in Mary O'Dowd and Sabine Wichert (eds), *Chattel, servant or citizen: women's status in church, state and society* (Belfast, 1996), 91–113.

[22] Cited in O'Dowd, 'Adolescent girlhood', 58–9.

[23] O'Dowd, 'Adolescent girlhood', 58.

[24] O'Dowd, 'Adolescent girlhood', 59.

25 O'Dowd, 'Adolescent girlhood', 59.

26 O'Dowd, 'Adolescent girlhood', 64–5.

27 Based on a search of the records of the Society of Friends available on www.find-mypast.co.uk. For the role of single women in the Society of Friends see, Sheila Wright, '"I have no horror of being an old maid": single women in the religious Society of Friends, 1780–1860', *Quaker Studies* 16(1) (2011), 85–104.

28 Cited in O'Dowd, 'Mary Leadbeater', 142–3.

29 Sarah Shackleton's Journal.

30 This account of the journey through England and Wales is based on Sarah Shackleton's Journal.

31 Sarah Shackleton's Journal.

32 Sarah Shackleton's Journal.

33 Department of Special Collections, Davidson Library, University of California, Santa Barbara, Ballitore Collection, MS 4, Sarah Shackleton to Margaret Grubb, 30 September 1798. Consulted on microfilm in NLI.

34 As 33.

35 For Sally's return to Ballitore see, Mary Leadbeater, *The Leadbeater papers*, vol. 1, 271, 278, 295. Sally's life can also be traced through NLI, MSS 9292–9346, Journal of Mary Leadbeater. See also, Sarah Shackleton's book of medical recipes (Department of Special Collections, Davidson Library, University of California, Santa Barbara, Ballitore Collection, MS 4); for Deborah Carleton's interest in herbal medicine see, Mary Leadbeater, *The Leadbeater papers*, vol. 1, 60.

36 Department of Special Collections, Davidson Library, University of California, Santa Barbara, Ballitore Collection, MS 4, Sarah Shackleton to Margaret Grubb, 2 February 1807, 16 Feb. 1810. Consulted on microfilm in NLI.

37 Geoffrey Watkins Grubb, *The Grubbs of Tipperary: studies in heredity and character* (Cork, 1972), 87–99.

38 Shackleton, *Memoirs*, ed. Leadbeater, 186.

39 David M. Butler, *The Quaker meeting houses of Ireland* (Dublin, 2004), 238.

40 Of the four Shackleton sisters, Deborah is the least well documented. Future research on her correspondence in the Religious Society of Friends in Ireland Historical Library will enable us to trace the chronology of her life in more detail.

41 O'Dowd, 'Mary Leadbeater', 143–4.

42 O'Dowd, 'Mary Leadbeater', 147–50.

43 Leadbeater, *The Leadbeater papers*, vol. 1, 116.

44 Shackleton, *Memoirs*, ed. Leadbeater, 137–8. See also, 102–4.

45 O'Dowd, 'Mary Leadbeater', 137, 150–51.

46 Leadbeater, *Annals of Ballitore*, ed. Stouthamer-Loeber.

'More than kin and more than kind': The Owenson sisters, Lady Sydney Morgan and Lady Olivia Clarke

CLAIRE CONNOLLY

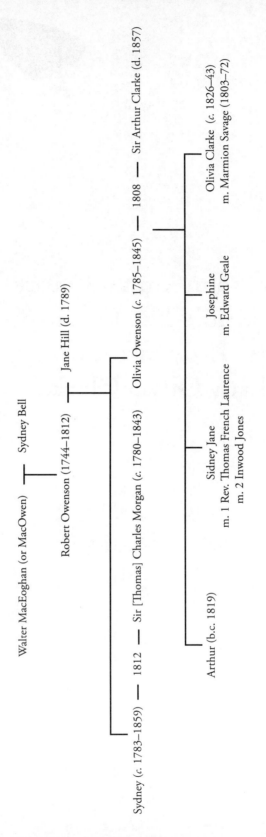

OWENSON FAMILY TREE

Walter MacEoghan (or MacOwen) — Sydney Bell

Robert Owenson (1744–1812) — Jane Hill (d. 1789)

Sydney (c. 1783–1859) — 1812 — Sir [Thomas] Charles Morgan (c. 1780–1843)

Olivia Owenson (c. 1785–1845) — 1808 — Sir Arthur Clarke (d. 1857)

Arthur (b.c. 1819)

Sidney Jane
m. 1 Rev. Thomas French Laurence
m. 2 Inwood Jones

Josephine
m. Edward Geale

Olivia Clarke (c. 1826–43)
m. Marmion Savage (1803–72)

Have I from childhood then, been writing,
And erst I well could write, inditing,
In scribbling ever still delighting;
        Since first the muse
Did kindly string my infant lyre,
And o'er my mind poetic fire
        As kind infuse;

Since first young fancy's meteor beam,
Did on my dawning genius gleam,
And wrapt me in poetic dream;
        As oft I strove
To sing, a sigh, a smile, a tear,
Or haply, an idea dear
        of infant love!

What! and no lines to thee addrest,
Thou longest known, and loved the best,
In no frail garb of fiction drest,
        not one to thee;
For whom I've oft wept, sigh'd, and smil'd,
My sister, mother, friend, and child,
        thou all to me!

– Sydney Owenson, 'To Olivia' (*c.* 1800)[1]

Sydney Owenson (*c.* 1783–1859) began at an early age to draw around herself the 'frail garb of fiction', claiming for herself a Celtic temperament that licensed a score of liberties with her life story. Mocking references to her desire to conceal her date of birth recur, but feminist critics have noted the gains she made via fiction: as Kathryn Kirkpatrick puts it, 'by constructing for herself the role of professional writer, Owenson crossed boundaries of class and gender, rescuing herself and her immediate family from penury and enjoying a professional and economic success usually reserved for men'.[2] To tell that personal, family and professional story more fully, it is vital to grasp the role of younger sister Olivia Owenson (*c.* 1785–1845) in her life and writings.

'To Olivia' (*c.* 1800), composed when Owenson was in her late teens, is addressed to her sister, but in fact celebrates Sydney's own burgeoning commitment to a life illuminated by literature. The lines do linger on the dark spot that is her 'poetic dereliction' of a beloved sibling, with Olivia imagined as 'more than kin and more than kind'.[3] The line paraphrases Hamlet's description of his uncle Claudius as 'A little more than kin, and less than kind'.[4] In Shakespeare's play, the line is delivered as an aside to the audience, signalling both Hamlet's resentment of his uncle Claudius and his determination to command the stage. Owenson's reworking of Shakespeare's line suggests a happier model of obligation, rooted in blood relationships, but shades of age and death are evident too: the 'Associate of my infant plays, / Companion of my happiest days' becomes the 'Sweet friend too of my riper years, / Who kindly shares my hopes, my fears'.[5] The poem ends on a bold image of death as a continuation of sisterly life: 'Nor e'en with life, to part with you, / For in my heavens, Utopia too, / I placed you high'.[6] Placed highest of all in the poem is Sydney's blazing ambition for authorship – a 'poetic dream' of lasting literary fame. Both women went on to lead lives characterised by display and performance, but it is to the older sister's writings that we most often look for evidence of their lives and relationships.

Background and family life

Sydney and Olivia Owenson (who became Lady Morgan and Lady Clarke, on marriage) made their way from backstage life and rented lodgings to dining rooms and salons. Their talents, work and connections came to define Irish romantic culture. They grew up in Ireland, the daughters of actor-manager Robert Owenson, a Roman Catholic from Mayo who converted to Protestantism, and Jane Hill, the daughter of a respectable Shrewsbury merchant who practised an evangelical Methodism. The pair met while Robert Owenson was on a theatrical tour of the Marches. The marriage was marked by their differences in background and outlook, and came under strain as Owenson continued to live the precarious wandering life of a jobbing actor.

In Lady Morgan's *Memoirs*, their early life is depicted in terms of laughter and fun, the girls singing sentimental tunes with their mother, and Jacobite songs with their father, all part of an ambient 'jingle of rhyme' that included religious recitations, 'the sublime Universal Prayer of Pope', the 'nursery rhyme of little Jack Horner', and 'tags of plays from Shakespeare to O'Keeffe'.[7]

Harder times came, but Sydney Owenson went on to achieve literary fame for her novels (mostly published under her married name). If her reputation dimmed in the early twentieth century, it enjoyed a revival following the feminist recovery of her writings in the late twentieth century. As Lady Clarke, Olivia also wrote songs and a play, but the work has received relatively little scholarly attention. Much of what we know comes from Lady Morgan's later life, when she published an impressionistic selection of family and other correspondence in her *Passages from my autobiography* and *Memoirs* (the latter prepared with the help of novelist Geraldine Jewsbury and edited by W.H. Dixon).[8]

We catch another glimpse of the two sisters in a late eighteenth-century poem by their friend Thomas Dermody, 'Advice to two adopted sisters'. The poem imagines young women whose close ties to one another are endangered by their own beauty and the charms of fashionable life. Putting on the patriarchal manner of an older poet, Dermody exhorts the girls to protect and secure their precious bonds, suggesting that friendship is fragile in the face of pride, and that praise may give rise to affectation:

> Dear girls, in youth and beauty's prime
> Despise not friendship's graver rhyme;
> Friendship, that marks your early bloom
> Perfection's brightest tints assume.
> The tints of modest worth divine,
> When sense and harmless wit combine,
> Prompt each low passion to control,
> Or bind in rosy chains the soul.
> Oh, ever charming! let not Pride,
> Usurper bold, your breasts divide,
> Nor fashion beauteous nature hide.[9]

Dermody goes on to mock his own presumption, sounding a welcome note of self-awareness in an otherwise strained and sententious poem, and suggesting real fondness behind the boyish bluster: 'Yet, sure, this idly-moral strain / Is both presumptuous and vain'.[10]

The stern moral of Thomas Dermody's poem belies the bonds that tied these young people together. In 1784 Robert Owenson, having previously performed at the Crow Street and Smock Alley theatres, opened his own rival establishment in the old Fishamble Street music hall, with the support and backing of the Irish Volunteers. Sydney later described it as 'The National Theatre Music Hall' though it was in fact known as the City Theatre. She also tells us that, as a result of a dispute about licensing, Owenson was bankrupted and went to work for Richard Daly, manager of the Theatre Royal at Crow Street.[11] While rehearsing there, Robert Owenson met a young and talented poet, employed by Daly as a stagehand. He brought Thomas Dermody home, introducing him to his wife as 'the greatest prodigy that has ever appeared since Chatterton, or your own Pope, who wrote beautiful poetry at fourteen'.[12] At eleven years of age, Dermody had already run away from his home in County Clare, intending to make his way as a writer. Sydney Owenson remembered that her mother was shocked at the young man's 'Papist name', but recalls that the entire family came to admire his literary taste and sympathise with his plight.[13] James Grant Raymond's *The life of Thomas Dermody* (1806) suggests that Owenson went to considerable lengths to boost the young poet's chances: he took up residence in 'an eminent bookseller's shop, and offered the books for sale to persons who entered, sometimes relating the doleful history of the luckless bard; and even assailed the passengers that passed the door ... by this mode he procured him considerable relief'.[14] Robert Owenson gave Dermody lodgings, food and clothing, but also arranged for the young poet to meet wealthy prospective patrons wearing rags.

The three young people grew close. In her first published book, a collection of poems, Sydney recalled the genius of her 'some-time brother' and his influence on her own taste: 'from thy lips, / My mind imbib'd th'enthusiastic glow; / The love of literature, which thro' my life / Heighten'd each bliss, and soft-en'd every woe'.[15] The poem in question is titled 'Retrospection', bearing the subtitle 'Written on the author's visiting the home of her childhood, after an absence of ighte [sic] years'. In it, she remembers a family group that included Dermody:

> Oft does my mem'ry sketch the social group,
>   At closing eve, that circled round the fire;
> Sweet hour that fondly knits each human tie,
>   Unites the children, mother, friend and sire![16]

Sydney can only have been about twenty years of age when she wrote this poem of 'dear scenes' and a former 'cot',[17] but by then the family group had already broken up, following the death of their mother. Dermody continued to correspond with the sisters, but died in 1802, aged only 27.

The two girls were educated by their mother at their home in Drumcondra until her death in 1789. Financial difficulties were ever present, but the successful novelist stops only occasionally to give readers a look back at the troubles of her childhood, which is almost always presented in terms of japes and jollity, amusing stories that often feature the family servant, 'the faithful Molly'.[18] What kind of household did Robert Owenson run after the death of his wife? Later commentators are sometimes defen-sive, as if rebutting accusations of slipshod parenting. A coun-sellor, George Stowell, admired 'the undeviating regularity with which Owenson, twice a day, would take his little daughters, Olivia and Sydney, out to walk. With a child tenderly held by each hand, Owenson, every inch a model widower, would daily leave the gaities of the city behind, and treat his tiny daughters to a healthful walk in the calm country'.[19] Reports of Robert Owenson's tender care for his children may reveal a pull between his busy professional stage life and domestic duties:

> Although Mr. Owenson was a true Irishman in the
> art of getting into difficulties, he was a careful parent
> in all that concerned his daughters. … He had kept
> them carefully from all contact with whatever was

undesirable in his own position and environments as an actor. In his own manners and bearing he was, by the testimony of all who knew him, a polished Irish gentleman. But, though full of the social talents which made him a delight at every mess-table and barrack-room of the places where he played, he had always been very careful with whom he allowed his daughters to associate. As children, he seldom allowed them to go to the theatre, and was strict in obliging them to go regularly to church, whether he accompanied them or not; he considered it a sign of steady and correct deportment … There never was the most passing thought of allowing either of his daughters to go upon the stage.[20]

That last comment is telling, implying the need to maintain respectability for Sydney and Olivia, and to remove the social taint of association with the stage. Certainly the girls often travelled with their father, and there are some suggestions that Sydney Owenson may have acted on the stage: a Dr Joseph Burke recalled seeing her father play Major O'Flaherty in Richard Cumberland's 'The West Indian' in Castlebar, on his tour of Connacht theatres in the 1780s, with his daughter acting alongside him.[21]

Following the death of their mother, Sydney and Olivia attended a Huguenot school in Clontarf while their father continued to pursue his career on the stage. At Madame Terson's establishment in Clontarf, they spoke French, read the bible and the works of Oliver Goldsmith and took walks by the sea. Their singing voices and ability to perform in front of audiences earned them friends: the two girls' popularity was secured on their first day at the school – 12 July – by their rendition of a ballad about the Battle of the Boyne. After three years, and following the closure of Madame Terson's academy, the young women went to a 'finishing school'[22] run by Mrs Anderson on Earl Street, built on lands newly laid out by Henry Moore, 3rd viscount Moore, 1st earl of Drogheda, whose daughters she had taught. Sydney did not enjoy this change 'from the sea-shore of

Clontarf to the most fashionable and fussy part of Dublin'.[23] The sisters mixed with 'the daughters of wealthy mediocrities', and walked out every Sunday with their father.[24]

The two girls and Molly lived without their father for periods of time, as he toured Irish theatres. The 'Early girlhood' chapter of the *Memoirs* includes fascinating letters from Sydney Owenson to her father, detailing the adventures of the small household he has left behind while travelling, giving an insight into precariously lived years. By Sydney's own account, the letters in this chapter are copies of 'old (or rather young) letters' kept by the family servant Molly and rescued from that 'Pandora's box, after her death, with many curious relics'.[25] A letter with the editorial date of 'probably 1796' regales Sydney's father with a story of a golden bird falling from the sky, glimpsed from their lodgings in St Andrew's Street in Dublin just as their father left them to set off on his theatrical travels. As Sydney tells it, the girls craned out the window to wave their father off. The wheels of his carriage had no sooner turned onto Trinity Street than the clouds opened up above them, and a golden bird descended from the sky. 'See what God has sent to comfort ye,' shouted Molly, though in the event the bird turned out to be a pigeon painted yellow by an upstairs neighbour. 'Olivia made great game of Saint Molly and her miracle', and the sisters returned to their usual occupation of socialising, singing and reading.[26] A later letter in the collection gathered in 'Early girlhood' tells of an experiment with phosphorous that went wrong, resulting in a scorched table, a burnt arm for Sydney and a scolding from the landlady.[27]

Amidst the tales of fun and flirtation can be found ongoing concerns relating to the future of the two young women, called upon by soldiers (despite the best efforts of Molly) and left to negotiate their own school bills. Their father was bankrupt once more, and Sydney worried over the immediate future of 'Miss in her Teens', her arch description of her younger sister.[28] One solution was for them to return to Mrs Anderson's school before the start of term (presumably they had to move out of their existing lodgings), but their father's failure to pay the bills from the previous year proved an obstacle to this plan. Mrs Anderson further refused to take in Molly 'on any terms'.[29] Sydney's response to the situation was to write: outlining their situation to their father, she assured him that she had 'two novels nearly finished', and that she intended 'to go as instructress or companion to young ladies'.[30] With the help of a few of her father's friends, Sydney secured employment with the Featherstone family in Bracklin, County Westmeath.[31] She began her working life as a governess in the winter of 1798, reading widely and beginning to draft her novels.[32] She remained with the family for about three years, including time sociably spent at their Dublin house on Dominick Street.

In her *Memoirs*, Sydney described a meeting with Thomas Moore as a key moment in the lives of the two sisters. Sydney met Sir John Stevenson at Dominick Street and heard him perform Moore's racy song, 'Anacreontic'.[33] Stevenson, himself newly acquainted with Moore, arranged an invitation for Mrs Featherstone, Sydney and Olivia to a musical evening at Moore's mother's house on Aungier Street, where polite Dublin society gathered to hear the young celebrity perform on his return from legal studies in London. Sydney's *Memoirs* give a breathless account of the effect of Moore's voice and presence, recalling how she and her delighted sister 'both went to bed in delirium, actually forgetting to undress ourselves'.[34]

Olivia at this time attended a school run by a former governess at Madame Terson's establishment, a Madame Dacier, who had opened a new school in 'Richmond, near Ballybaugh Bridge', and who was willing to take on Molly 'as upper children's maid to the establishment'.[35] The house was 'within a half an hour's drive' of the Featherstone's home in Dominick Street, and the two sisters saw each other regularly.[36] Yet the question of what would happen to Olivia and their family servant, Molly, was a perpetual matter of concern. Sydney gave this 'home picture' of family life in Dublin in 1801:

> *September 12th.* – Indisposition confines Olivia to her room; it is, thank God, but slight, yet sufficient to awake my anxiety and tenderness. We are seated at our little work-table, beside a cheerful turf fire,

and a pair of lights; Livy is amusing herself at work, and I have been reading out a work of Schiller's to her, whilst Molly is washing up the tea-things in the background, and Peter is laying the cloth for his master's supper – that dear master! – in a few minutes we shall hear his rap at the door and his whistle under the window, and then we shall circle round the fire and chat and laugh over the circumstances of the day.[37]

Other letters suggest that Olivia was prone to illness, suffering from 'a delicacy that has terrified us with the apprehension of a consumptive habit'.[38] In June 1803 Sydney wrote to her former pupil Miss Featherstone, letting her know that Olivia was unwell: 'a shadow of herself'.[39] Six months later she told her friend Alicia Le Fanu that Olivia was 'paying the tribute of a rheumatic complaint for having too closely adhered to the fashionable costume of the day'.[40] Recommended exercise and goat's milk by her doctor, Olivia was already recovering well enough for her sister to plan a trip to see the walls of Londonderry along with a trip to the races.[41]

It is difficult to reconstruct the exact whereabouts of this fragile family of three during these early years of the nineteenth century, but letters suggest that they continued to visit each other and spend time together, even while Sydney governessed and Olivia remained at school in Dublin. Robert Owenson continued to travel around Ireland and perform in regional theatres, becoming 'for some time stationary at Coleraine'.[42] Sydney visited Olivia and her father there, and continued to write warm and enthusiastic letters to her sister, addressing her as 'my dearest darling pet'.[43] In the late 1930s, as part of the national project run by the Irish Folklore Commission, school teacher Susan Irwin collected a story in Carricknahorna that bears on these years:

> Theatrical performances were frequently given in Ballyshannon and Lady Morgan then a young girl accompanied by her father Owenson performed in the town. After one of these entertainments in the

spring of 1802 a dispute arose between Lieutenant Mc. Govern of the Northumberland Regiment of Infantry, then stationed in Ballyshannon and George Henderson an attorney. The quarrel resulted in a duel in a field on the riverside at Laputa in which Mc. Govern was killed.[44]

In the summer of 1802 Robert Owenson took his daughters with him to Kilkenny for the first season of the city's famous private theatricals (1802–19), described by Michael Dobson as 'Shakespeare's finest hour on the Georgian private stage'; 'an important halfway stage between the private theatricals of the eighteenth century and the emergence of amateur dramatic organizations as Britain still knows them'.[45] While Owenson was busy managing actors and performances, Sydney made herself at home in an 'old diocesan library', 'fluttering over a quantity of genuine old Irish books' and laying the groundwork for *The wild Irish girl* (1806).[46]

Publishing and marriage

Already by 1800, Sydney had published her *Poems*, dedicated to the countess of Moira, including verses addressed to her father, her sister and her sometime brother, Thomas Dermody. She wrote fondly of her father in a poem titled 'The picture: on receiving a miniature likeness of my father'. The poem is gushing and repetitive, but evocative in its depiction of a household of three, united in loss but bravely facing the future.

> These shoulders too I've climbed to steal a kiss,
>   These locks my infant hands have oft carest;
> These arms I oft have fill'd, and shared the bliss,
>   For ah! with me, these arms a sister prest!
>
> Twin objects of the tenderest father's care,
>   A mother's loss we rather knew than felt;
> Twin objects still of every ardent prayer,
>   On whom each thought, each fear, each fond hope dwelt![47]

The poem imagines a living father already framed in memory and the household depicted here continued to be a precarious one.

Around 1807, enjoying the success of *The wild Irish girl* but still on shaky financial ground, Sydney arranged a job for Olivia as a governess with the family of General Brownrigg in Dublin. In the Brownriggs' home, Olivia met Arthur Clarke (later Sir Arthur Clarke), an apothecary turned physician and 'in those days one of the curiosities and celebrities of Dublin'.[48] Later nineteenth-century accounts stress Olivia's 'delicate health, sensitive nature and remarkable beauty', and present the marriage as her escape from a life as a domestic dependant.[49] 'He kept a carriage,' recalled Sydney, 'an advantage which a woman must have lived in Dublin thoroughly to understand'.[50] They married in 1808 and she moved into her husband's house in North Great George's Street, joined by her father and Molly. Robert Owenson died there on 27 May 1812. Arthur Clarke's reputation grew on marriage, helped (at least according to her *Memoirs*) by his sister-in-law's fashionable acquaintances, and he was knighted in 1811. Clarke earned fame for his advocacy of bathing and other hydropathic cures, and founded a 'Medicated Bathing Institution' on Lower Temple Street. Clarke's *Essay on warm, cold and vapour bathing, with practical observations on sea bathing* (1816) went into subsequent editions, and he followed it with *The mother's medical assistant, containing instructions for the prevention and treatment of the diseases of infants and children* (1820).

Sydney meanwhile continued to make her way in the world of books. Her career captures some of the complexities of a period that saw a transition from older forms of literary patronage to the burgeoning commercial world of publishing. The permission obtained (via her father) to dedicate a volume of poems to Lady Moira did not equate to the kind of financial support offered to Dermody some years earlier. Sydney continued to work as a governess while she wrote, making the most of the connections afforded in her roles, and famously (as she tells the story) sneaking out from the Featherstone home in Dominick Street with the manuscript of her first novel hidden under the 'market bonnet and cloak' of the family cook, her ambitions 'quickened into development by the success of Moore, the grocer's son'.[51] That novel, *St Clair,* was one of the few Dublin-published fictions in the years immediately following the Act of Union. Sydney went on to publish *The novice of St Dominick* (1805) and the aforementioned *The wild Irish girl.* All three share elements of historical romance, with sentimental modes, and served to fashion a new fictional model, summed up in the subtitle that she appended to *The wild Irish girl*: 'a national tale'. When *The wild Irish girl* was published and enjoying success, Sydney visited their maternal uncle and aunt in Shrewsbury in July of that year. She informed Olivia of a warm reception:

> Every indulgence, every tenderness, even respect that is possible for a human being to receive, is paid to me here. I am carried about as a show, worshipped as a little idol, and my poor aunt says she cannot help crying for joy, when she thinks she has such a niece![52]

It was not only in Shrewsbury that Sydney was 'carried about as a show'. She visited London following the novel's publication and appeared 'en princesse' at the salons of Lady Cork, meeting such celebrities as Lord Byron and Charles Kemble and finding herself at one party spending 'an evening seated on the second flight of stairs between Lady Caroline Lamb and Monk Lewis'.[53]

Sydney's ability to catch and repurpose literary fashions while making her own literary innovations was helped along by her canny dealings with publishers. No doubt her early experience of impecunious family finances left her determined to make the best of her prospects. Where contemporaries such as Jane Austen or Maria Edgeworth relied upon male family members to assist in negotiations with publishers, Sydney struck out on her own, taking advice from her father and a growing range of literary and cultural acquaintances but remaining solely responsible for her fortunes. Perhaps she was relieved to have some of this burden lifted when, in 1808, she accepted an invitation to live with Lord and Lady Abercorn at Baron's Court, in Campbell, County Tyrone, and later at Bentley Priory, Stanmore, Middlesex.

The Abercorns took a hand in her publishing arrangements and also her romantic life: through them, she met (Thomas) Charles Morgan, physician to the Abercorns and friend of Edward Jenner (praised by him for 'lashing the anti-vaccinists').[54] The story of their marriage is much mythologised but the resulting union was a long and happy one, with Sir Charles returning to live in Dublin and the couple setting up home on Kildare Street. Later he travelled alongside his wife, supporting all of her endeavours. As Lady Morgan, she published *O'Donnel* (1814), *Florence Macarthy* (1818) and *The O'Briens and the O'Flaherties* (1826), along with travel books on France and Italy and the ironically titled *Woman and her master* (1840), a sweeping historical review of the subjugation of women across the centuries. In 1837 Sydney was granted a civil-list pension of £300 per year in acknowledgement of her literary role (the first such pension ever given to a woman), and the couple moved to 11 William Street, Lowndes Square in Knightsbridge, London.

Olivia's story is less easy to track, though it also had some public dimensions. There was much social traffic between the two households in Kildare Street and North Great George's Street. Along with Sydney, Olivia became part of the social circle that gathered around Alicia Sheridan Le Fanu (1753–1817), her sister Anne Elizabeth (Betsy) Sheridan Le Fanu (1758–1837), her daughter Alicia Le Fanu (1791–?) and Mary Tighe (1772–1810), author of *Psyche* (1811).[55] She was known for a singing voice characterised by 'infinite grace and humour', and her songs 'in the Irish vernacular set by Sir John Stevenson, long formed the *délices* of musical society in Dublin'.[56] An admiring letter from Maria Edgeworth to her brother in 1815 describes a party at 'Mrs. Power's' in Dublin with 'Lady Clarke (Lady Morgan's sister) as "Mrs. Flannigan, a half gentlewoman, from Tipperary," speaking an admirable brogue, by far the best character, and she had presence of mind and a great deal of real humor – her husband attending her with kitten and macaw'.[57]

Anne Plumptre's Irish tour gives another first-hand account of Lady Clarke in company, where we once again encounter her skills as mimic and *improvisatore*:

She is very musical, and possesses a singular talent, approaching to ventriloquism, of imitating in singing two very different voices, so that it is scarcely possible to suppose they do not proceed from separate performers. The first time that I was entertained with a specimen of this talent, was in a large party at the house of her sister Lady Morgan, a few days after my arrival in Dublin. The company were in two rooms; and I happened to be engaged earnestly in conversation in the different room from that where the music was, when I heard, as I thought, rather an extraordinary kind of duet, in the form of an eclogue between a man whose voice was become rough from advance in years, and a squeaking little girl. I own this appeared to me rather an odd performance to introduce, since there was nothing in the singing of either party very much to amuse or gratify the company. How was I astonished when I found the whole to be executed by the same person, and that a lady whose natural voice, unlike either of the characters she assumed, is pleasing and melodious![58]

As early as 1807 Sydney had sent some satirical verses (on the topic of shoeblacks) by Olivia to the Dublin actor Richard Jones.[59] In 1826 Olivia got some of her songs into print alongside Sir John Stevenson's arrangements: her *Parodies on popular songs, with a paradotical preface by Lady Clarke* was published by Henry Colburn. In a preface, she presents her work as partaking of the same musical culture as Burns and Moore, albeit with a shift of tone 'from the *major* to the *minor*', replacing 'the tear with the smile'.[60] The volume was prefaced with a lithograph that illustrated a cabin scene framed by a score of fashionable literary references. Among the songs is one ('A description of Dublin') that boasts of Lady Morgan's Whig sympathies and mocks the Tory reviews:

> We've a Florence Macarthy,
> So merry and hearty,

Tho' I shouldn't say it's an elegant artist;
　　　She paints to the life
　　　And she causes much strife
　　　For a radical slut and a great Bonapartist.[61]

A review from the *New Monthly Magazine* (reprinted in the *Freeman's Journal* later that month) praised the 'light gamesome music' of Olivia's songs, and recommended that she try her hand at further comic fare.[62] Such a puffing notice could be expected from a journal owned by the publisher of the *Parodies*, Henry Colburn, also Lady Morgan's publisher. A more critical review in the *Quarterly Musical Magazine* noted some merit to 'the fair parodist's style', but queried the success of parodies based on songs that were not widely known, at least not in London. The reviewer only knew six of the twelve presented; of these, he found two to be worthwhile, suggesting that 'any one could write the rest in twenty minutes'.[63]

That Olivia herself became the subject of satire is no surprise given the 1820s mania for performance, improvisation and parody. Thomas Moore complained in a letter that he was 'solicited from all quarters' to give permission for one of his songs to be used in her *Parodies*.[64] Patrick Maume has identified her as the 'Lady Clarke' mentioned in the popular Orange song 'The orange lily-o':

And did you go to see the show,
Each rose and pink a dilly, O!
To feast your eyes, and view the prize,
Won by the Orange Lily, O!

Chorus
Heigh, ho, the Lily, O!
The royal, loyal Lily, O!
Beneath the sky, what flower can vie
With Erin's Orange Lily, O!

The Viceroy there, so debonair,
Just like a daffadilly O!

With Lady Clarke, blithe as a lark
Approached the Orange Lily, O!

Maume suggests that the Viceroy mentioned is likely to be one of the Whig lord lieutenants of the 1830s, while a later reference to 'Sir Charlie' is presumably Sir Charles Morgan, Olivia's brother-in-law.[65]

Throughout these years, Sydney and Olivia were often separated. Even before the elder sister moved to London in 1837, frequent travels by Lady Morgan to London, France and Italy meant long periods spent apart. One such period, lasting about a year, is detailed in *Passages from my autobiography*, which reprints a series of letters written between 1818 and 1819. During this time, Sydney was en route to France and Italy via London, stopping only to work on final additions to the text of *Florence Macarthy*, correcting proofs and making arrangements for its publication. Olivia, meanwhile, was pregnant in Dublin, awaiting the arrival of a son, referred to by his aunt as 'young Sir Arthur'. There are few references to the boy in biographies of the two sisters, and he must have died at a young age.[66] Letters from Sydney to Olivia continue to be fond, addressing 'my dear and only sister', 'my darling Olivia', 'my dearest darling pet', 'my dear love' or 'my dearest Livy'. The letters blend fashion and family concerns, as in this example from 1818: 'Toques like yours are very much worn. Send me word all about the babies and yourself'.[67] Sydney sent books, scarves, sweetmeats, toys and gossip to her sister, always enquiring after the well-being of 'our children'.[68]

In an early letter written from Holyhead after 'a bad passage', Sydney complains of her own sea sickness but expresses greater concern for her pregnant sister, 'patiently expecting her *mauvais quart d'heure*'.[69] The breezy French phrase conceals an ongoing anxiety about Olivia's condition and circumstances. There are long gaps in the correspondence while Sydney worried about her sister's health and the wisdom of a further pregnancy: 'our anxiety for you embitters all our pleasure', she writes from Paris, informing her sister that 'French women never have more than 2 or 3'.[70] In another letter that summer, still waiting for news from Dublin, Sydney told Olivia that 'I dream incessantly that I am attending you, and trying to keep the children quiet; but that Molly will make a noise. That is my nightmare'.[71] Finally assured of the arrival of a healthy baby, a letter from Sir Charles Morgan to 'Livibus' begs Olivia to reflect upon further 'frolics' and to 'take the pains to read three thick volumes of Malthus and Population'.[72] A letter written from Paris and dated 'Christmas Day, 1818, 7 o'clock' looks forward to family groups reunited:

> Merry Christmas! and a thousand of them, if it were possible. I trust this is the last we shall spend asunder. We have just drunk all your healths in a bumper of *vin de chablais* and wish we could enclose you a hogshead of it.[73]

As these letters passed back and forth between Ireland and the continent, Olivia was preparing a play for the stage. Her five-act comedy 'The Irishwoman' was performed at the Theatre Royal Dublin in 1819, preceded by a prologue written by her brother-in-law, Sir Charles Morgan. A comedy of manners featuring secrets, disguise and inheritance, along with mocking references to the fashionable practice of craniology, the play opens in London with the cruel plans of Sir Toby to marry off his niece, Miss Timorous, to the aged Lord Ancestor. The uncle's plans are upset by the arrival of an Irish woman who pretends to be his sister, the mother of the heroine, but is actually her old nurse, Mrs O'Gallagher. Aided by a stage-Irish servant character named Terence Macwhack, the newly arrived Irish characters disrupt the planned wedding and enable Miss Timorous to marry a handsome soldier recently returned from the Peninsular wars.

The text of the play was published in London by Henry Colburn, who brought out *Florence Macarthy* (as well as Olivia's songs and her husband's essay on sea bathing). 'The Irishwoman' attracted some snide remarks in *The Theatrical Inquisitor*, which noted that the sisters shared a publisher and imagined that 'a certain set of journals, magazines, and reviews, hired to trumpet the praises of Lady Morgan, and her periodical publisher, will bedeck it with a set of "ink horn phrases" that mean no more than implicit obedience to their patron's behests, and a conscientious earning of their appointed stipends'.[74]

Later years and legacy

It is difficult to pick up the thread of the sisters' relationship after Sydney moved to London, though it seems that the Clarkes were regular visitors to London and part of Irish social circles there. Thomas Moore's *Memoirs* refer to dinner parties held by Lady Morgan, including a 'pretty party' at the novelist's house, where he heard 'some of Rossini's things sung very well by the Clarkes'. 'I sung also,' Moore continues, 'and with no ordinary success'.[75]

Sir Charles Morgan died on 23 August 1843, while Olivia Clarke died in Dublin on 24 April 1845, and was buried alongside her father.[76] Sydney felt these successive deaths deeply, writing to Edward Bulwer Lytton on 29 April 1845 that 'I ought to have been prepared for the worst & yet I was not! You were witness how *she* supported me under my greatest calamity! ... I am alone and my heart is breaking!'[77] Olivia left three daughters, Sidney Jane, Josephine and Olivia. In 1839 the youngest, Olivia, married Marmion Savage (1803–72), author of satirical novels including *The Falcon family; or, young Ireland* (1845). She died in 1843, aged only 26. Her elder sister Sidney Jane Clarke married twice, first the Rev. Thomas French Laurence, in 1834, and later Inwood Jones, in 1840. As a young widow, Sidney lived with her aunt during the final years of life, and among Lady Morgan's papers in the National Library of Ireland is a sketch by the niece depicting her aunt playing the guitar.[78] Josephine married Edward Geale in 1841 and became involved in founding an Irish Academy of Music.[79] On Friday, 6 December 1861, *The Freeman's Journal* noted 'a very sweet song that has just appeared in print' with words by Lady Clarke and dedicated to Mrs Edward Geale, Olivia's daughter, finding in the song 'much of that pathos and peculiar musical rhythm that distinguishes Moore as the greatest lyrical poet of the day'.[80] Lady Morgan had no children, and Sidney and Josephine, along with Olivia Savage's son, inherited the majority of their aunt's fortune, alongside bequests to the

Theatrical Fund for Actors and the Governesses' Benevolent Association. Her nieces assisted W.H. Hepworth Dixon in the compilation of her memoirs, published in 1862.

An early account of the story of the two siblings is found in *Some fair Hibernians* from 1897, written by Geraldine Penrose Fitzgerald under the penname 'Frances A. Gerard'. The account given is highly coloured, but has the merit of being written when memories of the two women were still fresh. Since then, we find only passing references to Olivia's part in her sister's life, and little notice of her own occasional role amidst the changing cultural scenes of pre-Famine Ireland and Britain. Perhaps new feminist scholarship on women's networks in nineteenth-century Ireland and Britain will recover more of the intimate texture of a fascinating sibling relationship that played out on private and public stages.

NOTE: Images of the Owenson sisters as young women and of Sydney in her later years may be seen in the picture section.

Endnotes

[1] Sydney Owenson, *Poems* (Dublin, 1801), 48–9.

[2] Kathryn Kirkpatrick, Introduction to *The wild Irish girl* (Oxford, 1999), ix.

[3] Owenson, *Poems*, 50.

[4] William Shakespeare, *Hamlet*, eds Ann Thompson and Neil Taylor (London, 2016), 200.

[5] Owenson, *Poems*, 49–50.

[6] Owenson, *Poems*, 51.

[7] Sydney Owenson, *Lady Morgan's memoirs: autobiography, diaries and correspondence* (2 vols; London, 1862), vol. 1, 72 ff; 34.

[8] Owenson, *Passages from my autobiography* (London, 1859), 235.

[9] Thomas Dermody, *Selected writings*, ed. Michael Griffin (Dublin, 2012), 212.

[10] Dermody, *Selected writings*, 212.

[11] Owenson, *Memoirs*, vol. 1, 23–4.

[12] Owenson, *Memoirs*, vol. 1, 88.

[13] Owenson, *Memoirs*, vol. 1, 88.

[14] James Grant Raymond, *The life of Thomas Dermody* (2 vols; London, 1806), vol. 2, 8.

[15] Owenson, *Poems*, 95–6.

[16] Owenson, *Poems*, 97.

[17] Owenson, *Poems*, 93–4.

[18] Owenson, *Memoirs*, vol. 1, 209.

[19] W.J. Fitzpatrick, *The friends, foes, and adventures of Lady Morgan* (Dublin, 1859), 22.

[20] Owenson, *Memoirs*, vol. 1, 209.

[21] Fitzpatrick, *Friends*, 13.

[22] Owenson, *Memoirs*, vol. 1, 110.

[23] Owenson, *Memoirs*, vol. 1, 110.

[24] Owenson, *Memoirs*, vol. 1, 110–11.

[25] Owenson, *Memoirs*, vol. 1, 123.

[26] Owenson, *Memoirs*, vol. 1, 124.

[27] Owenson, *Memoirs*, vol. 1, 132–3.

[28] Owenson, *Memoirs*, vol. 1, 133.

[29] Owenson, *Memoirs*, vol. 1, 137.

[30] Owenson, *Memoirs*, vol. 1, 134, 136.

[31] Sydney may have confused the spelling with the variant, Fetherston, more commonly found in Westmeath at this time.

[32] Peter Garside, 'Introduction', in Lady Sydney Morgan, *St. Clair; or, The heiress of Desmond* (London, 1995; reprint of 1803 edition), xiii.

[33] [Thomas Moore], *The poetical works of the late Thomas Little* (London, 1801).

[34] Owenson, *Memoirs*, vol. 1, 183.

[35] Owenson, *Memoirs*, vol. 1, 135, 152.

[36] Owenson, *Memoirs*, vol. 1, 181.

[37] Owenson, *Memoirs*, vol. 1, 211.

[38] Owenson, *Memoirs*, vol. 1, 235.

[39] Owenson, *Memoirs*, vol. 1, 235.

[40] Owenson, *Memoirs*, vol. 1, 238.

[41] Owenson, *Memoirs*, vol. 1, 235–6.

[42] Owenson, *Memoirs*, vol. 1, 205.

43 Owenson, *Memoirs*, vol. 1, 280.

44 The Schools' Collection, UCD, vol. 1028, p.355. https://www.duchas.ie/en/cbes/4428255/4388860. A story of a duel for Sydney's affections was also told to me by Maureen Temple, Maharabeg House, County Donegal. The inscription on the grave of Lieutenant McGovern at St Anne's Church Ballyshannon reads: 'Returned to his native land lieth all that was mortal of Lieutenant Taffe McGovern, late of Northumberland Regiment of the Fencible Infantry. He fell in a duel on the 2nd March 1802, in the 23 year of his age. If the esteem and regard of his brother officers who have erected this stone to the memory could assist his soul in its flight to heaven, its ascent must have been rapid and its reception good'.

45 Michael Dobson, *Shakespeare and amateur performance: a cultural history* (Cambridge, 2011), 53, 65.

46 Owenson, *Memoirs*, vol. 1, 119.

47 Owenson, *Poems*, 70–1.

48 Owenson, *Memoirs*, vol. 1, 319.

49 'Sydney Owenson, Lady Morgan', *Temple Bar: A London Magazine for Town and Country Readers* 97 (1893), 341–62: 346.

50 Owenson, *Memoirs*, vol. 1, 319.

51 Owenson, *Memoirs*, vol. 1, 184–5.

52 Owenson, *Memoirs*, vol. 1, 280.

53 Lady Morgan, *The book of the boudoir* (2 vols; London, 1829), vol. 1, 109–10.

54 Owenson, *Memoirs*, vol. 1, 381.

55 Julia Wright, '"All the fire-side circle": Irish women writers and the Sheridan–Lefanu coterie', *Keats–Shelley Journal* 55 (2006), 63–72: 63.

56 Fitzpatrick, *Friends,* 45.

57 Maria Edgeworth to Charles Sneyd Edgeworth, 10 May 1815; *Life and letters of Maria Edgeworth*, ed. Augustus Hare (2 vols; London, 1894), vol. 1, 247.

58 Anne Plumptre, *Narrative of a residence in Ireland during the summer of 1814, and that of 1815* (London, 1817), 46.

59 See Julie Donovan, *Sydney Owenson: Lady Morgan and the politics of style* (Bethesda, 2009), 103, 127n.

60 Sir John Stevenson, *Parodies on popular songs, with a paradotical preface by Lady Clarke* (London, 1826).

61 Stevenson, *Parodies*, 15.

62 Review of *Parodies on popular songs, with a paradotical preface by Lady Clarke, Freeman's Journal*, 9 October 1826, 4.

63 Review of *Parodies on popular songs, with a paradotical preface by Lady Clarke, The Quarterly Musical Magazine and Review* 8 (31 July 1826), 353–5: 355.

64 Thomas Moore to James Power [March 1826], *The unpublished letters of Thomas Moore* ed. Jeffrey Vail (London, 2016), 1, 129.

65 Thanks to Patrick Maume for sharing his unpublished paper; '"Blithe as a lark": in search of Olivia Owenson Clarke, Dublin Whig wit'.

66 Owenson, *Passages,* 235.

67 Owenson, *Passages*, 46.

68 Owenson, *Passages*, 123.

69 Owenson, *Passages*, 13–15.

70 Owenson, *Passages*, 60.

71 Owenson, *Passages*, 87.

[72] Owenson, *Passages*, 103.

[73] Owenson, *Passages*, 235.

[74] *Theatrical Inquisitor* 16 (1820), 143–5.

[75] Thomas Moore, 16 February 1831, *Memoirs, journal, and correspondence of Thomas Moore. Ed. by the Right Honourable Lord John Russell, M.P.* (8 vols; London, 1853), vol. 6, 172–3.

[76] See the notice of her death and her literary achievement in *The Athenaeum* (September 1845).

[77] Quoted in Donovan, *Sydney Owenson*, 223.

[78] Donovan, *Sydney Owenson*, 102.

[79] Fitzpatrick, *Friends*, 45.

[80] *Freeman's Journal*, 6 December 1861, 2.

'We have found
a better way, boys':
Anna and Fanny Parnell

DIANE URQUHART

PARNELL FAMILY TREE

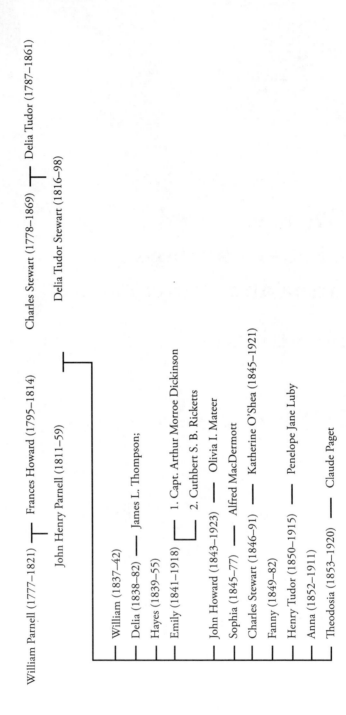

Penned in the opening phases of the Irish Land War (1879–81), Fanny Parnell's 1879 poem 'Hold the harvest' became her best-known work. Acclaimed by Michael Davitt as 'The Marseillaise of the Irish peasant',[1] Fanny's call for peaceful protest was symbolised by the lines:

> Hold your peace and hold your hands – not a
>   finger on them lay, boys
> Let the pike and rifle stand – we have found a
>   better way, boys.

In singling men out for instruction, Fanny highlighted the challenge to gendered mores that was omnipresent in the land campaign. Women's unprecedented involvement in this trans-national political movement that often defied both the law and gender expectations was controversial. However, not all female Land Leaguers received equal treatment at the hands of their critics; of the Parnell sisters, Anna was consistently depicted in the most extreme terms, even though Fanny, as a teenager, was the first of her family to support not only Irish independence but also the Fenians.[2] Fanny's sympathy with the Fenian cause mellowed as she matured into adulthood; she came to share Anna's view that physical-force nationalism should only be supported if it might succeed in freeing Ireland from British rule. She did not, however, approve of violence as a tactic in the Land War – hence, 'the better way' immortalised in 'Hold the harvest'.

The Parnell sisters were part of a large Anglo-Irish American family of eleven children. In the early nineteenth century Scottish political theorist, historian and psychologist James Mill offered a more precise definition of the family, one that inferred stability; it was 'The Group', a nuclear family that excluded servants.[3] Although outward appearances of the Parnells suggested gentility, the family was tried by early paternal and sibling death, as well as by economic instability. The Victorian period witnessed 'a greater degree of familial containment of women and children ... within the home ... [but] Family was the medium through which individuals entered society'.[4] This intersection of the domestic and public realms gave mothers a key function as 'the primary educator of children ... crucial to the ... shaping ... [of] self'.[5] The Parnells' American mother, Delia, inspired in some of her progeny an Irish nationalism that verged on Anglophobia. Delia took her elder daughters from the family estate of Avondale in Wicklow to London and Paris to pursue a finishing school education and spouses, whilst her sons and younger daughters, including Fanny and Anna, who were non-dowered and thus lacked marriage prospects, remained in Ireland.[6] Bookish, intelligent and schooled by governesses, the younger girls subsequently enjoyed more freedom than many women of their class.

Fanny Parnell (b. 1848) was described as 'a tall, intense, and handsome girl'.[7] A philanthropist, songstress and poet, she fulfilled some of the ideals expected of Victorian women. By comparison, Fanny's younger sister, Anna (b. 1852), was depicted as fragile in physical form but possessing a 'remarkable ability and energy of character, ... resoluteness of purpose ... together with a thorough revolutionary spirit'.[8] In 1864 Fanny, aged fifteen, began to contribute nationalistic poems to the Fenian paper, *The Irish People*. Writing under the pen name of *Aleria*, Fanny continued a pattern of female nationalist literary involvement evident from the Young Ireland movement of the 1840s.[9] Her poems were often rallying calls for Irish independence, sympathising with the labourers' plight. Fanny was greatly affected by the death of her father in 1859, and the lack of financial provision left for her mother. Devoted to her mother, Fanny moved to America to live with her on the family estate in Bordentown, New Jersey in 1874. Anna studied art in Dublin and London but later joined her mother and sister.

'Land League business is essentially women's business'

In 1878 the 'new departure' of Michael Davitt and exiled Fenian and Clan na Gael activist John Devoy conjoined physical force with constitutional nationalism to pursue land reform. It provoked Fanny and Anna to publish articles in the Irish-American press to counter criticism of the emergent land movement, and their brother Charles's involvement in it.[10] An 1879 letter by

Fanny to the editor of the *New York Tribune* entitled 'A sisterly defence' indicated that her political views could only be expressed under a familial banner.[11] Clearly aware of the gendered strictures that 'marked the most … distinctive indication of "one's place"',[12] Fanny 'regretted she was not a brother of Parnell to make it easier for her to help him in his battle for the rights of Ireland'.[13]

Fanny and Anna also helped to organise Charles's fund-raising tour of America in 1880. His address to the House of Representatives was a modified version of an article written by Fanny for the *North American Review*. However, intimating what lay ahead for women entering the political arena, the women's efforts were scorned by some male nationalists. Correspondence between Devoy and William Carroll of Clan na Gael, for instance, despaired of Fanny's 'interfering ways', suggesting that the Parnell sisters' work 'all smacked too much of a royal family'.[14] Undeterred, after Anna and Charles returned to Ireland, Fanny appealed to Irish-American women to support a female branch of the Land League to aid evicted Irish tenant farmers. The first Ladies' Land League was established in New York in October 1880, with Fanny as vice-president and her mother as president. To negotiate gendered strictures, the organisation was deliberately cast in the mould of a fundraising body. Its declared object was to collect 'funds for the Irish cause', but it also had a consciousness-raising mission, pledging 'to enlighten the members on the questions which now agitate Ireland'.[15] As noted, Fanny espoused peaceful protest as a tactic in the Land War, but she also supported the idea of Irish independence, which she envisaged as constituting a total break from the British connection. She was, however, socially conservative, and did not align the land question to the issue of social reform in the United States.[16] She also denied being a 'women's rights woman', portraying the organisation as an extension of women's proper role; 'Land League business is essentially women's business because it is … a work of philanthropy and humanity'.[17] This was persuasive; Fanny was described as lacking 'that unpleasant masculinity which is often seen in women who step outside of the home circle for any purpose', and her work was compared to that of Lady Jane 'Speranza' Wilde in the Young Ireland movement.[18]

Yet, this first incarnation of the Ladies' Land League was not above reproach. On St Patrick's Day 1881 Bishop Thomas Grace of St Paul, Minnesota condemned the 'repulsive' encouragement of women to leave their homes to establish political leagues that were 'foreign to their minds, their training, their duties, their womanly instincts and which were an infringement on the sacredness of the home'.[19] The women's organisation continued unabated, amassing over 225 branches and 17,000 members.[20] It was also defended by some male nationalists. Former Fenian Patrick Meledy denied it was 'a political organization ... it is a purely charitable one', reinforcing the prevailing separate spheres ideology by claiming that women were motivated by male activists 'entering their domain ... [of] clothing the naked, feeding the hungry, visiting the sick and in prison'. Meledy thus romanticised female activism: 'I do not want the ladies to fight ... it is the province of man, who represents superior strength and daring ... Woman's mission is to shed joy and gladness on all around'.[21] Further clerical condemnation came in the following year when Richard Gilmour, the Catholic bishop of Cleveland, excommunicated members of the local branch of the Ladies' Land League: 'Female modesty must be maintained ... No Catholic woman shall be permitted to forget her womanhood'. It was indicative of the organisation's, and more particularly Fanny's, growing sense of agency that she now publicly responded to the censure: 'We have done nothing against the Church. As Irishwomen we have organised a society to aid Ireland. If that be heresy, then we are heretics'. In the words of *The Nation*, the bishop was told 'to mind his own business'.[22]

Never a confident orator, Fanny began to deliver more public addresses, and became widely revered; lockets with her image, a poetry collection and song books of her poems were sold to raise money for the land movement. 'Hold the harvest' was also cited as evidence of incitement during the trials of Parnell and other male Land Leaguers in 1880. For Davitt the poem was 'the trumpet-call ... to the Celtic people to remember the hideous crimes of an odious system'. The reaction in court to the poem was certainly not what the prosecution intended: 'applause which could not be suppressed burst forth as the last stanza, with its final appeal to the God of the poor' was read. Davitt believed that this 'gave expression to Ireland's awakened hope to wrench the soil in one supreme struggle from the hands of their heirs to confiscations'.[23]

Anna Parnell: 'active to excess'

By comparison to its American counterpart, the Irish Ladies' Land League, with Anna, aged 29, at its head, was controversial from its establishment in January 1881. By that time, Anna's political views had already attracted criticism in republican circles. In 1879 Dr William Carroll, a leading figure in the Clan na Gael, wrote to John Devoy:

> Miss Parnell's opinions about … the Fenians [in the *Evening News*] … are not given as mere opinion but as facts … It will be news to all the Fenians … to learn that they would be satisfied with a Home Rule parliament and a British Queen. However it is not Irish to contradict a lady so we leave Miss Parnell to see what she will see of of 'Fenians['] love' for British Queens.[24]

An effigy of Anna (alongside one of the Pope) was burnt in Greenwich in the following year, and Katharine O'Shea recalled Charles Stewart Parnell's reaction: 'Poor Anna! Her pride in being burnt, as a menace to England, would be so drowned in the horror at her company, that it would put the fire out'.[25] The response to the creation of the Irish Ladies' League was also barbed; it was greeted with laughter by all but two members of the male Land League.[26] There were concerns that women's involvement would ridicule the land movement in its infancy, but Davitt averred: 'No better allies than women could be found for such a task. They are, in certain emergencies, more dangerous to despotism than men'. Nevertheless, he typecast politically active women as possessing 'more courage through having less scruples'.[27]

As in America, the Irish Ladies' League was legitimised by politicising the purported female domain of the home.[28] In a

February 1881 manifesto, a 'woman's mission' was epitomised in the following way:

> to feel for victims of affliction and oppression, to aid us in alleviating the sorrow and misery which ... threaten so many of our sex ... no more pure and noble duty could engage ... [women] than ... lightening the anguish of the prison, or dispelling the darkness of the desolate home.[29]

Anna shared Fanny's sense of gender difference, calling for 'the men and women of the country [to] take a manly and womanly attitude respectively' to fundraise for the land campaign, with men mobilising 'outside and the women and children inside'.[30] Attending the scenes of eviction, providing temporary shelter for the evicted and visiting tenants constituted key parts of the women's programme. They were, however, often depicted as a disruptive force, with particular emphasis on Anna's activities. Lord Belmore was informed, for example, that

> Miss Anna Parnell accompanied by the wives and daughters of publicans and country shopkeepers, visited a large property ... The visit ... caused ... much trouble, all the tenants have refused to accept bog tickets or give proposals for their waste bog fit for reclamation, and will only take the vacant grass farms if accepted as tenants.[31]

Indeed, as in America, the Irish Ladies' League was censured by Catholic clerics. The most extreme denunciation appeared in the pastoral letter of Archbishop Edward MacCabe, which was read at Mass in the Dublin diocese on 12 March 1881 and widely reprinted in the press. The women's organisation was portrayed as being headed by 'reckless leaders' operating 'under the flimsy pretext of charity' in a 'dishonouring attempt' to degrade 'the women of Ireland' by parading 'before the public gaze in a character so unworthy as a Child of Mary'.[32] However, other Catholic clerics and Irish Members of Parliament defended the organisation.[33] The latter group included A.M. Sullivan, whose wife was president of the London branch of the Ladies' Land League.

Although Anna shared her siblings' dislike of public speaking, she became an able and popular platform speaker, lecturing mixed-sex and all-male assemblies in Ireland, England and Scotland. In 1881, for example, an estimated audience of two thousand people paid admission fees ranging from a shilling to three pence to hear Anna speak at a Leeds Land League meeting.[34] *The Times* claimed Anna was lauded as '"The Queen of Ireland" ... [such is] the style and dignity now accorded to Miss Parnell by the Irish peasantry', but others were undoubtedly attracted by her increasing notoriety.[35] Her rhetoric intensified after the passing of the Land Act of August 1881, which she disparaged as a 'ridiculous mouse', and the widespread arrest of Land Leaguers, including Charles, in October of the same year.[36] Imprisonment compelled many male Land Leaguers towards negotiation with the Liberal administration, whilst Anna remained silent on the significance of the land courts established by the 1881 Land Act. She supported the no-rent manifesto, proposing nationwide tenant rent strikes, as a policy rather than as the political manoeuvre favoured by the men in the Land League:

> If the faintest suspicion had crossed my mind ... [that] the reason why ... [the male Land League] were not making preparations ... for a successful resistance to rent ... was simply that they did not intend to do it ... I would have had nothing to say to the Land League.[37]

The arrest of female Land Leaguers under legislation of 1361 which was used to prosecute women of ill fame further provoked Anna's ire. She castigated this 'female edition' of the Coercion Act as 'much worse than the male ... A new system of imprisonment without trial has been invented exclusively for women'.[38] Her platform addresses subsequently evoked memories of the Great Famine (1845–49), claiming that 'old Hypocrite Judas' Gladstone wanted to do away with the wooden shed [for the evicted]. If he did he would repair the way for another dying by thousands, called an Irish famine … then … the English people would send over a few thousand pounds and say 'Look how generous we are'.[39]

Anna's radicalism intensified the rift with male Leaguers; Charles was much vexed by her letter to *The Times* that criticised the outgoing Irish chief secretary William Forster's criminalisation of providing shelter for the evicted as evidence that 'the assassin's arm is not idle'. This appeared in the same edition of the paper as Charles's denouncement of the Phoenix Park murders of Forster's successor, Lord Frederick Cavendish, and his undersecretary, T.H. Burke.[40] William O'Shea consequently informed Gladstone of Charles's determination: 'to destroy the power of mischief … of Miss A. Parnell'.[41]

The press now deemed the Ladies' League 'a defiant sisterhood who have presumed to play the role of agitators', but Anna was singled out for particular reproach as a woman 'active to excess'. She was especially condemned for purportedly politicising children through the establishment of junior branches of the League.[42] The cartoon 'In bad company', published in the satirical English comic *Funny Folks*, depicted Anna as aggressive and armed (see picture section).[43] Schneller aligned this portrayal to the Elizabethan poet Edmund Spenser's depiction of a 'savage Irish woman', with Anna barefoot 'in a home spun outfit'.[44] However, this is a characterisation of 'Marianne', the symbol of the French Revolution subsequently adopted by French militant republicans. Marianne's image acquired heightened anarchical overtones following the 1871 Paris Commune, especially the violence of Louise Michel, who was transported to Nouvelle Calédonie for her actions. Wearing a Phrygian liberty cap, with Charles Parnell on the sidelines, Anna, portrayed with masculine features and a muscular frame, thrusts a rifle into the hand of 'Erin', the feminine allegory of Ireland.

Anna was also denied access to platforms due to her 'unbecoming language'; her recent description of Gladstone as a 'wretched, hypocritical, bloodthirsty miscreant' being the most likely cause.[45] Her denunciation of the Liberal administration prompted suggestions of irrationality, a claim that was often made of political women. Described as possessing the 'style of the Amazon and the spirit of the Spartan woman, who used to exhibit outward symptoms of joy when their husbands were slain in battle', Anna was again perceived as supporting violence, although she always claimed that it was a last resort.[46] The launch by Anna in 1881 of a Vigilance Committee to record and check Royal Irish Constabulary violence,[47] and her encouragement of white placard and platform decorations to underscore the ladies' peaceful work were also consistently overshadowed by her alleged extremism.[48]

Fanny Parnell: 'a stainless daughter'

Anna was soon troubled by more than press criticism. Suffering from recurring fever in mid-1882, Fanny cancelled travel plans and subsequently died, aged 33, on 20 July (see picture section). Her cause of death was 'paralysis of the heart',[49] but there were unsubstantiated claims of an overdose, as well as tuberculosis. Posthumous views of Fanny also varied. Publisher of the *Boston Pilot*, John Boyle O'Reilly, depicted Fanny in life as possessing 'the energy of a powerful man and the intellect and discrimination of a scholar',[50] but when she died he described her as so emotionally overwrought that she could not cope with the depth of her patriotism. Boyle O'Reilly thus claimed that Fanny died from the grief she felt for Ireland.[51] A short biography of Fanny with funeral obsequies and resolutions of condolence from representatives of the Land League in Ireland, England and America was published in America in the year of her death.[52] Ballads mourned her as a 'stainless daughter' and 'our chieftainess',[53] and a memoriam, given away with the *Weekly Freeman* newspaper, was published within weeks of her death.[54]

Many American Land Leaguers sought to repatriate Fanny's remains to Ireland, believing that her grave would become a rallying point and serve to unify the land campaign. Her brother Charles, however, would not allow it, averring that a person should be buried where he or she died.[55] Charles was undeniably distraught at his favourite sister's passing, allegedly avoiding the House of Commons in consequence. Anna would not leave home for weeks, and the press claimed that she was stricken with brain fever, an inflammation caused by acute emotional distress, and unable to 'recognize any one'.[56] Fanny's passing certainly impacted on Anna's fortitude. Unsurprisingly, there was little lament in the press at the Irish Ladies' Land League's enforced disbandment in August 1882 after Charles Stewart Parnell refused to stand by the female organisation's debts unless they ceased their work. The distaste that the women's association engendered lingered: one British newspaper later recalled the 'female patriots who mismanaged the affairs of the Ladies' Land League'.[57] It was never Anna's or Fanny's design to establish a permanent association of women. Thus, when Irish nationalism entered a new phase, with home rule rather than land reform as its primary object, it did so without women. As the *Wexford People* declared, 'the ladies will not take part' in the Irish National League, the successor of the Land League.[58] Anna certainly took no part. She went to live in the south of England, often under assumed names and in poverty so acute that friends arranged for her poems to be published.[59] She spent her time painting and, on occasion, redressed false claims made of the Ladies' League in the press, such as that by former ally Patrick Egan, who described the women as argumentative and 'obnoxious to the popular element'.[60]

An alternative Parnell legacy

Anna's estrangement from Charles for his part in the Ladies' Land League's demise stands in stark contrast to James Mill's avocation of the affection between brothers and sisters possessing 'most of the ingredients which go to the formation of Friendship'.[61] Anna rebuffed Charles's reconciliatory attempts, signifying that, as the historian Leonora Davidoff attested, sibling relationships 'can repel as well as attract'.[62] Anna agreed to write the introduction to Jennie Wyse Power's posthumous collection of Parnell's speeches, *Words of the dead chief*, published in 1892, although this was likely due to a sense of loyalty to the editor rather than to her brother. A despondent resignation regarding women's political power characterised Anna in the post-Land War era: 'If the men ... have made up their minds it shall not be done, the women cannot bring it about'. In 1907 she publicly censured the male Leaguers, especially with regard to their attitude towards the Women's movement: '... they were always ready to throw the responsibility of any failure on the shoulders of the women'.[63] In the same year she wrote that the Land League found 'fault with everything we did ... we could please nobody'.[64]

Anna drowned in Devon in September 1911. Unlike Fanny and Charles's ceremonial funerals, only seven people attended Anna's interment, none of them relatives. There was no clamour to return Anna's remains to Ireland; her grave remained unmarked for nearly 90 years before being restored by the Irish government in 2017.[65] Although some of her supporters wrote in tribute to the press, fearing 'that Ireland does not know, or appreciate, ... [her] priceless services', Anna could not escape the shadow of her brother.[66] The American press announced her death as that of 'a sister of the great Irish leader'.[67] John Redmond's condolences similarly stated that 'Ireland will never forget the noble part she played in ... [her] brother's heroic struggles in the Land League'.[68] But this was also Anna's struggle. She sought to end the land-lord system, which the Land War failed to secure, and wanted full independence for Ireland, which she depicted as 'a separate country by [an] act of nature'; she was thus far in advance of the home rule agenda embraced by her brother.[69] Feminism also played a part in Anna's political ideology; she wanted women to be enfranchised and autonomous, telling them 'you can mould your course of life anyway you please'.[70] This was embodied in the words that mark her grave: 'The best part of independence ... [is] the independence of the mind'. Anna had a sense of making history, but did not expect any acknowledgment. Rather, she wrote, 'when we are dead and gone and another generation grown up ... they will point to us as having set a noble example to all the women in Ireland'.[71]

Although Fanny's American Ladies' League is now being recast as providing 'a kind of political baptism for women', promoting reform and fostering political debate, history was slow to realise Anna's aspiration.[72] It is possible to read accounts of the Land War with either no reference to the Ladies' League or incorporating a barbed criticism being directed particularly at Anna. Jules Abels, for example, claimed that Anna was responsible for 'a hell broth of hate'.[73] In her memoir of Parnell, Katharine O'Shea aired similar views of her short-lived sister-in-law: 'The fanatic spirit in … this wild army of mercenaries … was extreme; in Anna Parnell it was abnormal'. She also claimed that Charles protected 'the country from … [Anna's] folly'.[74]

Anna's account of the Land War, written in reaction to Davitt's *Fall of feudalism* (1904), caustically titled *The tale of a great sham*, was written in 1907 but only published posthumously in 1986. Anna, never an impartial commentator, depicted her experience in the Land War as a 'long and uncongenial bondage'.[75] She mentioned neither Charles, Fanny nor the American Ladies' Land League, but her own organisation was not above reproach: 'People with aims so radically different and incompatible as the Land League and the Ladies' Land League had no business in the same boat'.[76] In straying from the bounds of feminine passivity, in wholeheartedly committing to the No Rent Manifesto and in showing profound political pragmatism, the Ladies' League was wrongly labelled extreme and extravagant, with Anna's radicalism castigated as the architect of women's undoing.[77] John O'Leary was confounded: 'What do you think of Healy's recantation about "no rent" manifesto and Miss P's contradiction? The last seems to me rather unintelligible'.[78] To unravel O'Leary's conundrum, the Parnell sisters need to be reassessed as integral to the Land War, and as women who, in life and in death, exemplified nineteenth-century gender expectations and the repercussions for those who transgressed these boundaries.

Endnotes

[1] Michael Davitt, *The fall of feudalism in Ireland; or, the story of the Land League revolution* (London and New York, 1904), 292. The French national anthem, 'La Marseillaise' was written in 1792 and adopted as the anthem of the French Republic in 1795.

[2] R.F. Foster, *Charles Stewart Parnell: the man and his family* (Hassocks (Sussex), 1976), 246.

[3] James Mill, *Analysis of the phenomena of the human mind* (2 vols, London, 1829), vol. 2, 176.

[4] Drew Lamonica, *We are three sisters: self and family in the writing of the Brontës* (Columbia (MO) and London, 2003), 12–13.

[5] Lamonica, *We are three sisters*, 17.

[6] The girls had an annual income of £100 each. For an account of the daughters of the family see, Marie Hughes, 'The Parnell sisters', *Dublin Historical Record* 21(1) (1966), 14–27.

[7] St John Ervine, *Parnell* (London, 1925), 1.

[8] Davitt, *Fall of feudalism*, 300.

[9] Aleria is on the eastern coast of Corsica but Fanny's choice of the name remains unexplained.

[10] The Irish republican organisation Clan na Gael succeeded the Fenian movement in America in 1869.

[11] *New-York Tribune*, 24 November 1879, 5.

[12] Lamonica, *We are three sisters*, 15.

[13] Robert Kee, *The laurel and the ivy: the story of Charles Stewart Parnell and Irish nationalism* (London, 1993), 206.

[14] Cited in Jane Côté, *Fanny and Anna Parnell: Ireland's patriot sisters* (London, 1991), 121.

[15] 'Ladies' branch of the Land League', *Worcester Daily Spy* [Worcester (Mass.)], 18 November 1880, 4.

[16] Ely Janis, *A greater Ireland: the Land League and transatlantic nationalism in gilded age America* (Madison (Wis.), 2015), 154.

[17] Cited in Tara M. McCarthy, *Respectability and reform: Irish American women's activism, 1880–1920* (New York, 2018), 74–5. Milwaukee's *Journal of Commerce* made an identical comment regarding Delia Parnell; see, 'The Parnell family', *Journal of Commerce* [Milwaukee], 22 December 1880, 2.

[18] 'The Parnell family', 2. Davitt also compared Fanny to 'Speranza' in his *Fall of feudalism*, 370.

[19] Bishop Thomas Grace of St Paul, Minnesota (cited in MacCarthy, *Respectability and reform*, 77).

[20] Janis, *A greater Ireland*, 143.

[21] 'A Ladies' Land League', *Indianapolis Sentinel*, 2 April 1881, 4. Meledy was imprisoned 1868–78 for the 1867 murder of Sergeant Charles Brett in Manchester but proclaimed his innocence.

[22] 'The Bishop of Cleveland and the Ladies' Land League', *The Nation*, 24 June 1882, 6.

[23] Davitt, *Fall of feudalism*, 292–3.

[24] NLI, MS 8,002/20/5, Dr William Carroll to John Devoy, 5 December 1879. Anna remained 'suspicious' of fenianism (see coverage of her lecture, 'Women's work in the Land League', *Freeman's Journal*, 5 December 1907, 15).

[25] In Eltham on 5 November 1880 (Katharine O'Shea, *Parnell* (London, 1973), 176).

[26] Michael Davitt and Patrick Egan.

[27] Davitt, *Fall of feudalism*, 299.

[28] Adrian N. Mulligan, '"By a thousand ingenious feminist devices": the Ladies' Land League and the development of Irish nationalism', *Historical Geography* 37 (2009),159–77: 168.

[29] 'The Ladies' Land League', *Reynolds's Newspaper*, 27 February 1881.

[30] Cited in Beverley Schneller, *Anna Parnell's political journalism: contexts and texts* (Dublin, 2005), 183. By mid-1881 there were 321 branches of the Irish Ladies' Land League.

[31] PRONI, D/3077/U/229, Hart papers, J.J. Benson to Lord Belmore, 29 April 1879.

[32] Cited in Côté, *Fanny and Anna Parnell*, 169–70. Local priests also sought to stem the spread of the Ladies' League in Britain. In Liverpool, for example, a number of clerics threatened to expel children from Catholic schools if they joined the children's League and a more sympathetic priest was threatened with removal (*Liverpool Mercury*, 28 March 1881).

[33] Archbishop Croke of Cashel denounced McCabe's 'monstrous imputations'. See, Archbishop Croke, 'The Archbishop of Dublin and the Ladies' Land League', *Freeman's Journal*, 17 March 1881, 5. Another hierarchical statement followed in June 1882 that Croke denied was a condemnation of the Ladies' League (Côté, *Fanny and Anna Parnell*, 175).

[34] 'Land League meeting in Leeds', *York Herald*, 11 October 1881, 5. Male Land Leaguers also addressed women's meetings.

[35] 'Ireland', *The Times*, 2 December 1881, 4. For a fuller discussion of Anna Parnell's British campaign see, Diane Urquhart, '"The Ladies Land League have [sic] a crust to share with you": the rhetoric of the Ladies' Land League British campaign, 1881–2', in Tina O'Toole, Gillian McIntosh and Muireann Ó Cinnéide (eds), *Women writing war: Ireland, 1880–1922* (Dublin, 2016), 11–24.

[36] Anna Parnell, *The tale of a great sham,* ed. Dana Hearne (Dublin, 1986), 99.

[37] Parnell, *Tale*, 89.

[38] 'Irish Ladies National Land League', *Manchester Times*, 28 January 1882. Thirteen women were subsequently arrested. Justice of the Peace Act (1361).

[39] 'Miss Anna Parnell in Huddersfield', Huddersfield Chronicle, 22 December 1881, 3; 'Irish demonstration in Manchester', *Manchester Courier*, 24 January 1882, 6.

[40] 'Miss Anna Parnell on Irish affairs', *The Times*, 9 May 1882, 6.

[41] Cited in Jane Jordan, *Kitty O'Shea: an Irish affair* (Gloucester, 2005), 79.

[42] 'To correspondents', *Liverpool Mercury*, 4 January 1882. Anna retaliated to charges like these claiming press partiality.

[43] *Funny Folks*, 18 June 1881, 1.

[44] Schneller, *Anna Parnell's political journalism*, 219.

[45] 'Mr Forster at Bradford', *The Times*, 13 May 1882, 9. Forster advised his constituents to ignore Anna's pronouncements in the same article.

[46] *Huddersfield Daily Chronicle*, 29 December 1881, 2.

[47] Côté, *Fanny and Anna Parnell*, 165.

[48] Evelyn Jenkins, The marginalization of revolutionary sisters: the betrayal of Fanny and Anna Parnell. Unpublished Doctor of Arts and Letters thesis, Drew University, Madison (NJ) (2006), 97.

[49] 'Death of Miss Fanny Parnell', *Cincinnati Daily Gazette*, 21 July 1882, 3.

[50] Cited in Côté, *Fanny and Anna Parnell*, 224.

[51] Jenkins, 'The marginalization of revolutionary sisters', 25.

[52] Aurelius MacSwynie, *A condensed history of the life of the late Miss Fanny Parnell…* (Hartford (Conn.), 1882).

[53] P. Hanley, 'Lines on the death of Miss Fanny Parnell' (1882) https://digital.nls.uk/english-ballads/archive/74893081?&mode=transcription, accessed 18 July 2020.

[54] NLI, EP PARN-FA (1) 111, W.E.P., 'In memoriam Miss Fanny Parnell' (James J. Lalor [printer], Dublin), 5 August 1882.

[55] Fanny's American grave became a site of pilgrimage. See, Foster, *Charles Stewart Parnell*.

[56] 'Personal', *Boston Daily Journal*, 29 July 1882, 1.

[57] *Sheffield and Rotherham Independent*, 9 December 1882, 6.

[58] 'Mr. Parnell, MP and the Ladies' Land League', *Wexford People*, 2 August 1882, 10.

[59] Dillon gave £50 in support; Anna was unaware of the gesture (Donal McCartney and Pauric Travers, *The ivy leaf: the Parnells remembered* (Dublin, 2006), 75).

[60] Anna used the names of Cerisa Palmer and Cecilia Garland (Jules Abels, *The Parnell tragedy* (London, 1967), 323).

[61] Mill, *Analysis*, vol. 2, 226.

[62] Leonore Davidoff, 'Kinship as a categorial concept: a case study of 19th-century English siblings', *Journal of Social History* 39(2) (2005), 411–28: 413.

[63] 'Lecture by Miss Anna Parnell', *Freeman's Journal*, 6 December 1907, 15.

[64] Parnell, *Tale*, 90.

[65] Dublin City Council erected a plaque to honour Anna at the former headquarters of the Ladies' Land League, now the Allied Irish Bank in O'Connell Street, in September 2021.

[66] Rev. D. Humphrys, 'The late Miss Anna Parnell', *Freeman's Journal*, 29 September 1911, 10.

[67] 'Anna Parnell drowned', *Baltimore American* [Md.], 24 September 1911, 13.

[68] *The Times*, 25 September 1911, 9.

[69] Parnell, *Tale*, 178.

[70] Côté, *Fanny and Anna Parnell*, 167.

[71] Parnell, *Tale*, 168. The Ladies' Land League was later seen as an example of women needing to be free from male control.

[72] McCarthy, *Respectability*, 71. See also, Janis, *A greater Ireland*.

[73] Abels, *Parnell tragedy*, 203.

[74] O'Shea, *Parnell*, 167.

[75] Parnell, *Tale*, 152.

[76] Parnell, *Tale*, 96.

[77] The Irish Ladies' League was £5,000 in debt at the time of disbanding. The women altered the wording of their agreement to disband so only those applications for relief which they, as opposed to the male Land League, had approved would be granted (see, Côté, *Fanny and Anna Parnell*).

[78] NLI, MS 18,009/46/1, John O'Leary to John Devoy, undated.

'Two girls in silk kimonos':
Constance and Eva Gore-Booth,
childhood and political
development

Sonja Tiernan

GORE-BOOTH FAMILY TREE

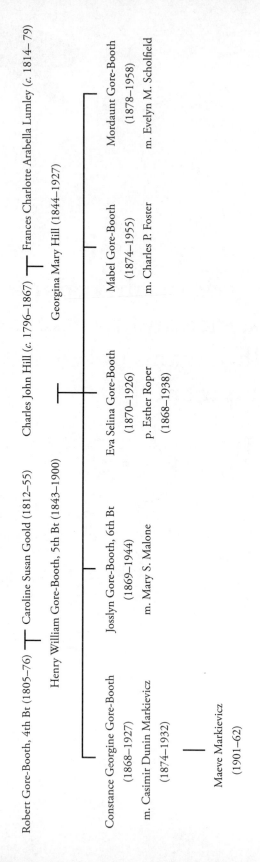

Robert Gore-Booth, 4th Bt (1805–76) ⊤ Caroline Susan Goold (1812–55)   Charles John Hill (c. 1796–1867) ⊤ Frances Charlotte Arabella Lumley (c. 1814– 79)

Henry William Gore-Booth, 5th Bt (1843–1900)   Georgina Mary Hill (1844–1927)

Constance Georgine Gore-Booth
(1868–1927)
m. Casimir Dunin Markievicz
(1874–1932)

Josslyn Gore-Booth, 6th Bt
(1869–1944)
m. Mary S. Malone

Eva Selina Gore-Booth
(1870–1926)
p. Esther Roper
(1868–1938)

Mabel Gore-Booth
(1874–1955)
m. Charles P. Foster

Mordaunt Gore-Booth
(1878–1958)
m. Evelyn M. Scholfield

Maeve Markievicz
(1901–62)

W.B. Yeats's admiration of youth is perhaps most evident in his celebrated poem 'In memory of Eva Gore-Booth and Con Markievicz'. In the first verse the poet recalls his early years, recounting autumn days spent at the Gore-Booth estate, Lissadell in County Sligo. An idyllic image is completed by the presence of the two sisters, 'both beautiful, one a gazelle'. In stark contrast with the splendour of youth, Yeats continues by describing how, as women, their beauty is ravaged due to their involvement with political affairs:

> The older is condemned to death,
> Pardoned, drags out lonely years
> Conspiring among the ignorant.
> I know not what the younger dreams –
> Some vague Utopia – and she seems,
> When withered old and skeleton-gaunt,
> An image of such politics.[1]

The Gore-Booth family

Although Yeats's poem may be read as a condescending portrayal of female activism, his imagery poses an interesting question. Why did two privileged women reject their aristocratic heritage so dramatically? Certainly, the image of the two women when they lived at Lissadell House reflects not only the beauty that Yeats idealised but also the affluence that provided them with rich clothing and pristine grooming. See picture section which includes a photograph taken around the time that Eva and Constance were presented at the Court of Queen Victoria in 1887.[2] The presentation to the monarch during her jubilee year was of course the ultimate testimony to the high social status of the Gore-Booth family. However, the image provides us with an insight into the sisters' developing radical ideals – each wears an armband emblazoned with the words 'Drumcliffe Co-operative Creamery'.

The creamery co-operative was an initiative started by their brother Josslyn, who worked with fellow Anglo-Irish landlord Horace Plunkett, credited with disseminating the ideals of the co-operative movement throughout Ireland. Josslyn had spent two years on farms in Canada and America learning about livestock management and was committed to the ideals of the co-operative movement. The Drumcliffe Co-operative Creamery became one of the most successful of such initiatives in Ireland.[3] *The Sligo Champion* newspaper commended the enterprise, noting how 'it is gratifying to find a gentleman so young as Mr. Josslyn Gore-Booth, so vigorously exerting himself to elevate and improve the condition of the Industrial Classes'.[4]

There were five Gore-Booth siblings, and it is clear that the eldest three – Constance, Josslyn and Eva – all demonstrated a propensity for helping others less fortunate than themselves. This social responsibility was undoubtedly first learnt during the wave of famine that hit Sligo during the winter of 1879.[5] The youngest two siblings, Mabel and Mordaunt, were born in 1874 and 1878 respectively, and may well have been too young to appreciate the gravity of the famine. Certainly, there are no records of the two youngest Gore-Booth siblings becoming involved in social reform; in their later years they appear to have led more traditional lifestyles. Mabel married Charles Foster, who had served in the Royal Scots Greys, and the couple lived near Falmouth in England until her death in 1955.[6] Mordaunt married Evelyn Scholfield and lived in London until his death in 1958.[7] Constance and Eva were the only two of the siblings who rejected their heritage and social status in order to pursue lives of social reform among the poor and dispossessed. By examining the Gore-Booth family background, it is possible to understand Eva and Constance's unease with their unearned privilege.

The origins of the Gore-Booth family in Ireland date to 1599, when Paul Gore arrived to serve in the Elizabethan army. Four years later, he escorted the defeated Irish chieftains, Donough O'Connor Sligo and Rory O'Donnell, to surrender to English forces in Athlone. Gore was rewarded for his military service with a grant of lands in the north-west of Ireland by James I, who had recently been crowned king of England and Ireland. In the aftermath of the rebellion of Sir Cahir O'Doherty in 1608, Gore was dispatched by Lord Deputy Sir Arthur Chichester to attack O'Doherty's remaining supporters on Tory Island. Exploiting a dispute between the Irish forces on the island, Gore intervened to slaughter the victors. Gore was created a baronet in 1622, and thereafter he resided in Ireland and built a castle in Sligo.[8]

The Gore-Booth sisters were direct descendants of Paul Gore. It is apposite to say that Eva and Constance learnt to despise this heritage. As children they appeared embarrassed by their family's wealth and privileged status, while in adulthood they resented the behaviour of many Anglo-Irish landowners. In 1904 Eva published a poem entitled 'The land to a landlord', belittling the egotism of the landed gentry:

> You hug to your soul a handful of dust,
> And you think the round world your sacred trust –
> But the sun shines, and the wind blows,
> And nobody cares and nobody knows.[9]

The activities of the Gore-Booth family during the Great Famine in Ireland (1845–49) continue to provoke controversy into the twenty-first century. One account maintains that Sir Robert, grandfather to Eva and Constance, forcibly evicted starving tenants from his land and boarded them onto a rotting ship, the *Pomano*, bound for Canada. Tragically, the *Pomano* sank in clear sight of Lissadell House, and all passengers on board were drowned. The Irish Folklore Commission, established in 1935 to collect folklore and stories of Ireland, includes accounts relating to this supposed mass eviction of tenants in the townland of Ballygilgan, known as the Seven Cartrons. The local folklore, recounted by two different contributors to the folklore project, describes how Sir Robert's evicted tenants 'were put out to sea in a ship which was so constructed that the bottom would fall out of it when it reached a certain distance from the shore'.[10] This tale of tenants drowned off the coast of Sligo retains a resonance locally, and indeed was the focus of debate in the pages of the *Irish Times* as recently as 2005.[11]

Although the facts of this case have never been proven, a ballad featuring the tale and blaming their grandfather for the tragedy was popular during Eva and Constance's childhood.[12] In more recent times, through an examination of the Lissadell estate papers in the Public Record Office of Northern Ireland, historian Gerard Moran and others have identified Sir Robert's assisted emigration scheme as a charitable project undertaken to alleviate suffering and hunger.[13] However, it is easy to understand why such local memories remain strong. The records of Saint John Almshouse in New Brunswick, Canada highlight an appalling situation: 172 passengers from a ship sent by Sir Robert were admitted to the institution over the course of twelve months after their arrival, and many of them died there.[14]

The scars caused by the Great Famine are still felt in many parts of rural Ireland. Sligo is an example of a county that never recovered its pre-famine population. The quay in Sligo town witnessed the exodus of tens of thousands of people who emigrated during and after the famine. The memory of this time is evidenced by the positioning of three famine memorials in the county established by the Sligo Famine Commemoration Committee. Moreover, the 2019 National Famine Commemoration was held on Stephen Street in Sligo town, an event that highlighted the impact that the famine had on the county. When Eva and Constance were born, the actions of their grandfather were still viewed with suspicion by the local community. This was an ambiguous legacy for the young Gore-Booth sisters to inherit.

Childhood: social and cultural influences

Constance was born in 1868 at her grandfather's London residence in Buckingham Gate. Her grandfather was then a member of parliament for Sligo; his entire family and a large household staff moved to London each year when the House of Commons was in session. While Sir Robert was an elected official, this does not necessarily reflect his popularity amongst the local Sligo population. He was first elected in 1850, topping the polls with a large vote from his Catholic tenants. It is possible that many tenants on the Lissadell estate felt compelled to vote for their landlord, as the secret ballot had not yet been introduced. He continued to represent County Sligo as a member of parliament until his death in 1876. Sir Robert's contribution to parliamentary debate was, however, undistinguished. He rarely attended House of Commons sessions, and Hansard only records four contributions made by him to debates over his 26 years as an MP for Sligo.[15]

The family's main residence at this time was Lissadell House, a 72-roomed Greek Revival mansion on 32,000 acres of land. It was here that Eva was born in 1870, just two years after her sister, Constance. Lissadell was then the largest landed estate in the west of Ireland. When Eva and Constance were children, hundreds of tenant families were dependent on the small patches of land they farmed at Lissadell, although their houses were not situated close to the main house. As a leading landowner in the county, Eva's and Constance's father, Henry, played a prominent role in local government: he served as high sheriff, justice of the peace and deputy lieutenant for the county.

When Eva's and Constance's grandfather died in 1876 their father took over management of the Lissadell estate. Within five years Sir Henry had reduced his tenants' rents below the level of Griffith's valuation, a national guide to the appropriate rents which tenant farmers should pay. The Irish Land League, founded in 1879 by Michael Davitt, campaigned for rents to be charged at the valuation rate. Sir Henry reduced his tenants' rents accordingly, without any legal obligation to do so. Whatever his reason for reducing the rents, this action no doubt impacted on the moral development of his young children. Numerous reports in local and national newspapers describe Sir Henry as a compassionate and good landlord. The London *Times* noted how:

> few owners or agents have such intimate knowledge of their tenantry, their holdings or their necessities. The people have been wont to come to Sir Henry as their adviser and friend, as their arbiter in family feuds and as their depository for wills and marriage settlements.[16]

The activities of Sir Henry's wife, Lady Georgina, on the Lissadell estate must also have inspired her daughters in their later campaigns for social reform. Their mother's charitable undertakings highlighted for Constance and Eva the importance of women's work. In 1860 Lady Georgina opened a school in an office building on the estate, where she taught women how to crochet, white embroider and do drawn thread work. Originally the women produced ladies' and children's handmade under-clothing; children's frocks, robes and pinafores; and tea cloths and handkerchiefs, in drawn thread work and embroidery. By 1895 the work of the Lissadell School of Needlework was officially recognised, and received a grant from the Congested Districts Board. In that year a total of 35 women were enrolled in the school. The produce was sold at reasonable prices, which provided the women with an independent income, crucial at a time of great poverty and deprivation in the Sligo area.

The work of the Lissadell School was highly commended in *The Pall Mall Gazette*. The paper recognised Lady Georgina's endeavour as a cottage industry that would contribute towards the 'regeneration of Ireland'. The article added that 'three or four members of the same family have by their work been able easily to increase the family income by £100 a year, a great contrast to the time when the whole burden fell on the solitary bread-winner'.[17] Lady Georgina's philanthropic activity provided her daughters with a positive example of economic reform through education and training. The fact that their mother also aimed to achieve financial independence for women would resonate with her daughters in their later labour campaigns.

When famine revisited Ireland during the winter of 1879–80 Sir Henry helped re-constitute the Carney and Drumcliffe Relief Committees. Conscious of the devastation caused by the Great Famine, the Gore-Booth family at once opened their food store and supplied meal to any tenant in need. The food was provided free, and the family, including the three eldest siblings, became involved with the distribution. Through this act of kindness, the local community once again warmed to the family. Years later, a former secretary of the Relief Committee in Sligo wrote to an Irish newspaper recounting the importance of Sir Henry's food donations during this time of hardship. He describes how Henry gave food 'to the starving poor, free to all, at his own cost'.[18] This sense of responsibility made a deep impression on the Gore-Booth children, and this was most clearly evident during the 1913 Dublin Lockout, when twenty thousand labourers were out of work. In a move reminiscent of food support given at Lissadell, Constance, along with Delia Larkin, organised soup kitchens at Liberty Hall to feed starving locked-out workers and their children.

The Sligo environment, with its wealth of history and legend, also served as a rich source of inspiration for the sisters. In their teenage years, Constance and Eva enjoyed roaming the local countryside on horseback, regularly stopping at cabins to speak with tenant farmers. During these visits Eva became enthralled with tales of Celtic legends and the history of Sligo. Constance was more impressed by the faded pictures of Irish republican heroes, such as Robert Emmet, on the walls of the tenants' cabins. Both sisters thrived on folklore that recounted the legends of the High Queen of Connacht, Maeve, reputedly buried on the cairn of Knocknarea Mountain not far from Lissadell. Maeve later became an inspirational character for both women. Eva wrote many plays and poems in which Maeve featured as the main character, while Constance was frequently compared to the warrior queen, and she named her only daughter Maeve.[19] These early influences sparked Constance's interest in Irish republican history and Eva's dedication to the Celtic literary revival. Eva spent much of her early life at Lissadell writing poetry and reading the classics. Constance showed a flair for sketching and painting, often illustrating Eva's work with watercolour paintings or line drawings, a collaboration that was to continue into adulthood.

Beyond Lissadell: literary and artistic lives

Constance left Ireland in 1893 to attend the Slade School of Art in London. She later moved to Paris to further her studies at the Académie Julian. It was while there that she met Casimir Markievicz, a purported count of Polish descent, whom she married in 1900. The couple's only child, the aforementioned daughter, Maeve, was born in 1901. From 1908 Maeve 'lived almost exclusively' at Lissadell, where she was cared for by her grandmother.[20]

The Markieviczs settled in Dublin in 1903 and immersed themselves in the artistic and theatrical culture of the city. They were involved in the establishment of the United Arts Club in 1907. The aim of the club was to provide a social space for the discussion of topics relating to art, literature and music. Constance insisted that membership should be open to men and women equally.

The couple founded an amateur theatre company in Dublin in 1908, the Independent Theatre Company, with Casimir taking the role of chief playwright and Constance that of a main actor. Constance and Casimir separated amicably the following year and continued with their artistic collaborations. In January 1912 their company performed Eva's first play, 'Unseen kings', in the Abbey Theatre.[21] This one-act play, subtitled 'the enchantment of Cuculain', differed significantly from the versions of the Cuculain story penned by male Irish authors.[22] Eva often manipulated the traditional version of Celtic mythology in order to present female characters as central to the drama. In the performance, Constance played the role of the temptress, one of the daughters of Cailitin who convinces Cuculain to enter into battle with Maeve, ultimately leading to his death.

The Independent Theatre Company disbanded in 1912. Constance was by then dedicated to the cause of Irish independence: she had joined Sinn Féin and Inghinidhe na hÉireann [Daughters of Ireland] and was a regular contributor to *Bean na hÉireann* [Woman of Ireland], the nationalist journal. While she had less time to devote to dramatic pursuits, she continued to paint and sketch throughout her life. She used her artistic skills in the intense propaganda campaign during the Irish civil war from 1922 to 1923. She produced cartoons critiquing the Irish Free State and depicting atrocities perpetrated by them. IRA leader Ernie O'Malley recounted how these cartoons were 'pasted on letterboxes and lamp-posts; handbills, and small mimeographed typewritten sheets sent around by hand', during this time.[23] The cartoons also appeared in the anti-Treaty paper *Poblacht na hÉireann*.

Eva continued writing and publishing throughout her life. She published no fewer than nineteen volumes of poetry, plays and philosophical prose, although much of this work was out of print from the 1930s until more recent times. Eva was a highly respected author during her lifetime. George Russell, 'Æ', was so impressed by her poetry that he included a selection in his anthology, *New songs*, in 1904.[24] She achieved a certain measure of fame for one poem in that volume, 'The little waves of Breffny'. The *Manchester Guardian* described it as 'one of the most beautiful things any writer … in the new Irish movement has produced'.[25] This poem remains perhaps her best-known work, and exemplifies how her early poetry was inspired by the beauty and legends of the countryside of Sligo. The first verse of the three-verse poem is set in a townland in Sligo near Lissadell:

> The grand road from the mountain goes shining to
> the sea,
> And there is traffic in it and many a horse and cart,
> But the little roads of Cloonagh are dearer far to me,
> And the little roads of Cloonagh go rambling
> through my heart.[26]

Her later poetry and plays often included a political message, such as, for example, the promotion of the idea of Irish independence from Britain.

When Constance was imprisoned at Aylesbury Prison in England for her part in the Easter Rising, the sisters engaged in their most surprising creative collaboration. Eva gave Constance a section from a play – 'The triumph of Maeve: a romance' – which she had originally published in 1905.[27] In the play, the warrior queen Maeve unsuccessfully attempts to shield her daughter, Fionavar, from the atrocities of her brutal and bloody battles. When Fionavar witnesses the aftermath of the battle led by her mother, she dies from heartache. In the aftermath of the Rising, Eva resolved to publish the final three acts of the play separately, focusing on 'The death of Fionavar'.[28] Eva wrote the introduction in May 1916, dedicating it 'To the Memory of the Dead. The many who died for Freedom and the One who died for Peace'.[29] 'The triumph of Maeve' incorporated a strong pacifist message. Eva asked Constance to illustrate the play, and she agreed. While imprisoned she drew pen-and-ink illustrations to accompany the text. As Constance was not allowed art materials, she was said to have used quills fashioned from rook feathers to complete her task.[30]

The opening page of the publication is adorned with Constance's sketches of wingèd horses flying gloriously free. The remaining 85 pages of text are bordered with drawings of flowers, sunsets and horses. The volume was published in England and marketed in America. American reviewers were quick to note the obvious paradox with this publication. A play with a strong pacifist message was illustrated by a convicted armed rebel, from her prison cell. The *New York Times* dedicated an entire page to the curiosity of the publication, under the title 'Irish rebel illustrates non-resistance play'.[31]

Later that year, Eva established a radical journal, *Urania*, edited with her partner Esther Roper and three others.[32] The chosen title reflected the content of the journal as advocating something beyond mainstream feminism of the time. The term *urania* was first coined by the German sexologist Karl Heinrich Ulrichs to describe homosexuality, and was filtered into the English language by the writer and philosopher Edward Carpenter.[33] *Urania* was privately printed and circulated, supporting same-sex relationships and transgender rights.[34] The editors of the journal presented instances of female same-sex love as natural.[35]

Beyond Lissadell: activism and political involvement

The Gore-Booth sisters both became extraordinary political activists, each in her own right. Constance rejected her aristocratic heritage and ended her days living among the working classes in Dublin, where she had become deeply involved with labour and social reform movements. Following her marriage to Casimir Markievicz, Constance had used the title Countess Markievicz.[36] She ultimately devoted herself to the cause of Irish nationalism, taking up arms during the Easter Rising in 1916. She was second-in-command of a group of combatants, first in St Stephen's Green and later in the Royal College of Surgeons in Ireland. Constance was sentenced to death for her part in the Rising. The sentence was later commuted to life imprisonment on account of her sex after appeals by members of her family and others.

Two years after the Rising, Constance became the first woman to be elected to the British House of Commons following the passing of the Representation of the People Act that granted the vote to women over the age of 30 who met a property qualification. A second act, the Parliament (Qualification of Women) Act, permitted women over 21 to stand for election. Constance declined her seat on nationalist grounds. At the time of her election, like many of the other elected Sinn Féin candidates, Constance was in prison for her involvement in what became known as the German plot. She was arrested at her home in Rathmines in Dublin after a proclamation was issued by the recently appointed lord lieutenant, Viscount French, who maintained that the Sinn Féin members were engaging in 'treasonable communication with Germany'.[37] It is fair to deduce that the British authorities wanted members of the party out of the way. Sinn Féin politicians had been successfully organising national protests against extending the Military Services Act (1916) to Ireland, which would have conscripted Irish men into the British army.

Although incarcerated, Constance received a letter from the newly elected prime minister, Lloyd George, inviting her to attend parliament on the first day of the new cabinet's sitting. The envelope, addressed to Madame Markievicz, MP, was redirected from her constituency, St Patrick's ward in Dublin, to Holloway gaol in London, where she was being held. The letter sent to Constance was addressed 'Sir', based on the hitherto correct assumption that all elected MPs were male. Although Constance refused to take her seat in the House of Commons, her election as the first woman was a significant achievement. She went on to become the first female TD in Dáil Éireann and the first female cabinet minister in Ireland. She proved to be an effective minister for labour. Yet, Yeats demotes Constance's inspiring political career to a miserable depiction of her as 'condemned to death', she 'drags out lonely years, conspiring among the ignorant'.

The younger of the two Gore-Booth sisters, Eva, was the 'gazelle' to whom Yeats referred in his well-known poem; Yeats at one stage considered proposing marriage to her.[38] Like her older sister, Eva also rejected her aristocratic heritage. In 1896 she met a young suffragist from Cheshire, Esther Roper, while recuperating from illness in Italy. This meeting was a defining moment in the lives of both women; their relationship would last until Eva's death in 1926. Eva was inspired by Roper's political activities in Manchester, and she was captivated by her character. Dedicating a poem to Esther, Eva wrote, 'You whose Love's melody makes glad the gloom'.[39] Eva moved to Manchester the following year, and she and Roper lived together for the rest of their lives.

In her efforts to provide educational opportunities for women, Eva adopted a similar approach to her mother's when she first arrived in Manchester. She instantly supported the University Settlement, a movement that encouraged past students and staff of universities to provide classes for people of the local area who had little or no access to education. In 1899 she established a dramatic society, working with sixteen female textile factory workers. Eva empowered her group to perform classic works such as the 'Merchant of Venice', and later encouraged them to join the trade union to fight for better work conditions.[40]

She became active in the trade union movement, becoming co-secretary of the Manchester and Salford Women's Trade Union Council. She campaigned on behalf of working-class women, many of whom were Irish immigrants. She was especially concerned for the rights of women workers in occupations thought to be morally precarious, such as circus performers, pit-brow lasses and flower sellers. Eva's campaigns were often highly successful at a time when women had little political influence and remained excluded from voting in general elections.

One of Eva's most successful political campaigns resulted in ousting the future British prime minister, Winston Churchill, from politics, albeit for a short time. The Liberal government, of which Churchill was a member, planned to introduce a licensing bill that included a section banning women from working as barmaids. The Home Secretary, Herbert Gladstone, described public houses as 'sources of evil and danger', and not suitable working environments for women.[41] Barmaids were not unionised, and previously had no cause to organise themselves. Estimating that 100,000 women were employed in the occupation across Ireland and Britain, Eva established the Barmaids' Political Defence League. The debate surrounding the licensing bill escalated during the 1908 by-election campaign in Manchester North West, which effectively acted as a referendum on the issue. Churchill supported the ban on women working in public houses, while his opponent, the Conservative candidate William Joynson-Hicks, was opposed to the proposed legislation.

Eva launched a campaign in support of Joynson-Hicks, and invited her sister to Manchester to help; this was Markievicz's first serious political venture. The two sisters drove a coach with four white horses through the dull grey streets of Manchester, creating a great spectacle (see picture section). When the coach came to a halt, the women made rousing speeches against Churchill, the Liberal Party and the proposed bill. Constance's stepson Stanislaus recounted how his stepmother's quick wit and engaging oratorical style easily won over the crowd, recalling how when she stood up to speak, 'she was heckled by a man in the crowd, with the inevitable male query, "Can you cook a dinner?" "Certainly" she replied, cracking her whip. "Can you drive a coach-and-four?"'[42] Eva wrote to her brother, Josslyn, describing how 'we had a great show in the election and people got very enthusiastic about barmaids'.[43]

The 'great show' by the sisters was successful, and Churchill lost the by-election and was temporarily removed from political life; he later secured a constituency in the Scottish city of Dundee. The by-election was still remembered in the 1960s, when author Ronald Blythe described it as 'the most brilliant, entertaining and hilarious electoral fight of the century'.[44] Within months, the Barmaids' Political Defence League had overwhelmingly won its campaign, as 294 out of 355 MPs rejected the clause in the licensing bill banning women from working as barmaids. During a debate in the House of Commons, Conservative MP Wilfrid Ashley questioned whether 'a body of men elected entirely by men had any moral right to prohibit the employment of women in a certain trade purely on sentimental grounds'.[45] The barmaids' campaign was an unqualified success, and the parliamentary debate had also highlighted the issue of women's suffrage.

This campaign had a deep impact on Constance: labour issues would eventually come to dominate her life. In 1911, when the Irish Women's Workers Union (IWWU) was formed, Constance was an enthusiastic supporter. She was nominated as honorary president and, during a meeting to encourage women to join, she implored them 'if you join this union we will help you get an increase in wages but more than that it could help you get the vote and thus make men of you all'.[46] The main objective of the union was to 'improve the wages and conditions of the women workers of Ireland, and to help the men workers to raise the whole status of labour and industry'.[47] This was an objective welcomed by Eva.

During the First World War, Eva became a pacifist, supporting conscientious objectors and publishing highly controversial condemnations of the war. Adopting a pacifist stance in England at this time was a particularly defiant act. She was at risk of appearing unpatriotic or worse, being labelled as a German sympathiser. Eva was also a dedicated champion of Irish independence, and in the wake of the Easter Rising, she supported the families of men killed during the insurrection, most notably Michael Mallin's wife, Agnes, and Hanna Sheehy-Skeffington, whose husband Francis had been illegally shot on the orders of an officer of the Royal Irish Rifles, Captain John C. Bowen-Colthurst.[48]

Eva also initiated a campaign for the reprieve of Roger Casement's death sentence, a campaign that forced the government to launch an investigation days before Casement was due to be executed. Although ultimately unsuccessful – Casement was hanged at Pentonville Prison in August 1916 – Gore-Booth's campaign placed Britain's actions regarding Ireland under international scrutiny at a crucial time during the war. In 1918 when the government attempted to extend military conscription legislation to Ireland, Eva successfully supported Constance in resisting it. The conscription of Irish men into the British army was never legally introduced. Yet, Yeats belittles Eva's work as dreaming of 'some vague Utopia' until she becomes 'withered old and skeleton-gaunt'.

Conclusion

Historians can but speculate as to what drove the Gore-Booth sisters to reject their aristocratic heritage so dramatically. It is clear that this heritage was a problematic inheritance for them. The fact that the Gore-Booth family originally acquired their land and social status by violently overthrowing local Irish forces was a significant concern for the sisters. For generations, the Gore-Booth family upheld British rule in Ireland, holding positions of power at local and national level. When Constance was elected as an MP, she refused to swear allegiance to the Crown, rejecting her seat at Westminster. She held fast to the ideal of an independent, self-governing Ireland. This was in direct contrast to the position taken by her grandfather, Sir Robert, when he had served as a member of parliament.

Constance and Eva's parents provided them with influential role models as benevolent landlords. They instilled, in both sisters, a sense of responsibility for others less fortunate than themselves. This lesson appears to have impacted deeply on the sisters from a young age. It is clear that Eva was especially troubled by the family's wealth, at a time when many people in Ireland lived in extreme poverty. A Gore-Booth family story recounts how, when Eva was very young, she was discovered by the side of the road taking off her coat to give it to another child. Esther Roper maintained that this was because Eva 'could not believe it right to possess what others had not'.[49]

It was not, however, their concern for social reform that initially caused Eva and Constance to leave Lissadell. Constance's interest in art led her to London and later to Paris; she relished the lifestyle and culture in these capital cities. The rural environment of Sligo may indeed have been too dull for Constance in comparison. Eva was undoubtedly first attracted to live in Manchester to be with Esther Roper. When the sisters moved from a rural environment to large cities, their opportunities broadened considerably, and so too did their social networks. Dublin and Manchester at the turn of the twentieth century were hives of cultural and political activity. In Dublin, the cause of Irish independence sparked new possibilities for Constance, while Manchester was at the heart of suffrage activity in Britain, providing Eva with opportunities to become directly involved in a vibrant campaign.

Added to the excitement and opportunities offered by city life, the intimate relationships chosen by Constance and Eva became a factor that may have hindered them from returning to life in Sligo. Neither of the sisters' relationships was traditional. Casimir was a widower with a young son, and he had a dubious aristocratic background. Josslyn Gore-Booth was so concerned about Casimir's credentials that he sought advice from the British ambassador to the Russian Empire, Sir Charles Scott. Following an investigation, Scott informed Josslyn that in fact there was no such count of that name in Poland. He provided further details regarding Casimir's drinking and gambling.[50] The Gore-Booth family did not approve of the proposed marriage. Dismissing his disapproval, Constance wrote to Josslyn threatening to live at the Markievicz family estate near Kiev if the family attempted to stop the wedding ceremony.[51] Josslyn gave way to his sister's choice, but the marriage lasted for less than nine years. When the couple separated on friendly terms *c.* 1909, Constance was already heavily involved in the republican movement and had firmly established herself in Dublin.

Eva's lifelong partner was a woman from a working-class background. Crossing class divides at this time would certainly have caused concern for her family. It is also fair to suggest that a love relationship between two women was not socially acceptable in wider society at the turn of the twentieth century. In the large English cities of Manchester and, later, London, Eva could live with Esther without their relationship, it seems, attracting much controversy. It was certainly not uncommon for two women to share a house and even a bedroom, often for economic and practical reasons. The issue of class difference may have been more difficult to explain in Sligo, where the Gore-Booths were a prominent gentry family.

It is evident from Eva's diary that she found the departure of Constance from Lissadell to London unsettling. The bond between the sisters during their time at Lissadell was extremely close, and they tried to maintain it in later life. While living in urban environments, Eva and Constance had the opportunity to visit and stay with each other regularly. In 1913 Eva and Esther moved to London to escape the smog-bound industrial city of Manchester, due to Eva's weakening health.

In 1925 Eva was diagnosed with bowel cancer. In possibly the only emotional account ever written by Esther, she describes how, after suffering terribly for two days, death came suddenly to Eva. Esther was by her bedside until the end. Eva suddenly looked up at her 'with that exquisite smile that always lighted up her face when she saw one she loved, then closed her eyes and was at peace'.[52] Eva died on 30 June 1926, aged 56, in the home that she had shared with Esther. Esther later published the remainder of Eva's later writing, as well as a large number of Constance's letters to Eva.[53]

Constance had been unaware of the nature of her sister's illness, and was profoundly shocked when a telegraph arrived in Dublin with the news of Eva's death. Grief-stricken, she did not attend the funeral; in a letter of condolence to Esther she admitted, 'I simply could not face it all. I want to keep my last memory of her so happy and peaceful'.[54] She sent a wreath of Eva's favourite white and blue flowers. Constance's own health was by then delicate. In July 1927 she was operated on for appendicitis, but her condition subsequently deteriorated and she died in a public ward of Sir Patrick Dun's hospital, on 15 July. Esther maintained a vigil by Constance's bedside with a number of her friends, including Dr Kathleen Lynn, Helena Moloney and Maria Perolz. Constance's estranged husband and her stepson Stanislaus arrived from Warsaw. Her daughter Maeve had had a troubled relationship with her mother, but she too travelled to see Constance during her final days. Constance had only outlived her sister by one year. A Catholic bible was found by her hospital bedside; it was inscribed in her own hand 'to Mother and Eva 1927 – They are not dead, they do not sleep. They have awakened from the dream of life'.[55]

The Irish republican historian Dorothy Macardle attempted to summarise the bond between the sisters, describing how 'Constance had a way of talking about her sister as though Eva were her angel, and when the news of Eva's death came there came to some of us in Ireland a sharp apprehension that we would not have Madame long, for we knew how close and spiritual the bond between them had been'.[56]

Endnotes

[1] William Butler Yeats, *The winding stair and other poems* (London, 1933), 197.

[2] There has been some debate as to whether the woman on the left is Eva or her younger sister Mabel. See, Dermot James, *The Gore-Booths of Lissadell* (Dublin, 2004), 130. The original tinted photograph, provenance Éamon de Valera, was auctioned by Adams Auctioneers, Dublin, on 18 April 2012 and verified as 'Eva and Constance Gore-Booth'. Lot 521: '800 years of Irish history' (April 2012). https://www.adams. ie/archived-auction-catalogues-adams-irish-art-auctioneers/auction Accessed October 2020.

[3] For more details on the movement in Sligo see, Sonja Tiernan, 'Sligo co-operative movements (1895–1905)', in Shane Alcobia-Murphy, Lindsay Milligan and Dan Wall (eds), *Founder to shore: cross-currents in Irish and Scottish studies* (Aberdeen, 2009), 189–96.

[4] James, *Gore-Booths*, 106.

[5] Gerard Moran, 'Near famine: the crisis in the west of Ireland, 1879–82', *Irish Studies Review* 5(18) (1997), 14–21.

[6] Charles Mosley (gen. ed.), *Burke's peerage, baronetage & knightage: clan chiefs, Scottish feudal barons*. 107th edition (3 vols; Wilmington (DE), 2003), vol. 2, 1596.

[7] *Burke's peerage*, 1595.

[8] For further information on the family background see, Sonja Tiernan, *Eva Gore-Booth: an image of such politics* (Manchester, 2012).

[9] Eva Gore-Booth, *Eva Gore-Booth: collected poems*, ed. Sonja Tiernan (Dublin, 2018), 165.

[10] Now available through the National Folklore Collection, UCD, see, 'Local happenings – eviction – the Seven Cartrons', in 'The Schools' Collection', vol. 157, pp 398–9 and Kathleen Lavin, Ballymote, 'The landlord', vol. 186, pp 230–2. www.duchas.ie Accessed October 2020.

[11] Joe McGowan, 'Lisadell House, coffin ships, the Pomano and Sir Robert Gore-Booth' (2005). See, Sligo Heritage website: https://www.sligoheritage.com/archpomano.htm Accessed October 2020. For debate on the issue see, Dermot James, 'Drowning of Sligo tenants: legend or history', *The Irish Times*, 31 January 2005.

[12] A verse of this ballad is quoted by Joe McGowan, 'My curse be on Sir Robert and that he may lie low, Our rent was paid, We were not afraid, But still we were forced to go, When they banished the Roman Catholic, Aboard the Pomano'. Sligo Heritage website: www.sligoheritage.com Accessed November 2020.

[13] Gerard Moran, *Sir Robert Gore-Booth and his landed estate in County Sligo, 1814–1876: land, famine, emigration and politics* (Dublin, 2006).

[14] Saint John Almshouse Records database, available at https://archives.gnb.ca/Irish/Databases/Almshouse/?culture=en-CA Accessed November 2020.

[15] Contributions by Sir Robert Gore (1850–76) recorded in *Hansard 1803–2005*, https://api.parliament.uk/historic-hansard/people/sir-robert-booth/index.html Accessed 29 October 2020.

[16] *The Times* (London), 7 March 1881.

[17] 'The regeneration of Ireland', *Pall Mall Gazette*, 30 December 1895, 3.

[18] Eva Gore-Booth, *Poems of Eva Gore-Booth: complete edition* ed. Esther Roper (London, 1929), 5.

[19] Hanna Sheehy-Skeffington wrote of Markievicz: 'her militant spirit was that of Queen Maeve or Granuaile, her countrywomen', 'Constance Markievicz – what she stood for', *An Phoblacht*, 16 July 1932, 8.

[20] Senia Peseta, 'Markievicz, Constance Georgine Countess Markievicz Gore-Booth', www.dib.ie

[21] PRONI, Mic 590, Reel 10, L/9:102–3, Abbey Theatre Programme, 25, 26 and 27 January 1912.

[22] The spelling of Cuculain often varies; Gore-Booth's usage has been retained here.

[23] Ernie O'Malley, *The singing flame* (Dublin, 1978), 158.

[24] Æ, *New songs* (Dublin, 1904).

[25] As cited in Declan Foley (ed.) with Janis Londraville, 'Eva Gore-Booth', in *John Quinn: selected Irish writers from his library* (West Cornwall (CT), 2001), 158.

[26] Eva Gore-Booth, *The one and the many* (London, 1904), 73–4.

[27] Eva Gore-Booth, *The three resurrections and The triumph of Maeve* (London, 1905).

[28] Eva Gore-Booth, *The death of Fionavar from The triumph of Maeve* (London, 1916).

[29] The 'One who died for peace' can be identified as Francis Sheehy-Skeffington.

[30] Constance Markievicz, *Prison letters of Countess Markievicz* ed. Esther Roper, with Introduction by Amanda Sebestyen (London, 1987; reprint of 1934 edition, with Sebestyen introduction and revisions), xxxii.

[31] 'Irish rebel illustrates nonresistance play', *The New York Times*, 10 September 1916, 2.

[32] The other editors of the journal were Dorothy H. Cornish, a Montessori educator; Jessey Wade, an animal rights campaigner; Thomas Baty, an international legal scholar.

[33] Edward Carpenter, *The intermediate sex* (London, 1916), 108.

[34] For details of the establishment of *Urania* see, Sonja Tiernan, '"No measures of emancipation or equality will suffice": Eva Gore-Booth's radical feminism in the journal *Urania*', in Sarah O'Connor and Christopher C. Shepard (eds), *Women, social and cultural change in twentieth-century Ireland* (Newcastle, 2008), 166–82.

[35] For example, a story by Irish author Katharine Tynan from her memoirs *Twenty-five years' reminiscences* was reprinted in the journal: 'An Irish school-girl', *Urania* 14 (March–April 1919), 6–7.

[36] For more information regarding this relationship see, Lauren Arrington, *Revolutionary lives: Constance and Casimir Markievicz* (Princeton, 2015).

[37] 'Sinn Féin leaders arrested over alleged "German plot"', *Illustrated London News*, 25 May 1918, as cited by *Century Ireland* – https://www.rte.ie/centuryireland/index.php/articles/sinn-fein-leaders-arrested-over-alleged-german-plot Accessed August 2019.

[38] Denis Donoghue (ed.), *Memoirs of W.B. Yeats* (New York, 1972), 78.

[39] Gore-Booth, *The one*, 81–2.

[40] University of Manchester Archives, MUS/1/3/1, 'University Settlement Manchester: The Third Annual Report for year ending 30 June 1899', 20.

[41] 'Licensing Bill: barmaids deputation to Gladstone', *Manchester Guardian*, 19 November 1907, 7.

[42] NLI, MS 44,619, Stanislaus Dun Markievicz, 'Life of Constance de Markievicz by her stepson Stanislaus Dun Markievicz', 133.

[43] PRONI, Mic 590, Reel 10, L/13/121, Letter from Eva Gore-Booth to Josslyn Gore-Booth, 29 April 1908.

[44] Ronald Blythe, *The age of illusion: England in the twenties and thirties* (London, 1963), 25.

[45] 'House of Commons', *Manchester Guardian*, 3 November 1908, 10.

[46] Mary Jones, *Those obstreperous lassies: a history of the Irish Women's Workers' Union* (Dublin, 1988), 1.

[47] NLI, LOP: 113/123, 'Irish Women's Workers' Union call for members', September 1911.

[48] See pp.181–3 of this volume.

[49] Markievicz, *Prison letters,* Introd. Sebestyen, 7.

[50] Arrington, *Revolutionary lives,* 22.

[51] PRONI, D4131/K/1, Correspondence of Constance Markievicz.

[52] Gore-Booth, *Poems,* ed. Roper, 48.

[53] *Poems of Eva Gore-Booth: complete edition* in 1929 and *Prison letters of Countess Markievicz* in 1934.

[54] Markievicz, *Prison letters …,* Introd. Sebestyen, 311.

[55] Cited in Anne Haverty, *Constance Markievicz: Irish revolutionary* (Dublin, 2016), 229.

[56] Stanislaus Dun Markievicz, 'Life'.

Left: Chalice commissioned for the monastery of Craobh Liath, Dromahair, by Máire Ní Dhomhnaill in memory of her husband Tadhg Ó Ruairc in 1619. Photograph reproduced by permission of Monsignor Liam Kelly.

Below: Beginning of 'Truagh liom Máire agas Mairghréag' in Nualaidh's poem-book KBR MS 6131–3, f. 9r. © KBR. Reproduced by permission of the Koninklijke Bibliotheek van Belgie/Bibliothèque Royale de Belgique/Royal Library of Belgium.

Three of the earl of Cork's daughters as represented on the Boyle monument,
St Patrick's Cathedral, Dublin. Originally erected in 1632. Reproduced by permission of
Albert Fenton and St Patrick's Cathedral.

Double portrait of two unknown ladies. Traditionally thought to be Katherine Jones (née Boyle)
(1615–91), Viscountess Ranelagh, and her sister-in-law, Elizabeth Boyle (née Clifford) (1613–91),
2nd countess of Cork and 1st countess of Burlington. © The Devonshire Collections, Chatsworth.
Reproduced by permission of Chatsworth Settlement Trustees.

Portrait of Mary Rich (née Boyle), Countess of Warwick (1624–78).
Reproduced by permission of the Burghley House Collection.

Portrait of a lady by Charles Jervas (*c.* 1675–1739) considered to be Katherine Conolly. Reproduced by permission of the Castletown Foundation.

Portrait of Katherine Conolly with her great-niece, Molly Burton, painted by Charles Jervas (*c.* 1675–1739), formerly attributed to Michael Dahl. Reproduced by permission of the Castletown Foundation.

Modern photograph of Castletown House from the yew hedge.
Reproduced by permission of the Office of Public Works.

Modern photograph of 'Griesebank', the mill house where Mary, Sally
and Margaret Shackleton lived for some time with their aunt, Deborah Carleton.

COTTAGE DIALOGUES

Ex libris AMONG THE *Rob. Walsh*

IRISH PEASANTRY.

By MARY LEADBEATER.

WITH

NOTES AND A PREFACE

BY

MARIA EDGEWORTH,

AUTHOR OF CASTLE RACKRENT, &c.

LONDON:

PRINTED FOR J. JOHNSON AND CO.
ST. PAUL'S CHURCHYARD.

1811.

Left: Title page of Mary Shackleton Leadbeater's best-selling book, *Cottage dialogues*, published in 1811. Reproduced by permission of the Royal Irish Academy Library.

Below: Silhouette images of Mary Shackleton Leadbeater and her husband, William Leadbeater. The guidelines of the Society of Friends prohibited members from having their portraits painted, but silhouettes were not explicitly forbidden. Based on an image in *Journal of County Kildare Archaeological Society* 8 (1915–17), 177.

Above: Modern photograph of the Society of Friends' graveyard in Ballitore, where Deborah, Mary and Sally Shackleton are buried. Their gravestones have not survived.

Right: Portrait of Lady Sydney Morgan. Dilke Collection. Reproduced by permission of the Royal Irish Academy Library.

Portrait of Lady Sydney
Morgan. Dilke Collection.
Reproduced by permission
of the Royal Irish Academy
Library.

Portrait of Lady Sydney
Morgan. Dilke Collection.
Reproduced by permission
of the Royal Irish Academy
Library.

Portrait of a lady, possibly Lady Olivia Clarke. Dilke Collection. Reproduced by permission of the Royal Irish Academy Library.

Portrait of Lady Sydney Morgan by her niece, Sidney Clarke. Reproduced by permission of the Royal Irish Academy Library.

No. 342—Vol. VII.]   For the Week Ending Saturday, June 18, 1881.   [Registered at the General Post Office as a Newspaper. [Price ONE PENNY.

THE COMIC COMPANION TO THE NEWSPAPER.

"Our True Intent is all for your Delight."—*Shakespeare.*

IN BAD COMPANY.

Left: 'In bad company', *Funny Folks*, 18 June 1881.

Below: 'The state of Ireland: dispersing a Ladies' Land League meeting', *Illustrated London News*, 24 December 1881. Reproduced from *History Ireland* 8(1) (Spring 1999) by permission of the editor, Tommy Graham.

Opposite: W.E.P., In memoriam Miss Fanny Parnell (James. J. Lalor, Dublin, 5 Aug. 1882) (EP PARN-FA (1) 111 (NLI). Reproduced by permission of the National Library of Ireland.

SUPPLEMENT GIVEN AWAY WITH THE WEEKLY FREEMAN OF AUGUST 5th 1882 PRICE THREE HALF-PENCE

IN MEMORIAM
Miss FANNY PARNELL
Died 20th July 1882.

Left: Eva Gore-Booth and Constance Markievicz campaigning in defence of barmaids at the 1908 Manchester North West by-election. *Daily Graphic*, 23 April 1908. Photograph reproduced by permission of the Lissadell estate.

Below: Eva and Constance Gore-Booth with their dog, Satan, *c.* 1898. Image from Sterry Album. Photograph reproduced by permission of the Lissadell estate.

Above: Eva and Constance
Gore-Booth, *c.* 1887. Drumcliffe
Co-operative Creamery
marketing image. Copyright
permission kindly granted by
Sligo County Library.

Right: W.B. Yeats, *Two plays for
dancers*. Dublin: Cuala Press,
1919, title page. Reproduced
by permission of the Royal Irish
Academy Library.

TWO PLAYS FOR DANCERS
BY W. B. YEATS

MONOCEROS DE ASTRIS

THE CUALA PRESS
MCMXIX

TELEPHONE
No. 62435.

Letters to
Miss Elizabeth
C. Yeats.

CUALA INDUSTRIES, Ltd.

133 LR. BAGGOT ST.
DUBLIN

NOW READY

NEW PRINTS

**PRINTED ON IRISH MADE PAPER.
COLOURED BY HAND.**

	s.	d.
PICTURE BY JACK B. YEATS, R.H.A.		
Celtic Capital and Lettering by E. C. Yeats		
ST. PATRICK AT TARA.	3	0
Commemoration Picture		
PICTURES BY DOROTHY BLACKHAM.		
WATERFORD.	3	0
With Poem by W. M. Letts		
THE BLESSING OF COLMAN.	3	6
Translated from the Latin by Helen Waddell		
CASHEL.	3	0
With Poem by Olive Meyer		
GLENDALOUGH.	2	0
With Quotation from Emily Lawless		
DUBLIN BAY FROM TICKNOCK.	5	0
(Landscape without words)		
PICTURE BY ANNE PRICE.		
HYMN OF ST. COLUMCILLE.	1	6
Translated from the Irish		

NEW CHRISTMAS CARDS
NOW READY

2023

CUALA INDUSTRIES, LTD.,
133 LOWER BAGGOT STREET, DUBLIN.

EMBROIDERY . . . . LILY YEATS.
PRINTING . . . . . ELIZABETH YEATS.

RECEIVED FROM *Dr Best*

the Sum of _____ Pounds *Ten* _____ Shillings

Six Pence, being *amount due*

for one copy of "A Little Anthology"

£ 10/6   Dated *Dec 18 1928*

with thanks
E. C. Yeats

Hely's Limited, Printers, Dublin.

The Sheehy family 1895–6. Left to right, standing: Hanna, Richard, David, Margaret, Eugene, Mary; seated: Fr Eugene, Kathleen, Bessie.
Photograph reproduced by permission of the National Library of Ireland.

Hanna and her sisters. Left to right: Hanna, Mary, Kathleen, Margaret.
Photograph reproduced courtesy of the Sheehy Skeffington family.

MRS. SKEFFINGTON

Arriving for the court martial at Richmond Barracks, May 1916.
From left: Meg Connery, Mary Sheehy Kettle, Kathleen Sheehy O'Brien, Hanna Sheehy
Skeffington. Photograph reproduced by permission of the Library of Congress,
Prints and Photographs Division (LC-B2-3962-9).

'Who will ever say again that poetry does not pay': Susan and Elizabeth Yeats and the Cuala Press

LUCY COLLINS

YEATS FAMILY TREE

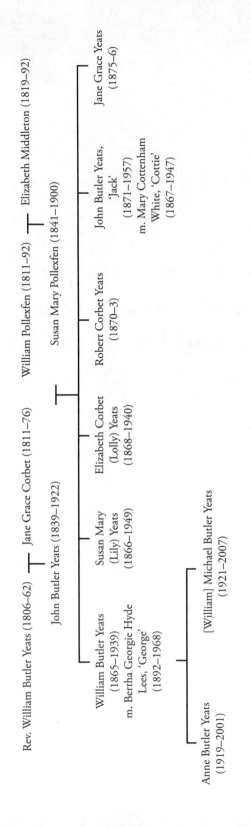

As members of Ireland's most remarkable artistic family, the Yeats sisters made a significant contribution to the Irish Revival and to the wider Arts and Crafts Movement in Ireland in the twentieth century. Their work in textile design, and especially in printing, shows the value of collaborative work in the arts and the importance of fully recognising the contribution made by women to these practices. The talents of Lily and Elizabeth Yeats complemented and intersected with one another, yet they struggled to create a productive and harmonious life together, not least because of the social and economic constraints they faced as unmarried women with little money behind them. Usually framed by their relationship to the men of their family, the Yeats sisters not only contributed to their family's artistic achievements across a range of visual and literary artforms but offered a medium by which their brothers could forge independent careers. In addition, the sisters were representative of the larger collaborative possibilities of the time, and especially of the importance of female education and labour in advancing the decorative arts both in Britain and Ireland. The conjunction between the Arts and Crafts Movement and the Irish Revival offered a unique opportunity to produce work that could be enjoyed widely, and to extend the boundaries of art for future generations. It is this commitment to craft over almost 40 years that marks the Yeats sisters' lasting achievement.

Family dynamics

Susan (Lily) Yeats (1866–1949) and Elizabeth Yeats (known in the family as Lolly) (1868–1940) were the middle siblings of the four children of John Butler Yeats (1839–1922) and Susan Pollexfen (1841–1900). William Butler Yeats (1865–1939), the eldest child, is Ireland's most famous twentieth-century poet, and was awarded the Nobel Prize for Literature in 1923. His younger brother, Jack Butler Yeats (1871–1957), would become one of Ireland's greatest modern artists. The two Yeats sisters, both in life and at work, functioned as part of this stimulating but unstable family, deriving their skills and inspiration from a large network of artists and writers, but also assuming additional family responsibilities brought about by their challenging economic circumstances and their father's privileging of artistic freedom over familial duties. The frequency with which the Yeatses moved between Ireland and England disrupted their personal lives but also demonstrated the creative potential that could be derived from these two environments in tandem – potential which all four siblings would realise in distinctive ways.

Lily, the elder daughter, was born in County Sligo, where her mother's family lived; Elizabeth was born in London. The family had relocated there from Ireland after John Butler Yeats had given up his early study of law at Trinity College Dublin and determined to become a full-time artist. Early life was difficult for the Yeats siblings, as their gifted father struggled to bring in a steady income to support the family; this was partly due to his lack of interest in the practical side of being an artist and partly to his laborious method of painting. These financial anxieties took a toll on their mother's health. She found it hard to adjust to life in London after the stable, supported situation of her Pollexfen home in Sligo, and felt alienated by her husband's wish to live a bohemian existence among English artists. These practical challenges prompted the Yeats children to adopt a strong work ethic, each being conscious that they might need to support the family as soon as they were of age. For Elizabeth, especially, awareness of the difficulties of her mother's life spurred her on to forge her own career, first as a teacher and then as a printer. Yet this situation created tensions, for both daughters, between the need to fulfil a role within the home and the desire to seek a career outside it.

In a period of transition for women, both politically and socially, the two sisters exemplify the challenges faced by women in families of artistic and ambitious men, where female achievements often went unrecognised. The Yeats sisters had very distinct personalities, and were temperamentally unsuited to the shared life that lay before them. Lily was the quieter of the two women, and the closest to her father: the letters between them testify to her anxiety for the family's future, and her father's attempts to set her mind at ease:

You must not bother about us. Even when lying awake with neuralgia you must not think of it, but just always assume that things will come right in the future as they have in the past. Some day Jack will be a substantial man with a cheerful kind hearted spouse and an openhanded way of welcoming friends … and Willie will be famous and shed a bright light on us all, and sometimes have a little money, and sometimes *not*.[1]

Lily also formed a strong childhood bond with her older brother William, sharing both his spiritual interests and his love of the west of Ireland landscape. By contrast, Elizabeth had a volatile temperament, and was prone to depression. The family perception of her as 'difficult' was not always shared by outsiders, however: she was a popular lecturer and a discerning craftswoman. The constraint of her circumstances would prolong family intimacies that would have been better discarded, and the closeness of her domestic and professional ties to Lily – they would live together for 38 years – led to profound discord in their adult lives.[2]

From the Arts and Crafts Movement to the Irish Cultural Revival

The family lived at various locations in London, but it was their time at Bedford Park, first in 1879 and again between 1888 and 1902, that offered a community with artistic interests within which the Yeats family could thrive. The two daughters became acquainted with the many writers, artists and political figures who came to see their father, including neighbours John Todhunter and Elkin Mathews, and Irish visitors John O'Leary, Katharine Tynan and Susan Mitchell. Though the sisters welcomed the opportunity to learn about art, literature and politics, they lacked the confidence to take a full part in the conversation. In November 1888 Elizabeth wrote in her diary that she and her sister felt 'dreadfully out of it. I wonder do all girls feel that way – as if the conversation when men talk was altogether beyond them'.[3]

In addition to their many Irish associates, the family had connections to English artists too, becoming acquainted with William Morris – pioneer of the Arts and Crafts Movement – and his family. The scale and emphasis of this movement's work made it comparatively hospitable to women but, despite its apparent radicalism, the Arts and Crafts Movement perpetuated many existing gendered stereotypes in the fields of design and production. As Anthea Callen has noted, artwork was one of the few occupations considered acceptable for middle-class Victorian women. This was especially true of the decorative arts: to beautify the home, and ensure its comfort and elegance, affirmed woman's place in the domestic sphere.[4] Accordingly, there was a clear division of labour within the Arts and Crafts Movement, with ceramics, book illustration and needlework becoming the sphere of women. There were specific economic implications for these demarcations: 'certain tasks were given to women only to avoid bringing them into direct competition with men, which would threaten male jobs, male status and male "family" wages'.[5] C.R. Ashbee deplored the growing involvement of the woman artist in the movement for these reasons. He linked her versatility ('she makes jewellery, she binds books, she enamels, she carves …') to her supposed lack of artistic standards: 'she is perpetually tingling to sell her work before she half knows how to make it'.[6] In Zoë Thomas's assessment, however, women artists were innovative in their desire to reach a wider public – 'they regularly sold work at cheaper prices, wrote accessible manuals and articles, staged special workshop events, and curated their own exhibitions'.[7]

In 1888 Lily began working for William Morris at Kelmscott House under the direction of his daughter May. For William Morris, the character of a house was integral to the artistic vision of its inhabitants, and this close relationship between domestic and professional spaces was an important dimension of women's artistic development during this period. When she began work at the Morris studio, Lily enjoyed the environment of Kelmscott House and found the presence of figures such as Bernard Shaw,

Cunningham Graham and Emery Walker stimulating. As a talented needlewoman she was involved in a number of significant projects with Morris, including the construction of elaborate bed hangings for Morris's bed at Kelmscott Manor; these were later exhibited at the 1893 Arts and Crafts exhibition. She did not design her own pieces, however: training in the Morris studio required precision, and Morris's instructions to his daughters and workers had to be followed exactly, emphasising skill and discipline over creative freedom.[8]

After May Morris married in 1891 the workshop moved from Kelmscott House, and within three years, due to ill health, as well as an increasingly fractious relationship with May, Lily had decided to give up her job there.[9] The work had given her a valuable training, however, as well as insights into collaborative arts practice. The late nineteenth century was a time of major change in literary and artistic production: in Ireland, this was marked by a desire to represent a distinctive national identity, in both the subject matter and the style of creative work. This development was part of a larger popularisation of such materials in the 'Celtic Twilight' movement in Scotland and Ireland, and drew on an enduring interest in antiquarianism dating from the eighteenth century and indicating a widespread engagement with Celtic culture and identity. Through their brother William, the sisters were becoming aware of cultural activities in Dublin and may have felt that greater opportunities awaited them there. The Irish Arts and Crafts Society, like its English counterpart, drew attention to the aesthetics of everyday design; in this movement, handmade items – furniture, clothing and decorative objects – were preferred to industrially produced ones, ensuring that the method of production was aligned to the importance of Irish heritage and tradition. This desire to revive dying crafts and inculcate pride in the act of making was an important dimension of the movement, but there was novelty and originality in evidence too; the aim was not to copy an earlier aesthetic, but to be inspired by it. As T.W. Rolleston wrote:

> The age of tradition and authority is past – in their
> stead the individual has emerged, bringing all things

to the test of his own personality ... Don't imitate; don't conceal the qualities of your material. Study arts of the past, above all those of your own land, but remember that you do not live in the times of Brian Boru, but of Mr. Edison.[10]

As well as encouraging writers to use Irish themes and settings for their work, there was also a drive to seek Irish modes of printing and publishing as a crucial way of de-anglicising Ireland. The task was made more difficult by the conservative nature of the Irish publishing industry at the time: firms such as M.H. Gill and James Duffy did not want to take risks with new literary material since their businesses flourished on the production of prayer books and standard Catholic works.[11] However, W.B. Yeats had become especially engaged in book design during his time publishing with Elkin Mathews and A.H. Bullen, and was interested in promoting Irish aesthetics. For Yeats, the opportunities offered by close involvement with an Irish hand press printing business were attractive, including, as they did, increased aesthetic control over the production and dissemination of his poems, and the chance to promote the work of writers in his circle.

The founding of Dun Emer Industries

The experience of both Yeats sisters in the art world had alerted them to the close connections between spaces of living and artistic collaboration; both were keen to detach themselves from the burdens of the London household, as well as to sustain their imaginative engagement with Ireland. In 1902 Evelyn Gleeson (1855–1944), the English-born daughter of an Irish physician, came to the sisters with a proposal. As a suffragist with a commitment to the Irish language as well as to traditional crafts, Gleeson wished to link developments in the Arts and Crafts Movement in London to the aims of the Irish Cultural Revival. She regarded Ireland as 'behind-hand in the matter of artistic industry ... Is there any distinctive school of [Irish] art? If so, where can one find it?'[12] She championed the power of the visual arts, wishing to 'nationalise through the eyes' as well as the ears.[13] The business she proposed to start was to have two distinct fields – embroidery, that Lily would run, and printing, led by Elizabeth. Though Elizabeth had, at that time, no formal instruction in this area, she was encouraged to train at the Women's Printing Society, where she learned the basics of composition and proofreading.[14] Acquaintance with Sydney Carlyle Cockerell, typographical advisor to William Morris, and with Thomas J. Cobden Sanderson, who set up the Doves bookbindery, made both sisters familiar with the aesthetics of hand printing and the role of the book in a wider Arts and Crafts Movement. So while they possessed the skills and inclination to embark on such a project, money worries made them anxious to ensure it had a strong foundation as a viable business. Notwithstanding these practical challenges, Elizabeth's father, John Butler Yeats, encouraged her to become involved in the enterprise, feeling that it would give an outlet for her talents and her powers of reasoning and intellect, though he was unable to offer financial support.[15] A period of negotiation with Gleeson ensued, and finally, with the help of her friend Augustine Henry, an agreement was reached in 1902.[16]

The relocation from London to Dublin required significant work on the part of the sisters; they had to agree a location for the business and find a house where they could live with their father, their mother having died in 1900. Gleeson secured a large house in Dundrum that was renamed 'Dun Emer' in reference to the wife of the hero Cúchulain, renowned in Irish folklore for her beauty and artistic skills. The association of Celtic symbolism with nationalist ideals was prevalent from the 1860s onward, and became even more explicit as Celtic style was further interpreted in the 1890s by groups working for Ireland's cultural and political independence. Dun Emer looked to a more poetic but progressive form of Irish art, sharing the same aspirations as the other European Art Nouveau movements.

The craft collective at Dun Emer was formed under the medieval guild model favoured by William Morris, and its aim was to 'find work for Irish hands in the making of beautiful things'.[17] This vision emphasised not only the beauty and utility of the art object but the importance of the creative process itself. In particular, the education of women was an important part of Evelyn Gleeson's vision for the enterprise; the girls who worked for Dun Emer Industries would be trained by Lily in needlework and by Elizabeth in typography, book design, printing and bookbinding. Language and music classes were integral to the education programme – an Irish tutor, Mr Hamilton, was hired,[18] and visits to the National Library and the National Museum forged a close connection between Ireland's material and intellectual heritage and the production of the Dun Emer workshops:

> Everything as far as possible is Irish: the paper, the books, the linen of the embroidery and the wool of the tapestry and carpets. The designs are also of the spirit and tradition of the country. The education of the work girls is also part of the idea – they are taught to paint and their brains and fingers are made more active and understanding. Some of them, we hope, will become teachers to others, so that similar industries may spread through the land.[19]

These progressive plans marked Dun Emer as a significant enterprise in Irish women's history; many of the young women trained there were talented artists in their own right, and some, such as Abbey actress Máire Nic Shiubhlaigh, were involved in other branches of cultural nationalism. The time devoted to education and artistic development at Dun Emer threatened the economic viability of the business, however, and placed a considerable burden on the Yeats sisters in sustaining production themselves, leaving them less time to publicise and sell the objects they made, though they did this through exhibitions and sales both at home and abroad.

Early challenges in printing and publishing

The first book printed by the Dun Emer Press, W.B. Yeats's *In the seven woods* (1903), signalled the poet's centrality to the project, despite the Yeats sisters' independence of mind. The book also exemplified the simplicity of design and execution that would be a hallmark of the Dun Emer and Cuala presses. In establishing her printing enterprise, Elizabeth had taken advice from Emery Walker; she had purchased an Albion hand press and some type in Caslon, an eighteenth-century font, signalling the importance of tradition rather than innovation to the project. This equipment, together with her choice of unbleached paper for printing and plain covers for binding, confirmed the fact that the materials themselves would play an important role in Dun Emer's distinctive print aesthetic: the books, as designed and produced, featured wide margins but comparatively close spacing of lines, making the text itself the key visual feature on each page. The importance of text was further accentuated, in most of the books, by the absence of illustration or ornamentation. This emphasis on the visual effect of the printed word was an especially noteworthy feature in the context of Dun Emer's identity: Karen Brown notes the aesthetic divergence between the design of textiles and books: 'while embroidery, tapestry and carpet design may contain text, image and elaborate decoration, the books were very modest indeed'.[20]

In addition to printing books, both Dun Emer and Cuala produced a range of other work, including bookplates, Christmas cards and calendars, and the business aimed to offer a variety of designed objects to beautify the domestic space (see picture section). A 1904 publicity campaign urged Irish housewives: 'Decorate your house with Dun Emer tufted rugs, embroidered portieres and sofa backs, put Dun Emer tapestries on your walls and Dun Emer books in your bookcases. This is the duty of an Irish woman'.[21] Dun Emer's early prospectus links its aesthetic value to a long, and underappreciated, commitment to material culture in Ireland: 'Though many books are printed in Ireland, book printing as an art has been little practised here since the eighteenth century. The Dun Emer Press has been founded in the hope of reviving this beautiful craft'.

The lack of illustration in the books produced at the press gave special significance to recurring visual features such as the pressmark and colophons. Emery Walker designed the first pressmark, but this was soon felt to be too small, and was replaced by

Elinor Monsell's 'The Lady Emer', first used in Katharine Tynan's *Twenty one poems* (1907); this too was finally replaced in 1925 by the image of the fairy thorn tree. Other pressmarks, such as those designed by Robert Gregory – one for W.B. Yeats's *Stories of Red Hanrahan* (1905), one for Gregory's own mother's volume, *A book of saints and wonders* (1906), and his remarkable charging unicorn for *Discoveries* (1907) – made the layout of the title pages spare but elegant. The use of red ink on some title pages was repeated in the colophons at the back of the volumes. These colophons were highly distinctive: they were triangular in shape and were sometimes used to comment on contemporary events, as in the case of their very first book 'finished the sixteenth day of July, in the year of the big wind 1903'.[22] Elizabeth's skills as a printer developed quickly: *In the seven woods* was clearly the work of someone with little experience, but Dun Emer's second book – Æ's *The nuts of knowledge* – showed a marked improvement in control of the setting, especially in the use of leading and the placing of blocks. This volume was unusual in that it included an image of 'An Claidheamh Soluis' (the sword of light) from a drawing by the author.

From the beginning, the model of subscription purchase played an important role in sales: about half the first print run of *In the seven woods* was guaranteed in this way. However, it was clear that the enterprise as a whole needed to raise its profile with the public if the business was to be sustainable. Within the first two years, the workrooms at Dun Emer were transformed into showrooms that were open to the public on designated days, offering potential supporters the opportunity to see the craftswomen at work and to purchase directly from the workshop.[23] These changes were accompanied by a growth in the scale of Dun Emer's business. Originally, just thirteen girls were employed, but by 1905 the number had risen impressively, to around 30.[24] As it became better known, the potential for the press to contribute to revivalist culture, and to establish a readership both at home and abroad quickly became apparent. Dun Emer's educational programme showed its connection to the Irish language revival, and Gifford Lewis argues that Elizabeth was aware that Irish-language ephemera could become a source of income that would supplement some of the slower-selling books in English.[25] However, for reasons of expense and legibility, Irish type – due in part to its direct reproduction of penmanship – was not used in Dun Emer or Cuala books. Nonetheless, the decision to print new work by Irish writers was a significant one; most English hand press printers of the period chose not to print the works of their contemporaries but to reproduce classic texts that were already familiar to readers; these, since they were in the public domain, brought with them few printing challenges. Dun Emer, however, adopted a more forward-looking position, despite the inherent traditionalism of its printing processes.

The press quickly consolidated its activities: 1905 saw the publication of four volumes, including W.B. Yeats's *Stories of Red Hanrahan*, of which G.K. Chesterton remarked:

> I may call this book in some special sense, or rather, in some unusually actual sense, a book from Ireland, because it is written by an Irishman and printed by Irish people upon Irish paper ... This Dun Emer Press ... is a very interesting matter in itself, as a specimen of the new possibilities and the new works of Ireland.[26]

W.B. Yeats was content with the minimalist aesthetic of the Dun Emer enterprise, and though in other contexts he paid attention to cover design – collaborating with Anthea Gyles and Sturge Moore at different stages in his career – he did not advocate a more lavish approach to illustration in Dun Emer or Cuala books. In other respects, however, he brought his opinions to bear on the activities of the press – a fact that Elizabeth resented. She viewed herself as the press's sole director, and resisted her brother's increasing assertion of his editorial role. For W.B. Yeats the press represented an opportunity not only to publish his own work, but to ensure that his friends and associates got their work into print. Given the small scale of the books produced by Dun Emer in the context of British publishing as a whole, it was possible to do this without interfering with other publishing opportunities. Yeats's letter to William Allingham's widow seeking permission to make a selection of his poems emphasises the aesthetic value of the Dun Emer productions, and the small print run – 'it would be quite a small book, let us say twenty-five poems, and could not in any case interfere with the sale of the ordinary editions'.[27] In the event just sixteen poems were chosen for the edition, and in other cases too Yeats's idiosyncratic editorial approach would prove puzzling to some of his contemporaries. John Eglinton noted that he had 'no hand in the selection which Mr Yeats has done him the honour to make for the Dun Emer Press series and in particular, that if consulted he would hardly have approved of the inclusion of the last essay, written over twelve years ago'.[28]

Elizabeth resisted her brother's editorial authority, and in 1906 a specific reason for tension arose when W.B. sought to withdraw Æ's *By still waters* from publication, since he found it to be of an insufficiently high standard. Elizabeth's refusal to comply prompted her brother to step down from his role as editor for the press. Their father encouraged a reconciliation, urging Elizabeth to recognise her brother's usefulness, while warning the poet against being too dictatorial:

> I see that there is some friction between you and Lolly and I dare say there have been mistakes made – only don't let irritation or unreasonableness of any kind bear sway. To make Dun Emer a pecuniary success is a matter of life and death to Lily and Lolly … Dun Emer is as it appears to them their one chance of ever having any sort of support in life – that is why they are so keen about things – and everything devolves on them – they have to do the thinking and working in Dun Emer.[29]

While Yeats's desire to exert editorial control over the press stemmed from his status as a poet, the Yeats family network would play an important role in the Dun Emer business at many levels. The sisters' younger brother Jack and his wife, Mary Cottenham Yeats, were involved in the design of a series of banners made by the Dun Emer Industries for Loughrea

Cathedral, County Galway. In fact, though the growth in Irish Catholic church building in the late nineteenth century provided ecclesiastical commissions of decorative objects, this did not always result in patronage for the Irish arts community: Ann Wilson notes contemporary criticism of the Catholic Church's reliance on mass-produced religious art, much of it imported from abroad.[30] Jack Yeats's most significant collaboration with his sisters would be in the production of the Cuala broadsides, the first series of which was published monthly between 1908 and 1915. Each broadside normally comprised two written pieces and three illustrations by Jack himself, printed on a single sheet folded to produce four pages.[31] In style they resembled ballad sheets: the broad dark outlines of the images mimicked wood blocks, and were sometimes mistaken for them.[32] As Bruce Arnold has noted, Jack Yeats not only provided illustrations but functioned in an editorial capacity, sourcing texts for each edition.[33]

Conflict and independence

Notwithstanding the significant achievements of these early years, there were difficulties with the management of Dun Emer from the beginning, not least because of the imbalance between the sisters' level of commitment and their creative autonomy. The main financial contribution had been made by Evelyn Gleeson, and it was her vision that linked the ideals of the English Arts and Crafts Movement with those of the Irish Cultural Revival. Karen Brown has also noted the significance of Evelyn Gleeson's feminism in shaping Dun Emer's educational programme, suggesting that the cultural importance of the Yeats family has resulted in her relative exclusion from the later narrative surrounding Dun Emer.[34] Though this may be true, it was both financial and personality issues that caused Dun Emer to be divided (after formal arbitration in 1907) into two discrete parts, Dun Emer Guild and Dun Emer Industries – with Evelyn Gleeson heading the Guild and the Yeats sisters maintaining a separate unit, which they managed financially. This division paved the way for the eventual creation of Cuala Industries, which moved to new premises in Churchtown, County Dublin. The eleventh and last book issued under the Dun Emer imprint was W.B. Yeats's *Discoveries*, published on 12 September 1907. Just over a year later, the Cuala Press issued *Poetry and Ireland*, essays by W.B. Yeats and Lionel Johnson; in appearance the Cuala book was very similar to those issued under the Dun Emer imprint, so that readers and supporters could see continuity of subject matter and design between the two.

With the continuing involvement of various members of the Yeats family came ongoing sibling friction. For W.B. Yeats, careful editorial selection was an important part of the identity of the Cuala Press, making it the most significant Irish literary publisher of its time and setting it apart from Maunsel Press and from larger commercial enterprises. The small scale of the business meant that Yeats could publish his own work there comparatively quickly, and could control the circumstances in which it was printed and distributed. This allowed him to cultivate distinct readerships and identities, sometimes by publishing different versions of the same poem, first in the small press edition and later commercially. Yeats's painstaking attention to the process of editing his poems testifies to the importance of this relationship for him, and he frequently revised poems that had already been set in proof at Cuala; this necessitated the resetting of pages, which meant additional labour and cost for Elizabeth. Sometimes she wished to make this situation explicit, as was the case in the 1914 volume *Responsibilities*, which carried a brusque erratum note informing purchasers: 'these are alterations that our brother made after the book was printed – so are not our misprints'.[35]

The period of the First World War was an especially difficult one for the business, restricting both the availability of materials and demand from purchasers. Letters from Lily to her father in New York record the responses of the two sisters to the outbreak of war, in particular to the sinking of the *Lusitania* and the death of Hugh Lane. The Easter Rising in April 1916 also features in her letters, and this had a more immediate impact, given the close intersection between revivalism and revolution. The Cuala workshop remained open during and after the Rising, but the events had a serious impact on the mood of the workers.[36] Both sisters were dismissive of the rebellion, indicating the difference in their minds between cultural nationalism and its militant counterpart, as Lily wrote to her father:

> What a pity Madame Markievicz's madness changed its form when she inherited it – in her father it meant looking for the North Pole in an open boat, very cooling for him and safe for others – her followers are said to have been either small boys or drunken dock workers out of work called the Citizens Army – I don't think any others would have followed her – I would not have followed her across the road.[37]

These letters also reflect the changing attitudes of the Irish public towards the rebellion. After the execution of the rebels, Lily noted that 'a great mistake had been made',[38] and Elizabeth who, during the War of Independence, was out and about more than her sister, recorded the brutality of the Black and Tans with disgust, showing how alienated moderate Irish people had become from the English establishment.

Though the revolutionary period was one of challenge and upheaval, Cuala continued to produce high-quality work, committing to the printing of excerpts of Yeats's *Autobiography*, including *Reveries over childhood and youth* (1916) and *Four years* (1921), together with editions of their father's letters; the Yeats sisters were thus affirming the familial dimension of the enterprise. Their brother was also keen to have friends represented on the Cuala lists: the publication of *The post office*, a play by Rabindranath Tagore (1914), and Ernest Fenollosa's *Certain noble plays of Japan* were instances where the poet's personal conviction superseded the larger aim to publish the work of Irish writers.

For almost all its existence, Cuala Industries was in debt, despite many attempts to run the business more economically. Handmade artworks – including books – were necessarily expensive to produce and not always easy to sell. In times of particular financial hardship, the press took on the printing of more ephemeral material, such as theatre programmes, single poems and cards; this jobbing printing helped increase income and the profile of the business. By the early 1920s these items constituted a larger part of the press's output than the books themselves, reflecting the increasing financial instability of the press. The year 1923 would be a turning point: Lily became ill and the difficult relationship between the two sisters at last came to a head. Elizabeth's bouts of depression had long been a cause of tension, and Lily finally acknowledged that 'life with her for the past twenty years has been torture', though she had always felt there was nothing to be gained by direct confrontation with her sister.[39] Lily had no wish to return to their shared life but, once she had recuperated, she returned to Dundrum nonetheless, and lived with her sister until Elizabeth's death in 1940.[40] A lapse in Cuala's lease on the Churchtown property where the press was situated necessitated a relocation, and in 1923 the printing press was temporarily housed in the basement of W.B. Yeats's home on Merrion Square, significantly reducing overheads and allowing the poet to keep a closer eye on the workings of the business. The poet's wife, George Yeats, took over management of the embroidery division from Lily: she initiated new designs and worked to increase sales through attendance at a number of exhibitions and fairs in London, Birmingham and other English cities.[41]

Family involvement with the business changed in other ways too. In 1925 Jack Yeats withdrew his support from the Cuala broadsides series, wishing to devote more time to oil painting and concerned that continued illustration was compromising his reputation as a painter. He was especially concerned at Elizabeth's practice of reproducing his broadside work as single images: 'If I had the ready money I would try and buy up the copyrights of all the prints of mine which Cuala publishes'.[42] Despite this breach, the press continued to produce fine work, and a later series of broadsides featuring illustrations by Harry Kernoff and Maurice MacGonigal was published; in time, Jack would offer new work too. Things improved in the mid-1920s with a phase of increased book production: ten new titles appeared in five years, including W.B. Yeats's *October blast* (1927), which contained poems later printed in *The tower* (1928).

Other work, including poems by contemporaries such as Patrick Kavanagh, continued to appear from the press in the 1940s, and its reputation for fine design and significant poetry publication did not diminish. However, the Second World War and the deaths of W.B. Yeats in 1939, Elizabeth a year later and Lily in 1949 ushered in a new era. Though George Yeats would maintain aspects of the press over the next two decades, it was the earlier work in both textile and print that would constitute the vital legacy of the Cuala Industries and ensure the lasting reputation of the sisters who ran it.

Endnotes

[1] John Butler Yeats to Susan (Lily) Yeats, 10 June 1894, in William M. Murphy (ed.), *Letters from Bedford Park: a selection from the correspondence of John Butler Yeats* (Dublin,1972), 8.

[2] William H. Murphy, *Prodigal father: the life of John Butler Yeats (1839–1922)* (Syracuse (NY), 2001), 106.

[3] Joan Hardwick, *The Yeats sisters: a biography of Susan and Elizabeth Yeats* (London,1996), 56.

[4] Anthea Callen, 1985 'Sexual division of labor in the Arts and Crafts Movement', *Woman's Art Journal* 5(2) (Autumn/Winter 1984), 1–6: 2.

[5] Callen, 'Sexual division', 4. See also, J. Ramsay MacDonald (ed.), *Women in the printing trades* (London, 1904).

[6] Zoë Thomas, 'Between art and commerce: women, business ownership, and the Arts and Crafts Movement', *Past and Present* no. 247 (May 2020), 151–95: 162. See also, Zoë Thomas, *Women art workers and the Arts and Crafts Movement* (Manchester, 2020).

[7] Thomas, 'Between art and commerce', 155.

[8] A.S. Byatt, *Peacock and vine: Fortuny and Morris in life and at work* (London, 2016), 31.

[9] Hardwick, *Yeats sisters*, 88.

[10] Nicola Gordon Bowe, 'The book in the Irish Arts and Crafts Movement', in Clare Hutton (ed.), *The Irish book in the twentieth century* (Dublin, 2004), 16–35: 19.

[11] See, Clare Hutton, 'Publishing the Irish Cultural Revival, 1891–1922', in Clare Hutton and Patrick Walsh (eds), *The Oxford history of the Irish book* (Oxford, 2011), vol. 5, 17–42.

[12] Karen E. Brown, 'Evelyn Gleeson and the Irish cultural revival', in Éimear O'Connor (ed.), *Irish women artists 1800–2009: familiar but unknown* (Dublin, 2010), 71–83: 75.

[13] Brown, 'Evelyn Gleeson', 76.

[14] Hardwick, *Yeats sisters*, 118.

[15] R.F. Foster, *W.B. Yeats: a life 1865–1939* (2 vols; Oxford, 1997–2003), vol. 1: *The apprentice mage 1865–1914* (1997), 274.

[16] Jacqueline Genet,'The Dun Emer and the Cuala Press', in Jacqueline Genet, Sylvie Mikowski and Fabienne Garcier (eds), *The book in Ireland* (Cambridge, 2006), 48–74: 54.

[17] Dun Emer Prospectus, 1903.

[18] Gifford Lewis, *The Yeats sisters and the Cuala* (Dublin, 1994), 52.

[19] Publicity leaflet for Dun Emer Industries, 1904.

[20] Karen E. Brown, *The Yeats circle, verbal and visual relations in Ireland, 1880–1939* (Farnham (Surrey), 2011), 41.

[21] See, Simone Murray, 'The Cuala Press: women, publishing, and the conflicted genealogies of "feminist publishing"', *Women's Studies International Forum* 27 (2004), 489–506: 500.

[22] W.B. Yeats, *In the seven woods* (Dublin, 1903).

[23] This sales mode had limited success as people often visited the showroom for social, rather than commercial, reasons. See, for example, George Yeats to W.B. Yeats, 6 December 1932, in Ann Saddlemyer (ed.), *W.B. Yeats and George Yeats: the letters* (Oxford, 2011), 336.

[24] Murray, 'Cuala Press', 494.

[25] Gifford Lewis, '"This terrible struggle with want of means": behind the scenes at the Cuala Press', in Clare Hutton and Patrick Walsh (eds), *The Oxford history of the Irish book*, vol. 5, 529–47: 534–8.

[26] Brown, *Yeats circle*, 42.

[27] W.B. Yeats to Mrs Allingham, 7 December 1904, in Allan Wade (ed.), *The letters of W.B. Yeats* (London, 1954), 446.

[28] Cited in Liam Miller, *The Dun Emer Press, later the Cuala Press* (Dublin, 1973), 43.

[29] Cited in Lewis, *The Yeats sisters and the Cuala*, 69.

[30] Ann Wilson, 'Arts and Crafts and revivalism in Catholic church decoration: a brief duration', *Eire-Ireland* 48(3–4) (Fall/Winter 2013), 5–48: 5.

[31] Angela Griffith, 'Jack Yeats and fine art publishing', in Yvonne Scott (ed.), *Jack B. Yeats: old and new departures* (Dublin, 2008), 100–19: 106.

[32] Griffith, 'Jack Yeats', 114–15.

[33] Bruce Arnold, *Jack Yeats* (New Haven, 1998), 168.

[34] Karen E. Brown, 'Gender and the decorative arts: Evelyn Gleeson and the Irish cultural revival', in Éimear O'Connor (ed.) *Irish women artists 1800–2009: familiar but unknown* (Dublin, 2010), 71–83.

[35] Lewis, *The Yeats sisters and the Cuala*, 65.

[36] 'I have Cuala open and going on as usual, I don't discuss things at all with the girls. Eileen Colum has a silly elated look … two of the girls were gone yesterday when I went back after lunch, they both have Sinn Féin brothers, they both appeared again this morning looking happy, I asked no questions'. Susan (Lily) Yeats to John Butler Yeats, 26 April 1916, quoted in Lewis, *The Yeats sisters and the Cuala*, 133.

[37] Cited in Lewis, *The Yeats sisters and the Cuala*, 135.

[38] Lewis, *The Yeats sisters and the Cuala*, 131.

[39] Murphy, *Prodigal father*, 268.

[40] Brenda Maddox, *George's ghosts: a new life of W.B. Yeats* (London, 1999), 221.

[41] See, Letters between W.B. Yeats and George Yeats, in Saddlemyer, *W.B. Yeats and George Yeats*, 100–285 *passim*.

[42] Arnold, *Jack Yeats*, 234.

'A precious boon' in difficult times: Hanna Sheehy Skeffington and her sisters, Margaret, Mary and Kathleen

Margaret Ward

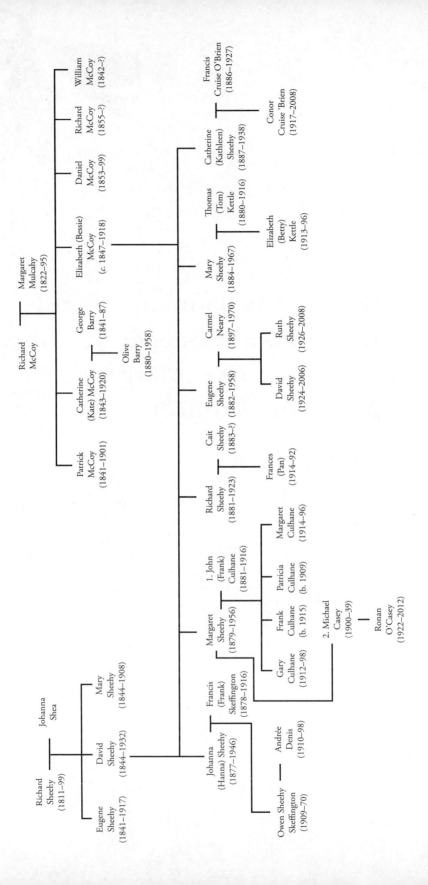

SHEEHY FAMILY TREE

Ireland in the Edwardian era was a country where social and political changes were promising to transform what had been a moribund state, in thrall to its British imperial masters, its economy skewed to support British rather than Irish needs. The land wars of the 1880s and 1890s had improved the position of many tenant farmers, and since then the Irish Parliamentary Party had been pursuing a strategy in Westminster to achieve a home rule that would give a native Irish parliament considerable power, even if imperial supremacy would be retained by Britain. A Catholic bourgeoisie waited for the era of self-government to arrive. Catholic girls were now benefiting from educational reforms that enabled them to pursue a broad range of academic subjects at secondary level. The Royal University of Ireland, an examining body only, was open to students of either sex. Victoria College in Belfast and Alexandra College in Dublin opened collegiate departments, enabling women to study at university level. In response, in 1893, the first Catholic women's college, run by the Dominican Order, began to provide a university-level education for their students. Other changes included improvements in the status of married women and gradual reform in voting rights, enabling women to become Poor Law Guardians and to stand for local government. By 1911 only the parliamentary vote was withheld. At the same time a younger generation was growing up, impatient with the slow pace of change and ready to embrace a whole host of new ideas: feminism, socialism, cultural nationalism. Literary societies blossomed, journals and newspapers sprang up and disappeared, while small theatres provided venues for plays beginning to redefine notions of Irish identity during this 'glorious Copper Age of Ireland', when cheap seats guaranteed audiences. Suffrage organisations had been formed in Belfast by Isabella Tod in 1871, and in Dublin in 1876 by Anna and Thomas Haslam. Nationalist women had been active in the Ladies' Land League of 1881–2. The new century would begin with the formation of the nationalist-feminist Inghinidhe na hÉireann (Daughters of Ireland), to be followed by numerous suffrage groups, most notably, in 1908, by the militant Irish Women's Franchise League, in which three of the four Sheehy sisters were involved.

The family lineage

The Sheehy sisters – Hanna, Margaret, Mary and Kathleen – were powerful characters from a formidable lineage, but with very different personalities (see picture section). R.M. Fox, who knew Hanna well, when writing of her in *Rebel Irishwomen*, praised the Sheehy Skeffington commitment to 'national freedom, internationalism, anti-militarism, feminism' and the bravery of Hanna's continued commitment to these 'ideas of light' in the years following the formation of the Free State. He also paid tribute to Mary and Kathleen: 'Mrs Cruise O'Brien and Mrs Kettle have each in their own way made distinctive contributions. The first was known as an exceptionally good Irish teacher and the author of admirable textbooks on Irish. The other was a member of the Dublin Corporation and was Chairman for some years of Rathmines Town Council'.[1]

Three out of the four Sheehy sisters would attend university. They were a tiny minority: in 1911 there were still only 280 female students in Ireland, compared with over 3,000 males. Their mother, Elizabeth (Bessie), valued education, and her influence was an important factor in the development of her daughters' lives. Bessie was the fourth of six children. It was said that she and her older sister Catherine (Kate) were sent to convent boarding school in Limerick rather than being kept at home to help with domestic chores. Their widowed mother, Margaret McCoy, ran two or three farms with the help of her older sons. Bessie was a strong-minded woman, intelligent and ambitious, who 'had the fighter in her too', as Hanna recalled with pride. When her brothers Dan and Pat were arrested as Fenians, and lodged in Mountjoy jail, Bessie defied the hostility of the local priest, managing to obtain the keys to the parish church, where she led the evening rosary 'to a packed congregation'.[2] Her sister Kate was also strongly political; she was a member of the Ladies' Land League in the 1880s and later, as a widow, was proprietor of Barry's Hotel, which was close to the Sheehy home in north Dublin. She was also a supporter of the suffrage cause, providing inestimable support, emotional and financial, to her goddaughter Hanna.

David Sheehy, their father, had been born into a mill-owning family at Broadford, County Limerick in 1844. He had an older brother, Eugene, and a sister, Mary. Their father, Richard, wanted both of his boys to become priests. Eugene became known as the 'Land League priest', and he was at one time a political prisoner with Parnell in Kilmainham jail. He was also Hanna's dearly loved godfather, a man who encouraged both her studies and her political activities. David Sheehy did not become a priest, returning instead to Ireland, where he joined the Irish Republican Brotherhood (IRB). He eventually moved into the mainstream of nationalist politics, becoming a mill owner like his father. He married Bessie McCoy in 1876 and they lived in Kanturk, County Cork, where Hanna was born the following year. They then moved to another mill, at Loughmore, County Tipperary, where the other Sheehy children were born in rapid succession. Margaret was born two years after Hanna, followed by Richard (Dick) in 1881 and Eugene in 1882. Mary was born in 1884 and Kathleen, the youngest, in 1887. The children's favourite game of 'Evictions and Emergency men' reflected the troubled society in which they lived. No one wanted to take the part of 'bailiff or peeler', because all wanted to be 'the evicted family guarding the home (it was an outhouse in the mill) against the crowbar, and fortified with water, hayforks and other means of defence'.[3]

As the oldest, Hanna was more exposed to the turmoil of the land wars. She remembered visiting her uncle Eugene in Kilmainham jail, going with Aunt Kate when she brought lunch to the prisoners. David Sheehy became a nationalist member of parliament for South Galway in 1885, taking part in the Plan of Campaign, another Irish Party initiative to force landlords to lower their rent demands. Another early memory of Hanna's was visiting her father in jail, 'dashing across the prison yard, as other children dash across the playground'.[4] This does not seem to have been an experience shared by her siblings. In 1887, when Kathleen was just one, the family moved to Dublin to make it easier for David to travel between London and Dublin.

Family life

In 1893 the Sheehys moved to 2 Belvedere Place, an impressively tall house with high granite steps leading to a majestic pillared door topped by a fanlight. The girls went to the Dominican school in Eccles Street, and Hanna stayed with the Dominicans when studying for her BA, but when the Loreto order of nuns set up their own university classes in St Stephen's Green, Mary and Kathleen decided to go there for their BA studies. These developments meant that they were able to benefit from an education that differed very little from that of their brothers, although they complained, with justification, that because of their sex they were denied attendance at University College lectures. Margaret was the only sibling who did not go to university. Her interest was in drama and theatrics, and she seems to have studied elocution, which she would later teach.

The Sheehy household was a woman-centred home, as David was in London for much of the time. It was always full of people, with a paying lodger (as the family never had much money), cousins visiting from the country and one live-in servant. Aunt Kate and her daughter Olive were frequent visitors. Hanna's description of leaving home in 1900 when she went to Paris as an au pair provides a glimpse of family life. It was 'awful leaving … Maggie retired at intervals to cry and Mary, Kathleen, mother, Minnie, Auntie were all in floods of tears'. She felt guilty at leaving Mary and Kathleen, now aged sixteen and fourteen, feeling very involved with their education and development as young women. Her room was let out to an Englishman, who paid £1, receiving breakfast and tea in return. It was a huge relief: 'I am not a burden … my room is contributing to the fund,' she wrote to Frank Skeffington, the man who would become her husband.[5]

A formal language exchange system for girls was organised in 1904, too late for Hanna, but Mary and Kathleen both benefited, enabling pupils from the Eccles Street school to spend a year at the Amiens École. Germaine Fontaine, who came to know the Sheehys very well, spent the Christmas of 1904 at Belvedere Place as an exchange student. Her reminiscences contain sketches of each family member;

Margaret, majestic and beautiful in a rather haughty way ... Mary, whom I knew and liked very much, gentle and lovely; Kathleen, very jolly and dynamic, about the same age as me ... Dick whom I admired greatly because he seemed to be a well of knowledge ... Eugene, very amusing with his deadpan humour, skinny and bony but full of vitality. I soon got to know the oldest daughter Hanna ... She too was very attractive because she knew how to incorporate more subtly all the qualities of the others.[6]

Mary was the one with looks. 'She is very handsome and wears an immense plait of soft black hair,' wrote Stanislaus Joyce in his diary.[7] Many agreed, but Mary was much more than merely a pretty face. James Joyce, who knew the family better than his brother, confided that in his opinion Mary Sheehy seemed to have 'a great contempt for many of the people she knew'.[8]

As the Sheehy children matured and developed their own friendships, their house became a notable venue for people from many different walks of life. Friendships between the sexes were not frowned upon in Belvedere Place, where Sheehy 'At Homes' were held on the second Sunday of each month. One of the young visitors recalled the 'genuine homeliness' of 'Old David and Mrs Sheehy [who] were open-hearted and had an old-style Irish welcome for everybody, young and old, rich and less rich'.[9] Entertainment was not lavish – refreshments were limited to tea and sandwiches – but attributes of wit and quick-thinking were highly prized. Germaine Fontaine, used to the formality of the French, found herself astounded by the 'heaps' of people who found seats where they could, from the basement to the staircase. Many years later Hanna recalled those days fondly: '[James] Joyce was then gay and boyish, flinging himself into topical charades. He loved to "dress up" and produce plays and parodies, and to sing old folk ballads in his sweet tenor'.[10]

Margaret was the instigator of many of their plays and charades. In 1901 'Miss Margaret M. Sheehy' gave a dramatic and musical recital at the Antient Concert Rooms, admission one shilling.[11] When she persuaded Joyce to write a paper on Ibsen for her literary group, Hanna commented wryly, 'Power of the smile!'[12] Margaret enjoyed clothes and drama and the gossip of everyday life, impatient with those who preferred conversations on politics. She and Hanna cooperated in writing a play called 'Cupid's confidante', with Joyce playing the part of the villain, Geoffrey Fortescue, at a public performance at the XL Café in Grafton Street.[13]

Politics

The United Ireland League was a support organisation for the Irish Party, and it developed a youth branch in Dublin – the Young Ireland Branch (YIBs) – which was made up mainly of former students. These included Richard and Eugene Sheehy, Tom Kettle, Frank Skeffington, Francis Cruise O'Brien and John Francis ('Frank') Culhane. Unusually, after a determined effort by Hanna and her sisters, the branch also accepted women as members. Hanna, Mary and Kathleen Sheehy were members, and in 1910 Kathleen became vice-president.

All four Sheehy sisters joined the Irish Women's Suffrage and Local Government Association in 1902. Margaret, with her sisters, paid her shilling subscription for the next three years, but when the Irish Women's Franchise League was formed by Hanna and Margaret Cousins, only Mary and Kathleen joined. Sheehy family and friends provided a significant proportion of the early League membership. At Mrs Barry's (Aunt Kate) on 26 January 1909 Kathleen Sheehy was reported to have made a 'brilliant debut' as a speaker; the other speaker on that occasion was Tom Kettle, who was becoming well-known in feminist circles as one of the few MPs to support suffrage delegations to Westminster.[14] Francis Cruise O'Brien, anxious for any opportunity to see Kathleen, was also a frequent attender at League events.

Marriage

The Sheehy sisters all married men who had been members of the YIBs. How did their marriages fit in with the plans of their parents, for a new political dynasty that would help shape the future of Ireland when home rule was achieved? Hanna was the first to marry. She and Frank Skeffington married in 1903, uniting their surnames to signify their commitment to equality within their marriage. They had been forced to endure a lengthy engagement until Frank was in a position to support a wife. At one stage, frustrated by the secrecy that had been imposed upon them, Frank decided the engagement had to be known publicly, suggesting that Hanna let her sisters into the secret before they left for school: 'tell Mary and Kathleen and show them the ring in your room ... that would be sufficient, I think, to ensure publicity!' However, Hanna was still a dutiful daughter, and the engagement would continue for another eighteen months. Frank, with his many controversial views, might not have been an ideal son-in-law, but he had potential, and when he became University Registrar for UCD he and Hanna were finally able to wed. However, within a year he had resigned that position in protest at attempts to curb his campaigning on behalf of women students. While Frank now earned a precarious living as a journalist, Hanna became the main breadwinner as a Catholic lay teacher. As the couple became more radical in their views, there was a gradual estrangement from the Sheehy parents, particularly from David Sheehy. When their son Owen was born in May 1909, their decision not to have him baptised caused a serious rift. Mary, who was strongly Catholic, disapproved. She had married Tom Kettle that year and Hanna noted in her diary: 'Gradual slackening of ties to Mary and all the rest. New ménage not friendly, definite religious departure re Owen'.[15] Despite this, Mary invited her sister and Frank to tea just before Christmas, while Father Eugene, still the loving godfather, visited them on Christmas Eve with Kathleen and Cruise O'Brien. Kathleen, although strongly Catholic also, had begun the battle with her parents for permission to marry the agnostic O'Brien, and she would receive unfailing support from her oldest sister, despite the difficulties this caused within the family. Hanna's diary entry for February 1909 had included 'Cruise O'Brien affair starts – fierce henceforth'. On 17 March she noted 'coolness in Belvedere still', while by the end of that year she wrote sorrowfully: 'the breach between family widens ever – nearly all ties gone'.[16]

At first Margaret did exactly what was expected of her. In 1907 she married Frank Culhane, a solicitor from a wealthy, conservative Catholic family, and had four children in quick succession. Although they lived in north Dublin, not far from the Sheehy home, Margaret does not seem to have become involved in any of the family disputes.

Mary married Tom Kettle in a smart society wedding in 1909. A report of the wedding said it was an event 'full of suffrage atmosphere'. The bride wore a 'Votes for Women' badge pinned to her white gown, and another mounted in her floral wreath. Many of the guests also wore badges. John Redmond, leader of the Irish Party, and many other Irish Party politicians were wedding guests.[17] Kettle was one of their most brilliant MPs, while the bride was a daughter of one of the most senior of the older generation of parliamentarians. The breach with Mary seems to have soon mended, despite Hanna's pessimism, and in June 1910 the two sisters travelled over to London as part of a united campaign to support a conciliation bill for suffrage. Mary was always feminist in outlook, and Tom was a notable suffrage ally. When signing his 1911 census return, he amended the form to read: 'One of the heads of the household'. However, once the Franchise League came into conflict with the Irish Party, both he and Mary were much less visible as League supporters.

Kathleen gained a BA in literature in 1908, followed by an MA. She volunteered in the Franchise League offices and supported the suffrage cause, but her great passion was the revival of the Irish language. She became a teacher of Irish and, as Caitlín Nic Shíothaigh, wrote an Irish grammar and a textbook. In 1929 she published an Irish-language version of Gregg shorthand, which Hanna praised as 'a big effort' that she hoped would add to her sister's prestige. Kathleen's defiance of her parents in wanting to marry Cruise O'Brien was out of character. She remained strongly religious, but she was in love. The Sheehys divided on predictable lines. Some, particularly Mary and the parents, were strongly Catholic; Margaret and Eugene were more easy-going in their views; while Hanna, Frank and Cruise O'Brien represented, in the family's view, the extreme of godless radicalism. It was a difficult time for the young woman, who had to 'put up with advice from three older sisters, each of whom knew better than she how to go about everything she did'.[18] At one stage during the months of argument David Sheehy wrote to Hanna to order her and her husband to stay away from Belvedere Place: 'I know it is the intention of yourself and your husband to come here this evening. I don't want him to my house. It pains me to have to say this to you, but I do so to avoid greater pain'.[19] This provoked an outraged response from Hanna, who accused her father of having become an eastern 'Pasha' with his dictatorial views.[20] However, as Conor, the child of the O'Brien marriage, wrote, 'A simple exercise in parental authority could not stand against the spirit of the age, incarnate in the Skeffingtons'.[21] In October 1911 Kathleen was finally able to marry the man she loved. Although it took a long while for the wounds to heal, there was no permanent difference between the sisters, and they retained their divergent views. Hanna's comment to her son, made nearly a quarter of a century later – 'Aunt Mary has gone to Lough Derg again … placating God, I guess' – made it plain that succeeding decades had not moderated anyone's opinions regarding religion.[22]

Years of trauma – Fall of the House of Sheehy

In her later years, interviewed by RTÉ, Hanna described her sisters as 'truly a precious boon'.[23] The four women needed to be that 'precious boon', as those golden years at the start of the century, when the inhabitants of Belvedere Place seemed to be on the cusp of a new age of self-government in which many would play prominent roles, came to an end. Tragedy upon tragedy would shake the family, but the siblings always rallied in support.

In March 1915 David Sheehy was declared bankrupt, with unsecured debts of £683 and assets valued at £65.[24] He and Bessie had to leave their home, and Belvedere Place, the scene of so much good companionship, became part of Trinity College women's war effort as the V.A.D. (Voluntary Aid Detachment) hostel for Belgian refugees.

In June 1915 Frank Sheehy Skeffington received a year's prison sentence because of his ceaseless protest against the war raging in Europe. He went on hunger and thirst strike. While his family and in-laws campaigned on his behalf, some individuals were put in a difficult position. On the outbreak of war Tom Kettle had enlisted in the army and was recruiting for Irish soldiers to fight in France. Eugene Sheehy had enlisted in the Royal Dublin Fusiliers and David Sheehy, as a loyal follower of Redmond, backed the Irish Party's support for Britain. As Hanna admitted, she and Frank 'were in a small minority' in the family.[25] Support for Frank required a determined suppression of personal views. Mary Kettle, on holiday in Wales, wrote immediately of her admiration for the 'splendid courage to support your ideas', which both Frank and Hanna so obviously possessed. Mindful of their past arguments over religion, she worded her goodbye with care: 'and – if you let me say – God help you, your loving sister'.[26] Kathleen, at home in Dublin, kept the various scattered members of the family informed of the latest developments, while Cruise O'Brien used all his contacts on behalf of his brother-in-law. On the seventh day O'Brien had good news. He wrote confidentially of his intervention with the Secretary of State – there would be no forcible feeding, and Frank should be out that evening: 'But do Hanna try to get him away after this. They are apt to be savage. Kathleen will tell you more … Cheer up. They are determined not to kill him this time'.[27] After Frank's release Mary wrote to say that, 'though we do not quite agree on politics – still you both fight splendidly. It is dreadful to think what you have both gone through. I have been very anxious and worried but Kathleen was good and wrote every day. Really I did not know how fond I was of Frank till this – but I am almost a pro-German now!'[28]

There was more heartbreak to come. In March 1916 Frank Culhane died of a brain aneurism. As this was during the First World War Margaret was able to secure employment as Welfare Superintendent in the National Shell factory in Dublin. She was now the family breadwinner.[29] The most traumatic event of all occurred the following month, with the murder of Frank Sheehy Skeffington.

Death of a pacifist

On the second day of the Easter Rising Hanna and Frank had walked into Dublin city centre to offer, in their distinctive ways, support to the insurgents. Hanna met her Uncle Eugene at the GPO. As a close friend of Tom Clarke, he had come there as confessor to the insurgents. She delivered messages and supplies to the Royal College of Surgeons outpost before returning home to their son. Frank, who supported the ideals of the Rising, but not its methods of warfare, had been horrified by the looting, and tried, unsuccessfully, to organise a citizens' militia to prevent further ransacking of shops. As he walked home to Rathmines he was arrested by a British patrol under the command of Captain Bowen-Colthurst. Later, he was taken out as hostage, where he witnessed acts of indiscriminate killing on the orders of Bowen-Colthurst. That night Frank and two other journalists were brought out to the yard of Portobello Barracks and shot dead, and their bodies were buried in the yard. Hanna was not informed of her husband's murder, and she spent the next few days trying to find out why he had not come home. On the Friday, by which time she said 'horrible rumours' had reached her, she tried to see a doctor connected to the barracks, but found herself stopped by the police. She discovered that she herself was being watched.[30]

The quest for justice

Mary and Margaret made enquiries on their sister's behalf. When they arrived at Portobello they first enquired for the whereabouts of their brother, Lieutenant Eugene Sheehy of the Royal Dublin Fusiliers, who was garrisoned somewhere in the city. They received a courteous reply, but when they asked about their brother-in-law they found themselves under arrest, accused of having been seen 'talking to Sinn Féiners'. After they were marched across the barrack square, Captain Bowen-Colthurst informed them that no information concerning Skeffington was available, and the sooner they left the premises the better. They were not only marched off by an armed guard and escorted to the tramway line but were also forbidden to speak to each other on the way. It was clear that something dreadful was being covered up. When Hanna found Mr Coade, the father of the boy who had been murdered near Rathmines Church, she finally knew the worst. He had seen Frank's body in the mortuary when he went for his son. The evidence led to only one conclusion, but Hanna could not let it rest there. She had to find out what had happened.

A court-martial of Bowen-Colthurst, in which the verdict was guilty but insane, took place in May (see picture section). That was insufficient for Hanna. She went to London, to see Prime Minister Asquith, turning down an offer of £10,000 compensation and succeeding in getting the promise of an inquiry into events in Portobello. This took place, under Sir John Simon, that August. Mary Kettle was one of the witnesses, giving evidence of the fruitless quest to the barracks. Kathleen was in London, reading all the newspaper reports of the inquiry; 'hard to follow it all,' she thought, as she praised her sister's performance. Mary's testimony was most 'characteristically given' in that decided manner typical of her.[31]

Hanna made out a will, to ensure that their son Owen would be brought up as she and Frank would have wished. Maurice Wilkins, who had often helped with the production of the *Irish Citizen*, was co-executor with Kathleen and Mary. He sympathised with Frank's views on organised religion, having no patience with sectarianism and 'narrowing cults'.[32] Owen's future concerned him very much. Hanna, while knowing that Kathleen and Mary were strongly Catholic, had no fears that they would not honour her wishes for Owen to be brought up in a secular manner.

Tom Kettle, still wearing the uniform of the British army, had to suffer the pain of seeing his daughter Betty and nephew Owen running away in fright at the sight of the khaki-clad man coming towards them. It was not long after the raid on the Sheehy Skeffington house by Bowen-Colthurst, who had worn the same uniform. The Easter Rising and the brutality of the British response ended Kettle's hopes of a peaceful solution to Ireland's struggle for independence. There was no further point in trying to persuade Irish men to enlist in the British army, so he volunteered himself for duty in France. He was killed at the

Somme on 9 September. Mary now joined her sister Hanna in trying to assuage grief through work. Tom Kettle's *The ways of war* was published in 1917, accompanied by Mary's long memoir of her husband, written, as she said, with 'the vision of love'.[33] Eugene Sheehy was posted to France in July 1916, serving at the Somme and Ypres, before being transferred to intelligence services. After the war he resumed his legal career as a barrister.

There were more deaths to come in the family: Father Eugene Sheehy died in July 1917; Bessie Sheehy died in January 1918; and Dick Sheehy died from tuberculosis in 1923. Conor Cruise O'Brien, the child of Kathleen and Cruise, was born on 3 November 1917. His birth was the only positive event in the Sheehy family during this time of immense tragedy.

Family life and public service

In 1921, at the age of 42, Margaret fell in love with Michael Casey, her godson, a 21-year-old poet. Disowned by the Culhane family, the couple emigrated to Montreal, where their son Ronan was born in August 1922. Margaret's son Gary Culhane was sent to join her that September, but her other three children remained in Ireland. She became part of a bohemian set in Montreal, an actress and elocutionist. Canadian academic Dara Culhane has written of her grandmother, portraying a larger-than-life character on and off stage: 'a gracious hostess, a successful competitive bridge and poker player, a hopeless housekeeper and a dreadful cook'.[34] Michael died in 1939 and Margaret, who was always homesick for Ireland, returned to Dublin soon after.

Hanna, Mary and Kathleen gathered together on Sundays, having lunch and outings, with friends coming in the evenings for games, charades and conversation, with the younger generation of Owen, Betty and Conor listening in. Even during the most hectic years of political involvement, when Hanna was in demand as a speaker in Britain and Ireland, she managed to attend many of the Sunday gatherings. Cruise O'Brien died suddenly of a heart attack on Christmas Day 1927, and Kathleen joined her sisters in widowhood. She struggled with debt, the bailiffs coming to the house on more than one occasion, and she worked hard as a teacher and superintendent of Irish exams. David Sheehy now lived with Mary, a lonely figure sitting by the fire, going to six masses a day – one for each of his children, it was thought. Eventually his children decided to create some variety in his life (and lessen the burden on Mary) by alternating where he would eat. Eugene, now the only son, had the honour of Sunday dinner; Mary had Tuesday; Hanna's turn was Thursday; while Kathleen had Saturday evenings.[35] David died in December 1932.

Mary remained a strong campaigner for women. She was an independent member of Dublin City Council, and in 1928 was elected its first female chair. In this capacity she became involved in the Hugh Lane Bequest Committee, which organised the reconstruction of Charlemont House as the home for the Hugh Lane collection of paintings.[36] Her dedication to public life was recognised in a ceremony in May 1932, when over 100 feminists came together in the Gresham Hotel to present her with a municipal robe and hat. It was cherry-coloured, fur-trimmed, poplin-lined and embroidered by the women of the Dun Emer Guild, with an inscription stating that the robe was presented to Mrs Kettle 'as a tribute for her unfailing loyalty and devotion to women'. Women from the Irish Citizen Army, the Irish Women's Franchise League, non-militant suffragists, the Women's Prisoners' Defence League and many women no longer active in political life came together, with sisters Hanna and Kathleen in the audience.[37]

When Hanna served a month in Armagh jail in 1933, for defying an order banning her from Northern Ireland, her siblings rallied round, despite their varying political views. Mary was the first to be contacted, as she sent out a request for clothes and other messages. In publicising this imprisonment Mary recalled the sacrifice that had been made by her husband Tom. If Hanna could not travel freely around Ireland, then the sacrifice of 50,000 Irishmen who had died fighting so that small nations could be free had been in vain.[38] Their brother Eugene, now a judge on the Monaghan circuit, used the old boys' network to secure a visit to his sister, explaining to the 'astonished' prison governor that 'the criminal of one generation became the judge and lawmaker of the next', such were the vagaries of Irish politics.[39]

Hanna and Mary made a formidable combination in the feminist campaign against the 1937 Constitution. Both were prominent in delegations, writing letters to the press and speaking at public meetings. The Women's Social and Progressive League was formed in the wake of that campaign, with both sisters in executive positions. While Hanna was in America Kathleen wrote to say Mary was 'working like the devil with that League',[40] as feminists attempted to mobilise women into a women's political party.

Last years

In February 1938, following a stroke, Kathleen died suddenly. Owen, recovering from TB in a sanitorium in Switzerland, wrote to his mother, still in America, about the 'horrible news about poor Aunt Kathy … I know this will be a terrible shock to you as it was to me; and as it must have been to all at home'.[41] Kathleen had been under the care of Dr Kathleen Lynn, who had put her on a diet, causing her to write humorously: 'You'll have to look for me with a microscope when you come back',[42] but, sadly, that was not to be. While the family was full of regret that they had not managed to persuade Kathleen to rest more, Owen tried to reassure Hanna: 'She hated resting & she loved her work, every minute of it; there had been talk of her retiring, but I feel glad she didn't'.[43]

Retirement or an easy life was not the Sheehy way. Hanna also remained active till the end, both as a teacher and as a political activist. In 1943 she stood, unsuccessfully, in elections to the Dáil, still hoping for the formation of a women's political party. She died in 1946.

Mary Kettle continued her activities for many more years. From 1936 to 1961 she served as Joint Chair of the Committee of Women's Societies and Social Workers. She died in 1967, aged 83. Margaret died in 1955. In their different ways all the Sheehy sisters had left their mark on the world.

Endnotes

[1] R.M. Fox, *Rebel Irishwomen* (Dublin 1935; reprint of 1967 edition), 73–4.

[2] Hanna Sheehy Skeffington, 'Unpublished memoirs', in Margaret Ward (ed.), *Hanna Sheehy Skeffington: suffragette and Sinn Féiner: her memoirs and political writings* (Dublin, 2017), 4.

[3] Ward (ed.), *Sheehy Skeffington memoirs*, 9.

[4] Ward (ed.), *Sheehy Skeffington memoirs*, 6.

[5] NLI, Sheehy Skeffington Papers (hereafter SSP), 40,464/1, Hanna Sheehy to Frank Skeffington, 7 January 1900. Minnie was the Sheehy maid.

[6] Germaine Fontaine, 'Unpublished reminiscences 1903–4', courtesy of Andrée Sheehy Skeffington. (Germaine's daughter Andrée Denis would marry Owen, son of Hanna and Frank Sheehy Skeffington.)

[7] Stanislaus Joyce, *My brother's keeper* (London, 1958), 123.

[8] Quoted in Bonnie Kime Scott, 'Emma Clery in *Stephen hero:* a young woman walking proudly through the decayed city', in Suzette Henke and Elaine Unkeless (eds), *Women in Joyce* (Brighton (Sussex), 1982), 62, n.33.

[9] Patricia Hutchins, *James Joyce's Dublin* (London, 1950), 72.

[10] NLI, SSP, 24,164, Hanna Sheehy Skeffington, RTÉ radio interview, incomplete transcript, 1945.

[11] NLI, SSP, 33,606/7, recital ticket, 1901.

[12] NLI, SSP, 40,464/1, Hanna Sheehy to Frank Skeffington, 14 October 1900.

[13] NLI, Joseph Holloway Papers, 23, 247. Richard Ellman claims that Margaret wrote the play (see, Richard Ellman, *James Joyce* (Oxford, 1982), 93); however, Andrée Sheehy Skeffington states that the play was written by Hanna and produced by Margaret (Andrée Sheehy Skeffington, *Skeff* (Dublin, 1991), 10. In conversation, Andrée Sheehy Skeffington stated her belief that Margaret would not have been capable of writing the play alone.

[14] *Votes for Women*, 18 February 1909.

[15] NLI, SSP, 41,183/5, Hanna Sheehy Skeffington, Diary, general comments, 1908–9.

[16] NLI, SSP, 41,183/5.

[17] *Votes for Women,* 17 September 1909.

[18] Donald Harman Akenson, *Conor Cruise O'Brien* (Montreal, 1994), 40.

[19] NLI, SSP, 41,176/5, David Sheehy to Hanna Sheehy Skeffington, 8 February 1910.

[20] NLI, SSP, 41,176/5, Hanna Sheehy Skeffington to David Sheehy, n.d.

[21] Conor Cruise O'Brien, *States of Ireland* (St Albans, 1974), 81.

[22] NLI, SSP, 40,484/7, Hanna Sheehy Skeffington to Owen Sheehy Skeffington, 8 September 1934.

[23] NLI, SSP, 24,164, Hanna Sheehy Skeffington, RTÉ radio interview.

[24] J.B. Lyons, *The enigma of Tom Kettle: Irish patriot, essayist, poet, British soldier, 1880–1916* (Dublin, 1983), 276. One family member speculated that gambling on horses might have been a factor in the Sheehy bankruptcy.

[25] Hayden Talbot, *Michael Collins' own story* (London, 1923), 97.

[26] NLI, SSP, 22,648, Mary Kettle to Hanna Sheehy Skeffington, n.d.

[27] NLI, SSP, 22,648, Francis Cruise O'Brien to Hanna Sheehy Skeffington, n.d., ('Monday').

[28] NLI, SSP, 22,648, Mary Kettle to Hanna Sheehy Skeffington, n.d.

[29] Padraig Yeates, https://www.historyireland.com/20th-century-contemporary-history/oh-what-a-lovely-war-dublin-and-the-first-world-war/
accessed 1 August 2019.

[30] For full details of the Sheehy Skeffington case and its aftermath, see Margaret Ward, *Fearless woman: Hanna Sheehy Skeffington, feminism and the Irish revolution* (Dublin, 2019), Chapter 8.

[31] NLI, SSP, 22,279, Kathleen Cruise O'Brien to Hanna Sheehy Skeffington, 28 August 1916.

[32] NLI, SSP, 22,279, Maurice Wilkins to Hanna Sheehy Skeffington, 7 September 1916.

[33] T.M. Kettle, *The ways of war* (London, 1917), 1.

[34] Dara Culhane, 'The Sheehy Skeffington Papers: treasure hunting at the National Library of Ireland archives', *Canadian Journal of Irish Studies* 39(1) (2015), 54.

[35] NLI, SSP, 40,484/6, Hanna Sheehy Skeffington to Owen Sheehy Skeffington, 9 November 1931.

[36] Charlemont House opened in 1933. With thanks to Mary McAuliffe for this information concerning Mary Kettle's involvement.

[37] *Irish World*, 9 July 1932.

[38] Quoted in Florence Underwood, Secretary to Women's Freedom League, letter to *Manchester Guardian*, 30 January 1933.

[39] Eugene Sheehy, *May it please the court* (Dublin, 1951), 146–7.

[40] NLI, SSP, 41,178/5, Kathleen Cruise O'Brien to Hanna Sheehy Skeffington, 10 February 1938.

[41] NLI, SSP, 40,483/3, Owen Sheehy Skeffington to Hanna Sheehy Skeffington, 23 February 1938.

[42] NLI, SSP, 41,178/5, Kathleen Cruise O'Brien to Hanna Sheehy Skeffington, 10 February 1938.

[43] NLI, SSP, 40,483/3, Owen Sheehy Skeffington to Hanna Sheehy Skeffington, 23 February 1938.

Bibliography

Ní Dhomhnaill sisters

Bergin, Osborn, 1970 *Irish bardic poetry: texts and translations, together with an introductory lecture*, eds Osborn Bergin and Fergus Kelly. Dublin. Dublin Institute for Advanced Studies.

Knott, Eleanor, 1960 'Mac an Bhaird's elegy on the Ulster lords', *Celtica* 5, 161–71.

Ó Macháin, Pádraig, 2007–8 'The flight of the poets: Eóghan Ruadh and Fearghal Óg Mac an Bhaird in exile', *Seanchas Ard Mhacha* 21–2, 39–58.

Walsh, Paul (ed.), 1916 *The Flight of the Earls by Tadhg Ó Cianáin, edited from the author's manuscript, with translation and notes*. Maynooth. St Patrick's College, Record Society.

Boyle sisters

Barnard, Toby, 2006 *Irish Protestant ascents and descents, 1641–1770*. Dublin. Four Courts Press.

Eckerle, Julie A. and McAreavey, Naomi (eds), 2019 *Women's life writing in early modern Ireland*. Lincoln. University of Nebraska Press.

Edwards, David and Rynne, Colin (eds), 2018 *The colonial world of Richard Boyle, first earl of Cork*. Dublin. Four Courts Press.

Walsh, Ann-Maria, 2020 *The daughters of the first earl of Cork: writing family, faith, politics and place*. Dublin. Four Courts Press.

Conynham sisters

Ashford, Gabrielle M., 2012 '"Advice to a daughter": Lady Frances Keightley to her daughter Catherine, September 1681', *Analecta Hibernica* 43, 17–46.

Ashford, Gabrielle M., 2012 Childhood: studies in the history of children in eighteenth-century Ireland. Unpublished PhD thesis, Dublin City University.

Conolly, Katherine, 2018 *The letters of Katherine Conolly, 1707–1747*, eds Marie-Louise Jennings and Gabrielle M. Ashford. Dublin. Irish Manuscripts Commission.

O'Dowd, Mary, 2005 *A history of women in Ireland 1500–1800*. Harlow. Pearson Education.

Shackleton sisters

Leadbeater, Mary, [forthcoming] *Annals of Ballitore by Mary Leadbeater*, ed. Magda Stouthamer-Loeber. Dublin. Irish Manuscripts Commission.

O'Dowd, Mary, 2016 'Mary Leadbeater: Quaker and modern woman?', in David Hayton and Andrew Holmes (eds), *Ourselves alone?: religion, society and politics in eighteenth- and nineteenth-century Ireland. Essays presented to S.J. Connolly*, 137–53. Dublin. Four Courts Press.

O'Dowd, Mary, 2018 'Adolescent girlhood in eighteenth-century Ireland', in Mary O'Dowd and June Purvis (eds), *A history of the girl: formation, identity and education*, 53–73. London. Palgrave Macmillan.

O'Neill, Kevin, 1996 '"Almost a gentlewoman": gender and adolescence in the diary of Mary Shackleton', in Mary O'Dowd and Sabine Wichert (eds), *Chattel, servant or citizen: women's status in church, state and society*, 91–113. Belfast. Institute of Irish Studies.

Pullin, Naomi, 2018 *Female friends and the making of transatlantic Quakerism, 1650–1750*. Cambridge Studies in Early Modern British History. Cambridge. Cambridge University Press.

Owenson sisters

Dermody, Thomas, 2012 *Selected writings*, ed. Michael Griffin. Dublin. Field Day.

Fitzpatrick, W.J., 1859 *The friends, foes, and adventures of Lady Morgan*. Dublin. W.B. Kelly.

The Freeman's Journal.

Owenson, Sydney, 1801 *Poems*. Dublin. A. Stewart.

Owenson, Sydney, 1859 *Passages from my autobiography*. London. Richard Bentley.

Owenson, Sydney, 1862 *Lady Morgan's memoirs: autobiography, diaries and correspondence* (2 vols), vol. 1. London. William H. Allen & Co.

Wright, Julia, 2006 '"All the fire-side circle": Irish women writers and the Sheridan–Lefanu coterie', *Keats–Shelley Journal* 55, 63–7.

Parnell sisters

Côté, Jane, 1991 *Fanny and Anna Parnell: Ireland's patriot sisters*. London. Macmillan.

Hughes, Marie, 1966 'The Parnell sisters', *Dublin Historical Record* 21(1), 14–27.

Mulligan, Adrian N., 2009 '"By a thousand ingenious feminist devices": the Ladies' Land League and the development of Irish nationalism', *Historical Geography* 37, 159–77.

Schneller, Beverley, 2005 *Anna Parnell's political journalism*. Dublin. Maunsel and Company.

Urquhart, Diane, 2016 "'The Ladies Land League have [sic] a crust to share with you": the rhetoric of the Ladies' Land League British campaign, 1881–2', in Tina O'Toole, Gillian McIntosh and Muireann Ó Cinnéide (eds), *Women writing war: Ireland, 1880–1922*, 11–24. Dublin. University College Dublin Press.

Ward, Margaret, 2001 'Gendering the Union: imperial feminism and the Ladies' Land League', *Women's History Review* 10(1), 71–92.

Gore-Booth sisters

Arrington, Lauren, 2015 *Revolutionary lives: Constance and Casimir Markievicz*. Princeton. Princeton University Press.

Gore-Booth, Eva, 1929 *Poems of Eva Gore-Booth: complete edition*, ed. Esther Roper. London. Longmans Green & Co.

Gore-Booth, Eva, 2018 *Eva Gore-Booth: collected poems*, ed. S. Tiernan. Dublin. Arlen House.

James, Dermot, 2004 *The Gore-Booths of Lissadell*. Dublin. Woodfield.

Moran, Gerard, 2006 *Sir Robert Gore-Booth and his landed estate in County Sligo, 1814–1876: land, famine, emigration and politics*. Dublin. Four Courts Press.

Tiernan, Sonja, 2012 *Eva Gore-Booth: an image of such politics*. Manchester. Manchester University Press.

Yeats sisters

Genet, Jacqueline, 2006 'The Dun Emer and the Cuala Press', in Jacqueline Genet, Sylvie Mikowski and Fabienne Garcier (eds), *The book in Ireland*, 48–74. Cambridge. Cambridge Scholars Press.

Gordon Bowe, Nicola, 2004 'The book in the Irish Arts and Crafts movement', in Clare Hutton (ed.), *The Irish book in the twentieth century*, 16–35. Dublin. Irish Academic Press.

Hardwick, Joan, 1996 *The Yeats sisters: a biography of Susan and Elizabeth Yeats*. London. HarperCollins.

Lewis, Gifford, 1994 *The Yeats sisters and the Cuala*. Dublin. Irish Academic Press.

Miller, Liam, 1973 *The Dun Emer Press, later the Cuala Press*. Dublin. Dolmen Press.

Murray, Simone, 2004 'The Cuala Press: women, publishing, and the conflicted genealogies of "feminist publishing"', *Women's Studies International Forum* 27, 489–506.

Sheehy Skeffington sisters

Culhane, Dara, 2015 'The Sheehy Skeffington Papers: treasure hunting at the National Library of Ireland archives', *Canadian Journal of Irish Studies* 39(1), 50–63.

Hutchins, Patricia, 1950 *James Joyce's Dublin*. London. Gray Walls Press.

O'Brien, Conor Cruise, 1974 *States of Ireland*. St Alban's. Panther Books.

Sheehy, Eugene, 1951 *May it please the court*. Dublin. C.J. Fallon.

Sheehy Skeffington, Andrée, 1991 *Skeff*. Dublin. Lilliput Press.

Ward, Margaret, 2019 *Fearless woman: Hanna Sheehy Skeffington, feminism and the Irish revolution*. Dublin. University College Dublin Press.

Contributors

Gabrielle (Gaye) M. Ashford completed a PhD at Dublin City University in 2012 on the history of children and childhood in eighteenth-century Ireland. She is co-editor of *The letters of Katherine Conolly 1707–1747*, published by the Irish Manuscripts Commission in 2018.

Lucy Collins is Associate Professor of Modern Poetry at University College Dublin. Her books include *Poetry by women in Ireland: a critical anthology 1870–1970* (2012) and a monograph, *Contemporary Irish women poets: memory and estrangement* (2015), both from Liverpool University Press.

Claire Connolly is Professor of Modern English at University College Cork. *A cultural history of the Irish novel, 1790–1829* (Cambridge Studies in Romanticism) won the Donald J. Murphy Prize. With Marjorie Howes (Boston College), Professor Connolly is General Editor of *Irish literature in transition, 1700–2020* (Cambridge University Press, 2020); and editor of Volume 2 of the series, *Irish literature in transition, 1780–1830*.

Siobhán Fitzpatrick served as Academy Librarian from 1997 to 2020; she has published mainly on Royal Irish Academy collections, and has co-edited several publications, including *That woman: studies in Irish bibliography: a Festschrift for Mary 'Paul' Pollard* (Dublin, 2005), *Treasures of the Royal Irish Academy library* (Dublin, 2009) and *Pathfinders to the past: the antiquarian road to Irish historical writing, 1640–1960* (Dublin, 2012).

Mary O'Dowd is Emeritus Professor at Queen's University Belfast. Her books include *A history of women in Ireland* (Harlow, 2005) and *Reading the Irish woman: studies in cultural encounters and exchange, 1714–1960* (Liverpool, 2013), co-authored with Gerardine Meaney and Bernadette Whelan. Her most recent book is *Marriage in Ireland, 1660–1925* (Cambridge, 2020), co-authored with Maria Luddy.

Pádraig Ó Macháin is Professor of Modern Irish at University College Cork. His recent publications include *Leabhar na Longánach: the Ó Longáin family and their manuscripts* (Cork, 2018) and *Paper and the paper manuscript* (Cork, 2019). Pádraig is editor of the journal *Ossory, Laois and Leinster* and co-editor of *An Linn Bhuí: Iris Ghaeltacht na nDéise*.

Sonja Tiernan is the Eamon Cleary Chair of Irish Studies and co-director of the Centre for Irish and Scottish Studies at the University of Otago, New Zealand. She has published in the area of gender and women's history in modern Ireland. She authored the first dedicated biography of Eva Gore-Booth and the first complete edition of Gore-Booth's poetry. Her most recent monograph is *Irish women's speeches: voices that rocked the system* (Dublin, 2021).

Diane Urquhart is Professor of Gender History in the School of History, Anthropology, Philosophy and Politics (HAPP) of Queen's University Belfast and President of the Women's History Association of Ireland (WHAI). Her publications include *Irish divorce: a history* (Cambridge, 2020); *The ladies of Londonderry:*

women and political patronage, 1800–1959 (London & New York, 2007); *Women in Ulster politics, 1890–1940: a history not yet told* (Dublin, 2000); and, with Lindsey Earner-Byrne, she co-authored *Irish abortion journey, 1920–2018* (London, 2019).

Ann-Maria Walsh was awarded her PhD (NUI) in 2017. Her monograph, *The daughters of the first earl of Cork: writing family, faith, politics and place* was published by Four Courts Press in 2020. Ann-Maria is a Marie Skłodowska-Curie postdoctoral fellow at Queen's University Belfast, and is currently working on an edition of the Boyle women's extant letters for the Irish Manuscripts Commission.

Margaret Ward is Honorary Senior Lecturer in History at Queen's University Belfast. Her many publications include *Fearless woman: Hanna Sheehy Skeffington, feminism and the Irish revolution* (Dublin, 2019). Her pioneering book, *Unmanageable revolutionaries: women and Irish nationalism* (1983), was re-issued in a revised and updated edition by Arlen House in 2021.

Acknowledgments

We acknowledge the support of the Academy Library staff in the administration and promotion of the original lecture series. Thanks to the Publications team for the excellent design and production, and to all the individuals, libraries, archives and institutions who have so generously provided images for this volume. We thank the anonymous reviewers for their constructive recommendations. Finally, we are very grateful to the contributors for their considered papers, their enthusiasm for the project and for their patience.

Index